NANNIE'S KITCHEN
KEEPSAKES
&
RECIPES

NANNIE'S KITCHEN KEEPSAKES & RECIPES

By Jeanette Walls

Published by
WINGS PUBLISHERS
3555 Knollwood Drive
Atlanta, Georgia 30305

Book design and composition by Melanie M. McMahon

Manufactured in the United States of America

10 9 8 7 6 5 4 3 2

ISBN 0-9668884-4-8

CONTENTS

JUST A HINT...   01

APPETIZERS, BEVERAGES, CANDIES, DIPS   05

THIS & THAT   27

SALADS, SAUCES, SOUPS, STEWS   45

MEATS, EGGS, ETC.   79

BREADS   93

KITCHEN HELPFUL HINTS   111

VEGETABLES   117

HOUSEHOLD HELPFUL HINTS   141

CAKES & DESSERTS   155

CASSEROLES & MAIN DISHES   227

HEALTHY HINTS   267

CANNING   273

JUST A HINT...

INTRODUCTION

The reader is invited to experience keepsakes and recipes of many sorts gathered and compiled by me—the Nannie. These keepsakes and recipes are from all aspects of life from the meats and vegetables of nutritional sustenance to the recipe for happiness and spiritual nurturing. The hints and recipes have all been tried and appreciated. Some of the remedies have been handed down for generations in the Appalachian Mountains of my home and may not be easily recognizable or provable. As you fill your household with these keepsakes, I hope you enjoy them as much as I have in the last 60 years.

NANNIE'S KEEPSAKES SAMPLINGS

Never place food on a paper towel or napkin for microwaving. Recycled paper products contain chemicals that may promote cancer.

After a big meal, pop a few fennel or anise seeds into your mouth. Italians and Greeks use these sweet herbs as an aid to digestion.

To keep a cake fresh; place 1/2 of an apple in the cake box. A slice of fresh apple fastened with toothpicks to the cut edge of the cake will keep the cake from drying out and getting stale.

When a drain is clogged with grease pour a cup of salt and a cup of baking soda into the drain, follow with a kettle of boiling water. Grease will usually dissolve immediately.

To keep windows and mirrors from steaming in winter: Mix 1/2 cup Isopropyl alcohol 70% (rubbing alcohol) and 1 quart of water.

To remove a splinter: Soak injured part in any cooking oil for a few minutes and the splinter can then be easily removed. Or you can apply an ice cube to the finger for several minutes. This will allow for painless removal of the splinter.

A good cup of coffee: One pinch of salt in the basket will remove some of the acid taste. For clear coffee, put eggshells in after perking; remember always start with cold water.

Cooking in iron pots adds iron to foods, which is a plus for nearly everyone, but especially for pregnant women and people who eat no meat, poultry, or fish. Foods high in acid, such as tomatoes, cause the most iron to leach out from the cookware.

Instant spot remover: Try shaving cream foam as a good spot remover, wash up with water or club soda.

Jerk up spongy lettuce by adding lemon juice to a bowl of water, soak for an hour in the refrigerator. Douse quickly in hot then ice water with a little apple cider vinegar added as another alternative.

To save energy use the electric skillet for baking cakes (place on a trivet or 3 pennies), dessert bars, potatoes, etc. can be baked inexpensively. Be sure to close the vent on the lid and bake the usual time.

Household odors can be killed for just pennies a day simply by putting a few drops of wintergreen oil on a cotton ball and placing it out of sight. Do this for each room and it will last for months.

A different flavoring for tea: Instead of using sugar dissolve old-fashioned lemon drops or hard mint candy in your tea. They melt quickly and keep the tea clean and brisk.

Marshmallows will not dry out if stored in the freezer. Simply cut with scissors when ready to use.

Thaw fish or wild game in milk. It will remove the strong odor and taste.

Ice cream that has been opened and returned to the freezer sometimes forms a wax like film on top. To prevent this, after part of the ice cream has been removed, press a piece of waxed paper against the surface and reseal the carton.

Grease your salad molds with mayonnaise before pouring your molded salads. They will come out more easily and the mayonnaise gives them extra nice flavor.

A little butter on the lip of a cream pitcher will eliminate the usual drip when pouring.

APPETIZERS
BEVERAGES
CANDIES
DIPS

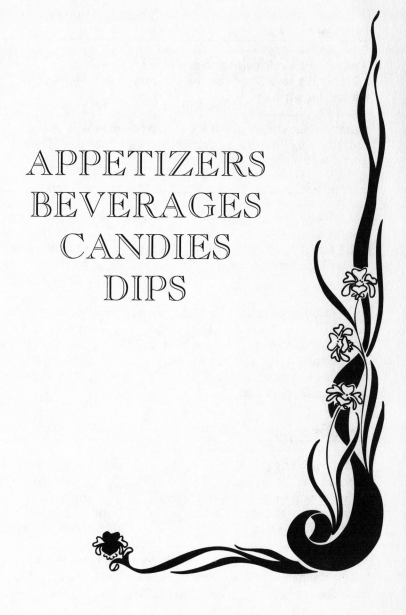

APPETIZERS

CHEESE PUFFS

1 pkg. (6 oz.) refrigerator biscuits
1/2 pound sharp Cheddar cheese, cubed in 1 inch cubes
Oil for deep frying

Separate biscuits and cut in half. Wrap dough around cheese cubes. Drop into hot oil and fry until browned, approximately 3 minutes. Drain.

CRABBIES

1 jar (5 oz.) Old English Cheese Spread
1 stick margarine, softened
1-1/2 tsp. mayonnaise
1/4 tsp. seasoning salt
1/4 tsp. garlic salt
2 cans (6 oz.) lump
   crab meat, drained (or 8 oz.
   fresh crab meat)
6 English muffins, split

In small bowl, mix cheese, margarine, mayonnaise, seasoning salt, and garlic salt until well blended. Stir in crabmeat. Spread on muffin halves and freeze for 30 minutes. Preheat oven to 350 degrees. Cut each half into 6 wedges and place on greased cookie sheets. Bake for 10-12 minutes until hot. Serve immediately. Muffins may be frozen for longer periods before baking. Yield: 72 servings.

NACHOS

1 lb. ground beef
1 onion
1 can cream of mushroom soup
1 can cream of chicken soup
1 can tomato soup
1 can Ro-Tel tomatoes
   (tomatoes with jalapeno
   peppers)
1 large bag of Doritos chips
Sharp cheddar cheese, grated

Brown beef and chopped onion. Add soups and Ro-Tel, bring to a boil and simmer a few minutes. Take Doritos chips and make layers alternating with other ingredients in casserole dish. Top ingredients with grated cheese. Bake at 350 degrees until cheese bubbles.

SAUSAGE BALLS

1 pound hot bulk sausage
3-1/2 cups biscuit mix
1 (10 oz.) pkg. shredded cheese

Combine all ingredients with hands. Shape loosely into small balls and bake at 350 degrees for 15-20 minutes. Yield: 100 balls.

CORNED BEEF BALLS
Delicious with crackers or by themselves

1 can corned beef
8 oz. cream cheese, softened
2 cups grated cheddar cheese
3/4 cup pickle relish
1 bunch parsley, snipped

2 tsp. horseradish
1-1/2 tsp. prepared mustard
1/2 tsp. Worcestershire sauce
3 Tbs. lemon juice

Combine all above ingredients (except parsley) together in large bowl. Form into small balls and roll in parsley. Refrigerate until serving time. A great party idea!

CHEESE BALL

1 pound mild or sharp Cheddar
   cheese, shredded
1 (8 oz.) pkg. cream cheese,
   softened to room temp

1 minced or shredded
   clove garlic
1 minced or shredded
   small onion
Pecan bits

Mix all ingredients well with hands. Shape into ball and roll in pecan bits. Garnish with a cherry.

BEVERAGES

WHOLE FRUIT SHAKE

1 can (6 oz.) or 3/4 cup pineapple juice
1/2 cup strawberries
1 ripe banana, peeled

Combine all ingredients in blender. Whip until blended. Pour into tall glass. Yield: 1 serving.

SWEETENED CONDENSED MILK

1 cup instant non-fat dry milk solids
1/2 cup boiling water
2/3 cup sugar
3 Tbs. melted butter

Combine all ingredients in blender container. Process until smooth. Store in refrigerator until ready to use. Yield: 1-1/4 cups.

RUSSIAN TEA

3/4 cup Lipton instant tea
1 Tbs. ground cloves
2 cups sugar
2 pkg. lemonade mix with sugar
2 cups orange drink mix
2 Tbs. cinnamon

Mix 2 or 3 teaspoons with 8 ounce cup of boiling water.

PARTY PUNCH

64 oz. pineapple juice
64 oz. Sprite
1 pkg. lemon-lime Kool-Aid
1/2 cup sugar

Mix Kool-Aid with sugar and 2 quarts water. Freeze pineapple juice and Kool-Aid in ice trays. Pour Sprite over frozen cubes when ready to serve.

SPRINGTIME PUNCH

1 cup fresh lemon juice (3-4 lemons)
(2-3 oranges)
2-1/2 cups water
1 can (6 oz.) frozen pineapple juice concentrate, thawed
2 cups sugar
1 cup fresh orange juice
2 quarts ginger ale, chilled

In a saucepan, bring sugar and water to a boil. Boil for 10 minutes; remove from the heat. Stir in the lemon, orange and pineapple juices. Refrigerate. Just before serving, combine with ginger ale in a large punch bowl. Yield: 16-20 servings (3 quarts).

TROPICAL PUNCH

1 can pineapple juice
3 quarts water
1 cup lemon juice
2 cups sugar
1 can orange juice
1 quart ginger ale (optional)

Mix all ingredients together. Chill bevfore serving.

HOLIDAY PUNCH

3 cans (6 oz.) frozen lemonade
1 pkg. frozen strawberries
1 quart ginger ale

Dilute lemonade concentrate according to directions on can. Pour into punch bowl. Stir in thawed strawberries. Just before serving, add ginger ale and ice. Yield: 1-1/2 gallons.

HOT CHOCOLATE MIX—I

5-1/2 cup nonfat dry milk   1 cup powdered sugar
1 cup non-dairy coffee creamer   1/2 cup cocoa
1-1/2 cup chocolate flavor mix (8 envelopes)

Mix together, store in airtight container. For one cup, use 1/2 cup (4 table-spoons) of mix to 3/4 cup boiling water.

HOT COCOA MIX—II

1/4 cup baking cocoa
2 cups powdered milk
1 cup confectioner's sugar
Dash of salt

Place 2 or 3 tablespoons of mixture in large cup and add hot water.

FRUIT YOGURT SMOOTHIE

1 medium banana, halved
1/2 cup milk
1 Tbs. sugar
1 container (8 oz.) strawberry-banana
     yogurt (or strawberry yogurt)

Combine all ingredients in blender container. Cover and blend on medium speed 30 seconds or until smooth. Pour into thermos bottles and add 1 to 2 ice cubes.

HELPFUL HINTS

You will not need sugar with your tea if you drink jasmine tea or the lighter-bodied varieties, like Formosa Oolong, which have their own natural sweetness. They are fine for sugarless iced tea, too.

Calorie-free club soda adds sparkle to iced fruit juices, makes them go farther, and reduces calories per portion.

A different flavoring for tea: Instead of sugar, dissolve old-fashioned lemon drops or hard mint candy in your tea. They melt quickly and keep the tea clean and brisk!

Most diets call for 8 ounces of milk and 4 ounces of fruit juice. Check your glassware. Having the exact size glass prevents overpowering.

Make your own spiced tea or cider! Place orange peels, whole cloves, and cinnamon sticks in a 6-inch square cheesecloth. Bring up corners and tie with string. Add to hot cider or tea for 10 minutes (longer if you want a stronger flavor).

Always chill juices or sodas before adding to beverage recipes.

When possible, float an ice ring in punch rather than ice cubs. This not only is more decorative, but also inhibits melting and diluting.

Try placing fresh or dried mint in the bottom of hot chocolate for a zesty taste.

Never boil coffee; it brings out the acid and causes a bitter taste. Store cof fee in the refrigerator or freezer to retain the fresh flavor.

Always use COLD water for electric drip coffee makers. Use 1 to 2 table spoons ground coffee for every cup of water.

When serving hors d'oeuvres on a silver tray, you may wish to protect it from acids by covering it with a layer of leafy green lettuce.

CANDIES

CORN FLAKE TREATS

1 cup sugar
1 cup peanut butter
1 cup corn syrup

9 or 10 oz. corn flakes
3 Tbs. cocoa
1 Tbs. butter

Butter sides and bottom of 9 x 13 inch pan. Crush corn flakes. Mix sugar, corn syrup and chocolate in sauce pan. Bring to a boil and remove from heat. Add butter and peanut butter. Mix well and pour over corn flakes. Stir to coat all the flakes. Let cool and cut into squares.

LADY FINGERS

4 Tbs. sugar
1-1/2 cups butter or oleo
2 cups plain flour

1 tsp. vanilla
1/2 cup finely chopped nuts

Blend ingredients well and add nuts. Shape into small rolls about the size of largest finger and bake on greased cookie sheet at 300 degrees for 45 minutes. When slightly cool, roll in confectioner's sugar.

CARAMEL POPCORN

6 quarts of popped corn
nuts (optional)
2 cups light brown sugar

2 sticks butter
1/2 cup white Karo syrup
1 teaspoon salt

Mix last 4 ingredients in saucepan and boil 5 minutes. Remove from heat and add 1 teaspoon baking soda and 1 teaspoon vanilla.

Pour over popped corn and work well. Bake in large pan one hour at 200 degrees stirring every 15 minutes.

PRALINE STRIPS

1 cup butter, salted
24 graham crackers (2_" x 2_" each)
1 cup light brown sugar, packed
1 cup chopped pecans

Arrange crackers one layer thick in an ungreased 15 x 10 x 1 pan. Heat butter and brown sugar over medium heat to boiling point. Boil for 2 minutes only. Stir in pecans and spread over crackers. Bake in a preheated 350 degree oven for 10 minutes. Cut while warm. Yield: 48 strips.

CORN FLAKE-PEANUT BUTTER CANDY

1/2 cup peanut butter
1 (6 oz.) pkg. chocolate bits
1 (6 oz.) pkg. butterscotch bits
5 cups corn flakes (add last)

Melt first 3 ingredients slowly and stir in 1 cup corn flakes at a time until all used up. Pour in pan, chill and set out 10 minutes, then cut into bars.

CHOCOLATE COATED PEANUTS

1 (6 oz.) pkg. semi-sweet chocolate chips
2-1/2 cups roasted shelled peanuts, skins on

Melt chocolate chips in top of double boiler over hot (not boiling) water. Add peanuts and stir to coat. Turn out on waxed paper, separate with a fork. Allow to cool. Yield: 1 pound.

PEANUT CLUSTERS

8 (2 oz.) vanilla candy coating squares, cut up
2-2/3 cups milk chocolate morsels
1 pound salted Spanish peanuts

Melt candy coating and chocolate morsels in a heavy saucepan over low heat, stirring constantly. Remove from heat; stir in peanuts.

CHOCOLATE FUDGE—I

2/3 cups cocoa
3 cups sugar
Pinch of salt
1-1/2 cups milk

1/2 cup butter
1 tsp. vanilla
1 cup chopped nuts

Combine cocoa, sugar, salt and stir in milk in a saucepan. Boil; cook to soft ball stage when tried in cold water. Remove from heat, add butter and vanilla and let it almost cool. Beat until mixture thickens. Add nuts and pour on greased dish. Cut in squares when cool.

CHOCOLATE FUDGE—II

2 cups sugar
3 Tbs. cocoa
1 cup evaporated milk, undiluted
3 Tbs. white corn syrup

1/2 cup butter
1 tsp. vanilla
1 cup chopped pecans (Optional)

Mix sugar, cocoa, milk and syrup in a heavy saucepan. Cook over high heat, stirring constantly, until mixture holds its shape completely when dropped in a cup of cold water. Add butter and vanilla. Allow fudge to cool slightly, then beat until candy can be dipped onto wax paper. (Optional: Top with 1 cup chopped pecans).

PEANUT & PRETZEL BARK

1 (24 oz.) pkg. chocolate or vanilla flavored candy coating
1 cup broken thin pretzels
1 cup coarsely chopped peanuts

In heavy saucepan, over low heat, melt candy coating, stirring frequently. Remove from heat; stir in remaining ingredients. Spread into thin layer on 2 aluminum foil-lined baking sheets. Chill 30 minutes or until firm. Break into chunks. Store covered at room temperature or in refrigerator.

Microwave: In 2-quart glass measure, melt candy coating on 50% power (medium) 5-6 minutes, stirring every 2 minutes. Stir until mixture is smooth. Proceed as above.

(Microwave ovens vary in wattage and power output; cooking times and power levels may need to be adjusted)

SUGARED PEANUTS

1 cup granulated sugar
1/2 cup water
2 cups raw shelled peanuts (with skins on)

Dissolve sugar in water in saucepan over medium heat. Add peanuts and continue to cook over medium heat, stirring frequently. Cook until peanuts are completely sugared (coated and no syrup left). Pour onto ungreased cookie sheet, spreading so that peanuts are separated as much as possible. Bake at 300 degrees for approximately 30 minutes, stirring at five minute intervals.

CHOCOLATE PECAN CLUSTERS

1 cup sugar
1/2 cup evaporated milk
1 Tbs. butter

1 tsp. vanilla
1 cup chopped nuts
1 pkg. chocolate pudding powder (do not use instant)

Cook and stir all ingredients except nuts to a full, all-over boil. Lower heat and keep stirring while mixture boils slowly for 3 minutes. Remove from heat, add nuts and beat until candy is thick and loses its shine. When candy starts to thicken, drop from teaspoon onto waxed paper. Work quickly. Yield: 24 clusters.

PEANUT BUTTER FINGERS

1/2 cup sugar
1/2 cup brown sugar, packed
1 cup all-purpose flour
1 cup quick cooking oats, uncooked

1/3 cup peanut butter
1 egg
1/2 tsp. vanilla
1/2 cup butter, melted

Combine sugars, flour and oatmeal in bowl. Cut in peanut butter. Add egg, vanilla and butter. Mix well. Press into a well-greased 9 x 11 inch pan. Bake at 350 degrees for 15-20 minutes. Top with icing. Yield: 20 pieces.

ICING

1/2 cup peanut butter
3 Tbs. Cocoa
1/2 box powdered sugar
1/3 cup milk

Combine peanut butter, cocoa, and sugar. Add milk gradually until creamy.

WONDERFUL PEANUT BUTTER FUDGE

4 cups sugar
1 cup milk
1 jar (18 oz.) smooth peanut butter
1 jar (7 oz.) marshmallow creme

Place sugar and milk in heavy 3-quart saucepan. Heat over medium heat, whisking frequently, until mixture comes to a boil. Boil for two minutes; remove from heat. Stir in peanut butter until smooth. Add marshmallow creme and continue to stir until well blended. Pour into a buttered 9 x 13 inch plan. Place on wire rack; let cool until firm. Cut into desired size pieces. Yield: About 4 pounds.

Variation: Crunchy peanut butter can be substituted for smooth to obtain a nutty taste.

Hint: To cut smoothly, dip a thin bladed knife in very hot water as often as necessary.

MOUND BALLS

1 large bag coconut
1 can condensed milk
1 pkg. confectioners sugar
Few drops vanilla
12 oz. semi-sweet chocolate bits

Heat the milk and sugar. Then stir in coconut. Grate a bar of paraffin wax, melt a 12 ounce Package of chocolate chips (semi-sweet); dip balls in chocolate mixture, put on wax paper.

PEANUT BUTTER BALLS

1-1/2 sticks butter, melted
1 (6 oz.) jar peanut butter
1 box confectioners sugar
4 cups Rice Krispies

Mix all the above, shape into balls, and put in refrigerator. Grate a bar of paraffin wax, melt a 12 ounce package of chocolate chips (semi-sweet); dip balls in chocolate mixture, put on wax paper.

PECAN BRITTLE

1-1/2 cups sugar
1/2 cup white syrup
1/2 cup boiling water
2 cups pecans

1/2 tsp. salt
1/2 tsp. soda
1 Tbs. butter

Cook sugar and syrup in water until syrup spins a thread. Add nuts and cook until golden brown. Syrup will look like it is burning. Remove from heat and add remaining ingredients. Stir while it is bubbling. Pour onto greased aluminum foil. Spread thin.

DIXIE PEANUT BRITTLE

2 cups granulated sugar
1 cup light corn syrup
1/2 cup water
1/2 tsp. salt

2 Tbs. butter
4 cups raw peanuts, skins on
2 tsp. baking soda

In a heavy saucepan heat sugar, syrup, water and salt to a rolling boil. Add peanuts. Reduce heat to medium and stir constantly. Cook until syrup spins a thread (293 degrees). Add butter, then baking soda. Beat rapidly and pour on a buttered surface, spreading to 1/4 inch thickness. When cool, break into pieces.

POTATO CANDY

1/2 cup cooked mashed Irish potatoes
1 tsp. vanilla flavoring
2 boxes powdered sugar (sifted)
1 jar chunky peanut butter

Combine vanilla and potatoes; slowly add sugar into stiff dough. Take small portions and roll out thin on wax paper. Spread desired amount of peanut butter; roll in jelly roll fashion. Cool 1 hour, cut into small bite-size pieces.

PEANUT BUTTER FUDGE

1 bag (12 oz.) milk chocolate chips
1 jar (12 oz.) crunchy peanut butter
1 can (14 oz.) sweetened condensed milk

Melt chocolate and peanut butter in top of double boiler. Remove from heat and stir in milk. Pour in an 8 x 8 inch pan lined with waxed paper. Refrigerate to chill. Cut in 1-inch pieces. Yield: 1-1/2 pounds.

ALMOST PEANUT BUTTER CUPS

1 cup smooth peanut butter
1/2 pound butter, melted
25 graham crackers, crushed

3 cups powdered sugar
2 cups semi-sweet chocolate chips, melted

Combine first four ingredients and spread in a lightly buttered 9 x 12 inch casserole. Pour melted chocolate over. Allow to cool. Cut in squares. Yield: 10 squares.

(**Note:** The peanut butter mixture can be mixed easily with the food processor.)

PEANUT BRITTLE

1-1/2 cups sugar
1/2 cup white corn syrup
2 Tbs. cold water

2 cups unblemished peanuts, raw
1-1/2 tsp. baking soda

Mix sugar, syrup, water and peanuts in a deep iron skillet. Cook over high heat, stirring occasionally until peanuts start to make a soft popping sound and the syrup begins to turn a light golden brown. Remove from heat and add baking soda. The mixture will foam. Pour out onto a heat-resistant surface that has been generously buttered. Spread out mixture into one layer of peanuts. When cool, break into pieces.

BORDEN'S ROCKY ROAD CANDY

1 (12 oz.) pkg. semi-sweet chocolate chips
1 (14 oz.) can sweetened condensed milk (not evaporated milk)
2 Tbs. margarine or butter
2 cups dry roasted peanuts
1 (10 1/2 oz.) pkg. miniature marshmallows

Line a 9 x 13 inch pan with wax paper and set aside. In heavy saucepan over low heat, melt chocolate chips with sweetened condensed milk and margarine; remove from heat. In large bowl, combine nuts and marshmallows; fold in melted chocolate mixture. Spread in prepared pan. Chill 2 hours or until firm. Remove from pan; peel off wax paper and cut candy into squares. Cover and store at room temperature.

UNCOOKED CHOCOLATE FUDGE

3 Tbs. cocoa, heaping
4 Tbs. butter or oleo
1/2 cup Karo
1 Tbs. water
1 box confectioners sugar
1/3 cup instant or powdered milk
1 tsp. vanilla
1 cup chopped nuts

Blend all ingredients well and beat until creamy. Add nuts and spread about 1 inch thick on wax paper. Let set for short while and cut in squares.

CHRISTMAS PARTY PINWHEELS

2 (8 oz.) pkg. Cream cheese softened
1 (4 oz.) pkg. Ranch salad dressing mix
1/2 cup minced sweet red pepper
1/2 cup minced celery
1/4 cup sliced green onions
3 or 4 (10-inch) flour tortillas

In a mixing bowl beat cream cheese and dressing. Mix until smooth. Add pepper, celery, onions and mix well. Spread about 3/4 cup on each tortilla. Roll up tightly and wrap in plastic wrap. Refrigerate for at least 2 hours. Remove wrap and slice into 1/2 inch pieces. Yield: 15 to 20 servings.

CINNAMON DIVINITY

2-1/2 cups sugar
1/2 cup light corn syrup
1/4 tsp. salt
1/2 cup water

2 egg whites
1 tsp. vanilla extract
cinnamon candy (optional)

Combine sugar, syrup, salt and water in 2 quart saucepan. Cook over high heat until mixture reaches 260 degrees (hard ball stage) on a candy thermometer; stirring only until sugar dissolves. Remove from heat; cool for 3-4 minutes. Meanwhile, beat egg whites to stiff peaks. Gradually pour syrup over egg whites in a thin stream, beating at high speed on electric mixer. Add vanilla and beat until candy holds its shape and starts to lose its gloss. Quickly drop from a teaspoon onto waxed paper. (Optional: Top with cinnamon candy.) Store in airtight container. Yield: 3 dozen pieces.

DIVINITY CANDY

Snowy white or tinted a delicate color, this is one of the prettiest and most popular of all candies

2 cups of sugar
1/4 cup water
1/2 cup white corn syrup

1 tsp. vanilla
Whites of two eggs

Mix sugar, syrup and water and let boil until it forms hard ball when dropped in cold water. Then pour the mixture slowly into well-beaten egg whites, beating gently. Add flavoring and nuts if desired. Beat until it loses its gloss, drop in balls on wax paper or pour into square pan and when cold cut in squares.

Sea Foam Candy
A very good variation of the above Divinity recipe is to use 2-1/2 cups brown sugar instead of the 2 cups white sugar. Make as Divinity. Add nuts and/or raisins if desired.

DIPS

MEXICAN BEAN DIP

Shredded lettuce
Chopped green onions
Tortilla chips for dipping
Diced tomatoes

Salsa (optional)
1 (8 oz.) pkg. Cream cheese, softened
1 can bean dip

Mix cream cheese and bean dip together and spread on serving plate.

Layer on lettuce, tomatoes and onions (enough of each to cover the previous layer). Arrange tortilla chips around the edge of the platter or tray. Serve with salsa, if desired.

TEX MEX DIP

Serve with corn chips or taco chips

Layer 1: 2 (10 oz.) cans refried beans
Layer 2: 3 mashed avocados
2 tsp. lemon juice
salt and pepper
Layer 3: 8 oz. sour cream
1/2 cup mayonnaise
1 pkg. taco seasoning mix

Layer 4: 1 bunch green onions, chopped
Layer 5: 3 tomatoes, chopped
Layer 6: 1 can pitted black olives, chopped
Layer 7: 8 oz. grated sharp cheddar cheese

Serve with corn or taco chips.

CHILI CHEESE DIP

1 medium onion chopped and sautéed
1 (15 oz.) can chili, with or without beans (without is preferred)
1 lb. Velveeta processed cheese
1 (10 oz.) can Ro-Tel diced tomatoes and peppers
3 slices bacon, cooked and crumbled

Mix together onion, chili, tomatoes, and bacon. Put in crockpot and heat on low until cheese melts. Serve with chips. Recipe can be doubled. Cheese can be plain or with peppers.

7-LAYER DIP

1 can refried beans
1 pint sour cream
1 envelope taco seasoning mix
1 cup mayonnaise
3 avocados
1 Tbs. lemon juice
1 (8 oz.) Monterey Jack cheese, shred
1 (8 oz.) Cheddar cheese, shredded

1 cup scallions, sliced
2 tomatoes, diced (slightly drained)
1 small can chopped black olives

Mix taco seasoning, mayonnaise, and sour cream together, set aside. Spread refried beans on the bottom of 13 x 9 pan. Spread sour cream mixture over beans. Mash avocados and mix with lemon juice and a little salt and pepper; spread over sour cream layer. Next layer—tomatoes; next layer—scallions; next layer—black olives; next layer—cheeses.

HOT ARTICHOKE DIP

1/2 cup mayonnaise
1/2 cup sour cream
1 can (14 oz.) artichoke hearts,
        drained, chopped

1/3 cup grated Parmesan cheese
1/8 tsp. hot pepper sauce

Stir all ingredients until well mixed. Spoon into small ovenproof dish. Bake at 350 degrees for 30 minutes or until bubbly. Yield: 2 cups.

GUACAMOLE DIP

1/2 cup mayonnaise
1 large avocado, peeled, mashed
1 small tomato, chopped
1/4 cup minced onion

1/4 cup drained chopped green
        chilies
1 Tbs. lemon juice
1/2 tsp. salt

Stir all ingredients until well mixed. Cover; chill. Yield: 2 cups.

BACON HORSERADISH DIP

1 cup mayonnaise
1 cup sour cream
1/4 cup real bacon bits
1/4 cup prepared horseradish

Stir all ingredients until well mixed. Cover; chill. Yield: 2 cups.

ROTEL DIP

1 can Ro-Tel tomatoes
1 pound Velveeta cheese

Heat slowly until cheese is melted. Can be microwaved. Good with corn chips or tortillas.

SHRIMP LOUIS DIP

1 cup mayonnaise
1 cup sour cream
1/3 cup finely chopped green pepper
1/4 cup chili sauce
1 Tbs. prepared horseradish
1/4 tsp. salt
1/8 tsp. freshly ground pepper
2 cups finely chopped cooked shrimp

Stir all ingredients until well mixed. Cover; chill. Yield: 3 cups.

HOT CRAB DIP

1 pkg. (3 oz.) cream cheese, softened
1/2 cup mayonnaise
1 can (6 oz.) crabmeat, drained
1/4 cup minced onion
1 Tbs. lemon juice
1/8 tsp. hot pepper sauce

Beat cream cheese until smooth. Stir in remaining ingredients. Spoon into small ovenproof dish. Bake at 350 degrees for 30 minutes or until bubbly. Yield: 1 cup.

HOT CHEDDAR BEAN DIP

**1/2 cup mayonnaise
1 can (16 oz.) pinto beans, drained, mashed
1 cup shredded Cheddar cheese
1 can (4 oz.) chopped green chilies
1/4 tsp. hot pepper sauce**

Stir all ingredients until well mixed. Spoon into small ovenproof dish. Bake at 350 degrees for 30 minutes or until bubbly. Yield: 2-1/2 cups.

PESTO DIP

**1 cup mayonnaise
1 cup sour cream
1 pkg. (10 oz.) frozen chopped
    spinach, thawed, well-drained
1/3 cup grated Parmesan cheese**

**1/4 cup walnut pieces
1 tsp. dried basil
1/4 tsp. salt
1 clove garlic, crushed**

In blender or food processor blend all ingredients until almost smooth. Cover; chill. Yield: 2 cups.

CUCUMBER DILL DIP

**1 pkg. (8 oz.) cream cheese, softened
1 cup mayonnaise
2 medium cucumbers, peeled,
    seeded, and chopped
2 Tbs. sliced green onion**

**1 Tbs. lemon juice
2 tsp. snipped fresh dill or
1/2 tsp. dried dill weed
1/2 tsp. hot pepper sauce**

Beat cream cheese until smooth. Stir in remaining ingredients until well mixed. Cover; chill. Yield: 2-1/2 cups.

GREEN ONION DIP

**1 cup mayonnaise
1 cup sour cream
1/2 cup sliced green onions**

**1/2 cup parsley sprigs
1 tsp. Dijon mustard
1 clove garlic, crushed**

In blender or food processor blend all ingredients until almost smooth. Cover; chill. Yield: 2 cups.

GINGER LIME DIP

1/2 cup mayonnaise
1/2 cup sour cream
2 tsp. grated lime peel

1 Tbs. lime juice
1 Tbs. honey
1/2 tsp. ground ginger

Stir all ingredients until well mixed. Cover; chill. Serve with fruit. Yield: 1 cup.

GREEN APPLE DIP

1 pkg. (8 oz.) cream cheese (softened)
1/2 cup brown sugar
1/2 cup white sugar

1 tsp. vanilla
Pecans (chopped)

Mix all ingredients. Serve with apple slices.

APPLE DIP

1 (8 oz.) pkg. cream cheese
1 cup brown sugar
1/4 cup butter
1 tsp. vanilla
Apples

Melt all ingredients. Cool. Slice apples and dip.

THIS-CAN'T-BE-TUNA DIP

1 (7-3/4 oz.) can white tuna, drained
1 (8 oz.) container sour cream
1 (.6 oz.) pkg. Zesty Italian dressing mix
Corn chips

In a small bowl, break tuna into small pieces. Add sour cream and dressing mix. Stir until blended. Refrigerate several hours, or overnight. Serve with corn chips. Yield: 1-1/2 cups.

SAUSAGE DIP

1 pound regular sausage
1 pound Velveeta Mexican hot cheese
2 cups broccoli, steamed and drained

Crumble and fry sausage and drain. Add all three ingredients together.
(**Hint:** I find it easier to melt cheese in the microwave before mixing together.)

THE BIG DIPPER

1 (15 oz.) can Hormel Chili No Beans
1 (10 oz.) can Ro-Tel tomatoes & Green Chilies (diced), reserving 1 Tbs.
   drained for garnish
1-1/2 cups (8 oz.) Velveeta cheese, cubed
1/2 cup sliced green onions
1/2 tsp. cayenne pepper

In saucepan, combine all ingredients. Heat just until cheese melts, stirring frequently. Serve warm with assorted raw vegetable dippers and toasted French
bread slices. Garnish dip with reserved tomatoes, red pepper and additional
green onion, if desired. Yield: 4 cups.

BACON & CHEDDAR DIP

1 (1 oz.) pkg. Hidden Valley Party Dip
1 pint sour cream
1/4 cup bacon bits
1 cup shredded cheddar cheese

Mix together and serve.

CRAB DIP

1 cup mayonnaise
1 cup canned crab meat
1 cup Cheddar cheese, grated
1 Tbs. horseradish
2 Tbs. French dressing

Mix ingredients and chill before serving.

THIS
&
THAT

RECIPE OF LIFE

1 cup of Good Thoughts
1 cup of Consideration for Others
2 cups of sacrifice for Others

3 cups of Forgiveness
1 cup of Kind Deeds
2 cups of Well Beaten Thoughts

Mix these ingredients thoroughly and add tears of Joy,
Sorrow and Sympathy for others.
Flavor with little gifts of Love.
Fold in 4 cups of Prayer and
raise the texture to great heights of Christian Living.
After pouring all this into your Daily Life,
bake well with heat of Human Kindness.
Serve with a smile.

"Today is the tomorrow you worried about yesterday."

∾

"Life is just a bowl of cherries, it depends on you whether they are sweet."

RECIPE FOR HAPPINESS

1 heaping cup Patience
2 handfuls Generosity
1 headful Understanding
1 heartful of Love
Dash of Laughter

Sprinkle generously with Kindness.
Add plenty of Faith. Mix well.
Spread over a period of a lifetime and serve everybody you meet.

HAPPINESS CAKE

1 cup Good Thoughts	**2 cups Sacrifices**
1 cup Kindness	**2 cups Forgiveness**
1 cup Kind Deeds	**3 cups well beaten Faults**
1 cup Consideration	

Mix thoroughly. Add tears of Joy, Sorrow and Sympathy. Flavor with Love and Kindly Service. Fold in 4 cups of Prayer and Faith; blend well. Fold in daily life. Bake well with the warmth of human kindness and with wisdom from above. Serve with a smile from above at any time.

RECIPE FOR HAPPINESS

Mend a quarrel; search out an old friend.
Dismiss suspicion, show your trust.
Write a letter, share some treasure.
Give a soft answer.
Encourage youth.
Manifest your loyalty.
Don't give up.
Keep a promise.
Find the time.
Forego a grudge.
Forgive an enemy.
Open your heart.
Apologize if you were wrong.
Try to understand.
Root out envy.
Think first of someone else.
Appreciate, be kind, and be gentle.
Laugh a little more.
Do a good job.
Deserve confidence.
Reach out.
Fight prejudice.
Express your gratitude.
Gladden the heart of a child.
Take pleasure in the beauty of nature.

RECIPE FOR A HAPPY HOME

4 cups of Love
2 cups of Loyalty
3 cups of Forgiveness
1 cup of Friendship

5 spoons of Hope
2 spoons of Tenderness
4 quarts of Faith
1 barrel of Laughter

Take Love and Loyalty, mix thoroughly with Faith.
Blend with Tenderness, Kindness and Understanding.
Add Friendship and Hope.
Sprinkle abundantly with Laughter.
Bake with Sunshine.
Serve daily with generous helpings.

RECIPE FOR A HAPPY FAMILY

1 Husband
1 Wife
Children
1 Bible for each
1 Home
Generous portion of Prayer
1 cup of Kisses

1 package of Work
1 package of Playing Together
1 Tbs. Patience
1 Tbs. Understanding
2 Tbs. Forgiveness
1 small paddle
3 cups of Love, packed

Mix thoroughly and sprinkled with Awareness.
Bake in moderate oven of everyday Life,
using as fuel all the grudges and past unpleasantness.
Cool.
Turn out onto platter of Cheerfulness.
Garnish with Tears and Laughter in large helpings.
Serve God, Country, and Community.

FRIENDSHIP CAKE

1 cup Greetings   **2/3 cup Love**
1/2 cup Smiles   **2 cups Hospitality**
2 large Handshakes   **1 Tbs. genuine Interest in Others**

Cream Greetings and Smiles thoroughly.
Add Handshakes separately.
Add Love slowly.
Sift in Hospitality and Interest in others carefully.
Bake in moderate oven.
Serve warm to all new acquaintances.

RECIPE FOR A GOOD DAY

Take two parts of Unselfishness and one part of Patience.
Work together.
Add plenty of industry.
Lighten with good spirits and sweeten with kindness.
Put in smiles as thick as raisins in a plum pudding and
Bake by the warmth that streams from a loving heart.

If this fails to make a good day,
the fault is NOT with the recipe,
but with the Cook!

RECIPE FOR THE GOOD LIFE

A heaping cup of Kindness
  Two cups of Love and Caring
    One cup of Understanding
      One cup of Joyful Sharing.

A level cup of Patience
  One cup of Thoughtful Insight
    One cup of Gracious Listening
      One cup of Sweet Forgiveness.

Mix ingredients together
  Toss in Smiles and Laughter
    Serve to everyone you know
      With Love forever after.

HOW TO COOK A HUSBAND

A good many husbands are utterly spoiled by mismanagement in cooking and so are not tender and good.

- ❖ Some women keep them constantly in hot water; others let them freeze by their carelessness and indifference.
- ❖ Some keep them in a stew with irritating ways and words.
- ❖ Some wives keep them pickled, while others waste them shamefully.

It cannot be supposed that any husband will be tender and good when so managed, but they are really delicious when prepared properly. Like crabs and lobsters, husbands are cooked alive. They sometimes fly out of the kettle and so become burned and crusty on the edges, so it is wise to secure him in the kettle with a strong silken cord called Comfort, as the one called Duty is apt to be weak.

Make a clear, steady flame of Love, Warmth and Cheerfulness. Set him as near this flame as seems to agree with him. If he sputters, do not be anxious, for some husbands do this until they are quite done.

Add a little sugar in the form of what confectioners call kisses, but use no pepper or vinegar on any account.

Season to taste with spices, good humor and gaiety preferred. Avoid sharpness in testing him for tenderness. You cannot fail to know when he is done. If so treated, you will find him very digestible, agreeing with you perfectly, and he will keep as long as you choose, unless you become careless and allow the home fires to grow cold.

Thus prepared, he will serve a Lifetime of Happiness.

RECIPE FOR PRESERVING A HUSBAND

Be careful of your selection.
> Do not choose too young.
When once selected, give your entire thought to preparation for domestic use.
> Some insist on keeping them in a pickle, others constantly get them in hot water
>> —this makes them sour, hard and sometimes bitter.
> Even poor varieties may be made sweet, tender and good
>> —by garnishing them with Patience,
>>> well sweetened with Love and seasoned with Kisses.
> Wrap them in a mantle of charity;
>> keep warm with a steady fire of domestic Devotion,
>>> and served with peaches and cream.

Thus prepared, they will keep for years!

SCRIPTURE CAKE

1 cup Psalms 55:21	1 cup Genesis 24:17
3 cups Jeremiah 6:20	1 Tbsp I Samuel 14:25
6 each Isaiah 10:14	2 cups I Samuel 30:12
3-1/2 cups I Kings 4:22	1 cup Numbers 17:8
1 Tbs. I Corinthians 5:6	2 cups I Samuel 30:12
1 little Levicicus 2:13	Season to taste with I Kings 10:10

Mix and follow advice in Proverbs 23:14 for making a good boy.

TAKE TIME

1. Take time to DREAM   * it hitches the soul to the stars.
2. Take time to SEE FRIENDS   * it is the source of happiness.
3. Take time to LAUGH   * it is the singing that helps with life's loads.
4. Take time to LOVE   * it is the one sacrament of life.
5. Take time to PLAY   * it is the secret of youth.
6. Take time to READ   * it is the foundation of knowledge.
7. Take time to THINK   * it is the source of power.
8. Take time to WORK   * it is the price of success.
9. Take time to WORSHIP   * it is the highway of reverence and washes the dust of the earth from your eyes.

10. Take time to PLAN   * it is the secret of being able to have time to take time for the first nine things.

HEAVEN'S GROCERY STORE

I was walking down life's highway a long time ago,
One day I saw a sign that read "Heaven's Grocery Store."
As I got a little closer, the door came open wide.
And when I came to myself, I was standing there inside.

I saw a host of angels, they were standing everywhere,
One handed me a basket and said, "My child, shop with care."
Everything a Christian needed was in that grocery store,
And all you couldn't carry, you could come back for more.

First, I got some patience, love was in the same row,
Further down was understanding, you need that wherever you go.
I got a box or two of wisdom and a bag or two of faith,
I just couldn't miss the Holy Ghost, for it was all over the place.

I stopped to get some strength and courage, to help me run the race.
By then my basket was getting full, but I remembered I needed some grace.
I didn't forget salvation, for salvation, that was free,
So I tried to get enough of that to save both you and me.
Then I started up to the counter to pay my grocery bill,
For I thought I had everything to do my Master's will.

As I swept up the aisle, I saw prayer and I just had to put that in,
For I knew when I stepped outside, I would run right into sin.
Peace and joy were all plentiful, they were on the last shelf,
Song and praises were hanging near, so I just helped myself.

Then I said to the angel, "Now how much do I owe?"
He just smiled and said, "Just take them everywhere you go."
Again, I smiled at him and said, "How much do I owe?"
He smiled again and said, "My child, Jesus paid your bill a long time ago."

FOOD FOR THOUGHT

Every minute you are angry you lose 60 seconds of happiness.

A good Christian should be like a good watch
    open faced
            busy hands
                  pure gold
                      well regulated
                          and full of good works!

God has given us two hands—one to receive and the other to give with.

WORDS IN THE ENGLISH LANGUAGE

The 6 most important words—*I admit I made a mistake.*

The 5 most important words—*You did a good job.*

The 4 most important words—*What is your opinion?*

The 3 most important words—*If you please.*

The 2 most important words—*Thank you.*

The most important word—*We.*

The least important word—*I.*

MORE WORDS IN THE ENGLISH LANGUAGE

Happiness is like potato salad—when you share it with others, it's a picnic.

Just about the time you think you can make ends meet, somebody moves the ends.

Be careful how you live—you may be the only Bible some people read.

A recipe that is not shared with others will soon be forgotten but when it's shared, it will be enjoyed by future generations.

BIRTHDAYS

Monday's child is fair of face.

Tuesday's child is full of grace.

Wednesday's child is loving and giving.

Thursday's child works hard for a living.

Friday's child is full of woe.

Saturday's child has far to go.

But the child that is born on the _Sabbath_ day is grave and bonny, and good and gay.

IMPROVISE IN THE KITCHEN

When you're out of an ingredient, improvise. It's more convenient than making a frantic trip to the store. To remember how, clip this chart and post in a kitchen cupboard.

* 1 tablespoon cornstarch (for thickening) equals 2 tablespoons all-purpose flour.

* 1 teaspoon baking power =1/2 teaspoon cream of tartar + 1/4 tsp. baking soda.

* 1 cup sugar equals 1 cup packed brown sugar or 2 cups sifted powdered sugar.

* 1 cup molasses equals 1 cup honey.

* 1 square (1 ounce) unsweetened chocolate equals 3 tablespoons unsweetened cocoa powder plus 1 tablespoon shortening or cooking oil, or one 1-ounce envelope pre-melted unsweetened chocolate product.

* 1 cup whole milk equals 1/2 cup evaporated milk plus 1/2 cup water, or 1 cup water plus 1/2 cup nonfat dry milk powder.

*   1 cup buttermilk equals 1 tablespoon lemon juice or vinegar plus enough milk to make 1 cup (let stand 5 minutes before using).

*   1 cup light cream equals 1 tablespoon melted butter plus enough whole milk to make 1 cup.

*   Buttermilk – 1 tablespoon vinegar or lemon juice plus enough milk to make 1 cup.

*   Shortening – peanut butter for pie crust.

*   Sour cream – 1-cup evaporated milk plus 1 Tbs. vinegar or 1-cup cottage cheese blended with 1 tablespoon of milk and 1 teaspoon lemon juice.

*   Giblet Gravy – use cream of chicken soup and your chopped egg, onion, meat and add chicken broth.

THIS AND THAT

If you run short 1 egg while making something, you can use 1 teaspoon of cornstarch or you can use 1 teaspoon of vinegar (I've used vinegar – it works!). But you will need to increase the liquid in your recipe at least 3 or 4 tablespoons or add 2 tablespoons of mayonnaise.

If you are cooking and add too much salt, add a pinch of sugar.

To give your Rice Krispies Treats a new taste, add some peanut butter or use Cocoa Krispies instead of Rice Krispies.

WORTH REMEMBERING

A pie crust will be more easily made and better if all the ingredients are cool.

The lower crust should be placed in the pan so that it covers the surface smoothly. And be sure no air lurks beneath the surface, for it will push the crust out of shape in baking.

Folding the top crust over the lower crust before crimping will keep the juices in the pie.

In making custard type pies, bake at a high temperature for about ten minutes to prevent a soggy crust. Then finish baking at a low temperature.

Fill cake pans about two-thirds full and spread batter well into corners and to the sides, leaving a slight hollow in the center.

The cake is done when it shrinks slightly from the sides of the pan or if it springs back when touched lightly with the finger.

After a cake comes from the oven, it should be placed on a rack for about five minutes. Then the sides should be loosened and the cake turned out on rack to finish cooling.

Cakes should not be frosted until thoroughly cool.

Kneading the dough for a half minute after mixing improves the texture of baking powder biscuits.

Keep a toothbrush around the kitchen sink – you will find it useful in cleaning rotary beaters, graters, choppers and similar kitchen utensils.

Instead of trying to iron rickrack on the right side of the garment, turn the article. The rickrack can be pressed perfectly.

When your hands are badly stained from gardening, add a teaspoon of sugar to the soapy lather you wash them in.

Use paper cups as handy containers for your "drippings" in the refrigerator as they take up little room and can be thrown away when empty.

Before emptying the bag of your vacuum cleaner, sprinkle water on the newspaper into which it is emptied, and there will be no scattering of dust.
To whiten laces, wash them in sour milk.

To remove burned-on starch from your iron, sprinkle salt on a sheet of waxed paper and slide iron back and forth several times. Then polish it with silver polish until roughness or stain is removed.

Dip a new broom in hot salt water before using. This will toughen the bristles and make it last longer.

Try waxing your ashtrays. Ashes won't cling, odors won't linger and they can be wiped clean with a paper towel or disposable tissue. This saves daily washing.

Plant a few springs of dill near your tomato plants to prevent tomato worms on your plants.

Marigolds will prevent rodents.

Spray garbage sacks with ammonia to prevent dogs from tearing the bags before being picked up.

You can clean darkened aluminum pans easily by boiling them in two teaspoons of cream of tartar mixed in a quart of water. Ten minutes will do it.

Fresh lemon juice will take away onion scent from hands.

Wash old powder mugs in soapy water, rinse well and dry thoroughly. Then use them for polishing silverware, copper and brass.

Soak colored cottons overnight in strong salt water and they will not fade.

To dry drip-dry garments faster and with few wrinkles, hang garment over the top of a dry cleaner's plastic bag.

If a cracked dish is boiled for 45 minutes in sweet milk, the crack will be so welded together that it will hardly be visible, and will be so strong it will stand the same usage as before.

To maintain natural juices, thaw meat until barely icy before cooking.

Thaw large frozen vegetables before cooking until just icy; small vegetables, like peas, need no thawing.

Do not thaw any product by leaving on a counter. Thaw in a cooler.

PLAY DOUGH

1 cup water
1-cup plain flour
1/2 cup salt
1 Tbs. cooking oil
1 tsp. Cream of tartar

Combine all ingredients in a pot and stir until well mixed. Cook until rubbery. When cool, add food coloring and knead into the dough.

CRAFT CLAY

4 cups baking soda
2 cups cornstarch
2-1/2 cups cold water

Mix ingredients in saucepan and cook over medium heat stirring constantly. Cook about 10 minutes until mixture is consistency of mashed potatoes. Remove from heat and turn onto plate and cover with damp cloth. After it cools, knead into a smooth ball. Store in tight plastic bag and refrigerate until ready to use. Can half the recipe.

HOMEMADE FINGER PAINTS

Mix 1/2 cup cornstarch with 2 cups cold water in a saucepan. Bring mixture to boil and continue to boil until it thickens. Let cool slightly. Pour equal amounts into clean (baby-food) jars and color each with food color.

FROZEN STORAGE PERIODS

Food – Maximum Storage Period at –10 degrees F.
Freezing not recommended for ham and luncheon meats.

Beef, ground and stewing	3-4 months
Beef, roasts and steaks	6 months
Cake batters	3-4 months
Cakes, prebaked	4-9 months
Cookies	6-12 months
Fatty fish (mackerel, salmon)	3 months
French-fried potatoes	2-6 months
Fruit	8-12 months
Fruit juice	8-12 months
Fruit pies, baked or unbaked	3-4 months
Giblets	3 months
Ice Cream	3 months, original containers
Lamb, roasts and chops	6-8 months
Other fish	6 months
Pie shells, baked or unbaked	2 months

Pork, ground	1-3 months
Pork, roasts and chops	4-8 months
Pre-cooked dishes	2-6 months
Pre-cut poultry	4 months
Shellfish	3-4 months
Vegetables	8 months
Whole chicken, turkey, duck	12 months
Yeast breads and rolls, baked	3-9 months
Yeast breads and rolls, dough	1-1.5 months

SIZE OF CANS

8 oz	= 1 cup
No. 1 flat	= 1 cup or 9 oz.
No. 1 tall	= 2 cups or 16 oz.
No. 303	= 2 cups or 16 oz.
No. 2	= 2-1/2 cups or 20 oz.
No. 2-1/2	= 3-1/2 cups or 28 oz.
No. 3 cylinder	= 5-1/2 cups or 46 oz.
No. 10	= 13 cups or 6 pounds 10 oz.

WEIGHTS AND MEASURES

3 tsp.	= 1 Tbs.
4 Tbs.	= 1/4 cup
5-1/2 Tbs.	= 1/3 cup
8 Tbs.	= 1/2 cup
10-2/3 Tbs.	= 2/3 cup
12 Tbs.	= 3/4 cup
16 Tbs.	= 1 cup
2 Tbs.	= 1 liquid ounce
1 cup	= 1/2 pint
2 cups	= 1 pint
4 cups	= 1 quart
4 quarts	= 1 gallon
8 quarts	= 1 peck
4 pecks	= 1 bushel
2 Tbs. Butter	= 1 oz.
1/2 cup butter	= 1/4 pound or 1 stick
2-1/4 cups granulated sugar	= 1 pound

2-1/2 cups firmly packed brown sugar	= 1 pound
3-1/2 cups sifted confectionery sugar	= 1 pound
4 cups sifted flour	= 1 pound
4-1/2 cups sifted cake flour	= 1 pound
3 cups corn meal	= 1 pound
1 Tbs. Cornstarch	= 2 Tbs. flour
2-1/8 cups uncooked rice	= 1 pound
1 square chocolate	= 1 oz.
3-1/2 Tbs. Cocoa & 1/2 Tbs. Butter	= 1 square chocolate
1 cup chopped nuts	= 1 pound
15 marshmallows	= 1/4 pound
4 cups grated American cheese	= 1 pound
6-2/3 Tbs. cream cheese	= One 3 oz. Package

EQUIVALENTS OF CAPACITY
(ALL MEASURES ARE LEVEL FULL)

3 teaspoons	= 1 Tbs.
1/2 fluid ounce	= 1 Tbs.
16 Tbs.	= 1 cup
2 gills	= 1 cup
1/2 liquid pint	= 1 cup
8 fluid ounces	= 1 cup
1 liquid pint	= 2 cups
16 fluid ounces	= 2 cups

KITCHEN WEIGHTS, MEASURES

4 large Tbs. = 1/2 gill
1 teacup = 1 gill
1 common sized tumbler = 1/2 pint
2 cups = 1 pint
2 pints = 1 quart
1 Tbs. = 1/2 ounce
1 large wine glass = 2 ounces
8 quarts = 1 peck
4 cups flour = 1 pound
2 cups solid butter = 1 pound
4 quarts = 1 gallon

2 cups granulated sugar = 1 pound
3 cups cornmeal = 1 pound
2-2/3 cups brown sugar = 1 pound
2 cups solid meat = 1 pound
2-2/3 cups powdered sugar = 1 pound
16 ounces = 1 pound
2 tablespoons butter, sugar, salt 1 ounce
16 ounces 1 pound
2 tablespoons butter, sugar, salt 1 ounce
4 tablespoons four = 1 ounce
16 Tbs. = 1 cup
60 drops = 1 tsp.
3 tsp. = 1 Tbs.
4 Tbs. = 1/4 cup
1 cup shelled almonds = 1/4 pound
1/4 pound cornstarch = 1 cupful

CUP MEASURES

1 cup granulated sugar = 1/2 pound
1 cup butter = 1/2 pound
1 cup lard = 1/2 pound
1 cup flour = 1/4 pound
1 cup rice = 1/2 pound
1 cup oatmeal = 5 ounces
1 cup raisins (stemmed) = 6 ounces
1 cup currants (cleaned) = 6 ounces
1 cup bread crumbs (stale) = 2 ounces
1 cup chopped meat = (1/2 pound)

SALADS
SAUCES
SOUPS
STEWS

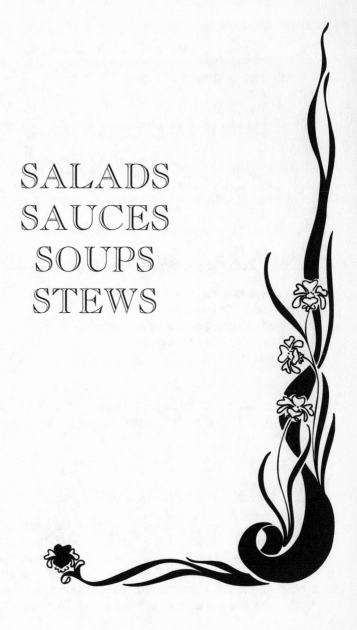

SALADS

SUNSET SALAD

1 (3 oz.) pkg. lemon or orange gelatin
1/2 tsp. salt
1 cup boiling water
1 (8-3/4 oz.) can crushed pineapple
   undrained

1 Tbs. mayonnaise
1 Tbs. lemon juice
1 cup grated carrots
1/3 cup chopped pecans
   (optional)

Dissolve gelatin and salt in boiling water. Add undrained pineapple, mayonnaise and lemon juice. Fold in carrots and pecans (if desired). Chill until firm. Cut into squares. Delicious served on lettuce with crackers.

TANGY TOMATO DRESSING

1/4 cup low-calorie, low-sodium catsup
2 Tbs. grated red onion
2 Tbs. olive or vegetable oil
2 Tbs. lemon juice or vinegar
2 Tbs. water

1 tsp. drained prepared
   horseradish
1/2 tsp. sugar
1/2 tsp. low-sodium
   Worcestershire sauce
1/8 tsp. black pepper

In a jar with a tight-fitting lid, combine all ingredients. Cover and shake well, then refrigerate (will keep for up to 1 week). Yield: About 3/4 cup (6 two-tablespoon servings).

CHICKEN SALAD

2 Tbs. oil
2 Tbs. vinegar
2 Tbs. orange juice
1 tsp. salt
1 chicken, cooked and cubed
1-1/2 cups mandarin orange slices

1-1/2 cups pineapple chunks
1-1/2 cups green grapes
1-1/2 cups diced celery
2-1/2 cups cooked rice
1 cup slivered almonds
1-1/2 cups mayonnaise

Combine first 4 ingredients; toss with chicken. Combine remaining ingredients and toss well. Refrigerate before serving. Yield: 8-10 servings.

PINK CLOUD FROZEN SALAD

1 (8 oz.) pkg. cream cheese, softened
1/4 cup honey
1 (10 oz.) pkg. frozen sliced strawberries,
   partially thawed
2 bananas, sliced
2 cups miniature marsh
   mallows
1 cup whipping cream,
   whipped

In large mixing bowl, beat cream cheese until smooth. Add honey; continue to beat until blended. Add strawberries, bananas and marshmallows. Stir with rubber spatula until coated. Gently fold in whipped cream until well mixed. Pour into a 9-inch square pan. Freeze until firm. Cover with foil for continued storage. To serve, let stand at room temperature for 20-30 minutes. Cut into squares. Yield: 9 servings.

ENGLISH PEA SALAD

2 (17 oz.) cans English peas, drained
2 hard cooked eggs, chopped
1 cup cubed Colby cheese
1 medium onion, finely chopped
1/4 tsp. celery salt
Dash of pepper
2 Tbs. blue cheese salad
   dressing, optional
Mayonnaise

Combine all ingredients in a large mixing bowl. Add mayonnaise as desired, using enough to mix well. Yield: 8 servings.

WILTED OR HOT LETTUCE

3 strips bacon
1 Tbs. bacon drippings
1/2 cup vinegar
1/2 cup water
2 Tbs. flour, dissolved
1 small onion
1/2 head lettuce, broken
   into small pieces
Salt and sugar to taste

Fry 3 strips of bacon crisp, drain off drippings. Crumble bacon, add 1 tablespoon of drippings to vinegar, water and flour. Let simmer a few minutes. Sprinkle with salt and sugar to taste. Then pour over lettuce. Delicious with roast beef.

WILTED LETTUCE SALAD

1 bunch of leaf lettuce, torn
6 to 8 radishes, thinly sliced
4 to 6 green onions with tops, thinly sliced

DRESSING:

4 to 5 bacon strips
2 Tbs. red wine vinegar
1 Tbs. lemon juice
1 tsp. sugar
1/2 tsp. pepper

Toss lettuce, radishes and onions in a large salad bowl; set aside. In a skillet, cook bacon until crisp. Remove to paper towels to drain. To the hot drippings, add vinegar, lemon juice, sugar and pepper; stir well. Immediately pour dressing over salad; toss gently. Crumble the bacon and sprinkle on top.
Yield: 6-8 servings.

THREE WEEKS SLAW

3 pounds white cabbage, chopped fine
1 green bell pepper
2 onions
2 cups sugar

DRESSING:

1 cup vegetable oil
1 cup vinegar
1 or 2 Tbs. celery seed
1 Tbs. salt

Chop cabbage, bell pepper, onions, add sugar, and set aside while preparing dressing. Bring dressing to a boil. While hot, pour over cabbage mixture and stir. This slaw will keep for three weeks in refrigerator.

CRANBERRY SALAD—I

1 cup water
1 (3 oz.) pkg. cherry gelatin
1 (16 oz.) can whole cranberry sauce

1/2 cup sour cream
1 (11 oz.) can mandarin oranges
1/2 cup chopped walnuts

Mix gelatin with one cup boiled water. Beat cranberry sauce and sour cream into gelatin mixture with rotary egg beater. Drain oranges. Fold oranges and walnuts into gelatin mixture. Spoon into a 5-cup ring mold. Chill. Yield: 8 servings.

CRANBERRY SALAD—II

1 cup cranberries measured after grinding
1 cup sugar
1 cup chopped nuts

1 (9 oz.) can crushed pineapple
Juice of one lemon
2 cups boiling water
1/2 cup celery chopped in small pieces
1 pkg. strawberry or lemon gelatin

Mix sugar and cranberries together and let stand overnight or several hours. Add gelatin to boiling water. Stir until dissolved. Add other ingredients and chill. Use the pineapple juice and less water if desired.

CRANBERRY SALAD—III

1 (16 oz.) can crushed pineapple, undrained
1/2 cup pineapple juice
1/2 cup water
1 (6 oz.) pkg. orange gelatin

1 (16 oz.) can cranberry sauce
1 cup nuts
grated peel from 1 orange

Drain juice from pineapple except for 1/2 cup. Heat 1/2 cup juice and water; dissolve gelatin. Break up cranberry sauce with fork and add to gelatin mixture. Add nuts and orange peel; mix. Pour into mold; let jell and serve. Yield: 6-10 servings.

CRANBERRY RELISH

1 pkg. cranberries
2 oranges
2 cups sugar
1 cup pecans

Chop all ingredients. Mix well. Refrigerate overnight.

TROPICAL CHICKEN SALAD

2 cups cubed cooked chicken
1 cup chopped celery
1 cup mayonnaise
1/2 to 1 tsp. curry powder
1 (20 oz.) can chunk pineapple,
    drained
2 large firm bananas, sliced
1 (11 oz.) can mandarin oranges,
    drained
1/2 cup flaked coconut
Salad greens, optional
3/4 cup salted peanuts or cashew
halves

Place chicken and celery in a large bowl. Combine mayonnaise and curry powder; add to chicken mixture and mix well. Cover and chill for at least 30 minutes. Before serving, add the pineapple, bananas, oranges and coconut; toss gently. Serve on salad greens if desired. Sprinkle with nuts. Yield: 4-6 servings.

"HOT CHICKEN SALAD"

2 cups chopped chicken
1 cup cracker crumbs
2 cups finely chopped celery
2 cans undiluted chicken soup
4 Tbs. grated onion
1 cup slivered almonds
1 cup mayonnaise
6 hard-boiled eggs, grated
salt to taste
4 Tbs. lemon juice

Mix together, put in buttered 8-inch glass baking dish. Add a few cracker crumbs and paprika on top. Bake at 350 degrees for 40-45 minutes. Serves 8 or more and may be prepared ahead of time. Bake until bubbly all over.

SUMMER SALAD

3 cups cooked macaroni
3 cucumbers, sliced
1 large green pepper, chopped
1 small onion, sliced

3 tomatoes, chopped
1/2 cup mayonnaise
1/4 cup cider vinegar
salt and pepper to taste

Combine first five ingredients. Combine mayonnaise and cider vinegar. Toss with vegetables and macaroni. Salt and pepper to taste. Yield: 6-8 servings.

BEAN SALAD—I

1 can cut green beans
1 can cut yellow wax beans
1 can red kidney beans, drained
1 medium onion, thinly sliced
1/2 cup celery, chopped

1/2 cup bell pepper
1/3 cup Wesson oil or other
   cooking oil
1/2 cup vinegar
1/2 cup sugar
1 tsp. salt

Combine vegetables.   Mix remaining ingredients and pour over salad. Refrigerate for several hours or overnight.

BEAN SALAD—II

1/2 cup chopped green pepper
1 small can slivered almonds
1/2 cup chopped onion
1 (1 lb.) can wax beans, drained
1 (1 lb.) can small whole green
   beans, drainedl
1 (1 lb.) can kidney beans, washed
   and drained

1/2 cup vinegar (may use wine
   vinegar)
3/4 cup sugar
1 tsp. salt
1/2 cup salad oi

Combine all ingredients, toss lightly. Refrigerate overnight. Drain before serving. Serves 12 and keeps several days.

FROZEN CRANBERRY SALAD

1 (8 oz.) pkg. cream cheese, softened
1 tsp. lemon juice
12 oz. whipped topping

1 (8 oz.) can crushed pineapple, drained
1 (16 oz.) can whole cranberry sauce
1/2 cup chopped pecans

Combine cream cheese, lemon juice and whipped topping; beat until smooth. Add remaining ingredients; stir to combine. Pour into mold and freeze until set. Yield: 12 servings. Each serving contains 258 calories.

WILD RICE EGG SALAD

1 (6 oz.) pkg. seasoned long grain and wild rice mix (cooked)
1/2 cup finely chopped onion
1/2 cup diced ham
2 Tbs. salad oil
1 cup finely chopped celery

2 Tbs. wine vinegar
1/2 cup finely chopped green pepper
1/2 cup mayonnaise
6 hard cooked eggs, finely chopped
1 envelope Knox gelatin
Salt and pepper to taste

Soften gelatin in 2 teaspoons water, then mix with other liquids and heat until the gelatin is dissolves. Combine the rice, ham, celery, onion, pepper and egg. Mix well and add the mayonnaise, then fold in the dissolved gelatin and add salt and pepper as desired. Pour into a prepared mold and chill until firm. Serve on a lettuce leaf. Yield: 6 servings.

TACO SALAD

1 or 2 lbs. ground round
1 pkg. taco seasoning
1 head lettuce
1 tomato, chopped
1 bottle Ranch dressing

1 (8 oz.) pkg. sharp cheese, shredded
1 medium onion, chopped
Salsa
Doritos

Brown beef, drain and/or rinse well. Prepare taco seasoning according to package directions. Cool. Layer shredded lettuce, onion, beef, Ranch dressing, salsa, tomatoes, and cheese in large bowl. Top with crushed Doritos before serving. Toss, serve immediately.

FRUIT SALAD WITH SOUR CREAM

1 can pineapple chunks, drained
2 oranges, cut in pieces
2 cups miniature marshmallows

1 cup coconut
1 cup sour cream
2 or 3 bananas

Combine pineapple and oranges. Stir in bananas to keep from turning dark. Add coconut and marshmallows. Stir in sour cream.

PEAS PLEASE

1 cup cooked English peas
1 cup chopped pecans
1 cup chopped celery
1 cup chopped cheese (American or pimento)

Mix all ingredients together with salad dressing.

BROCCOLI SALAD

2 large bunches broccoli, tops only
12 slices bacon, cooked and crumbled
1/2 cup chopped onion
3/4 cup raisins
1 cup sunflower seeds

DRESSING:

1 cup Miracle Whip
1 Tbs. white vinegar
1/4 to 1/2 cup sugar

Blend dressing ingredients and toss well with salad ingredients. I think dressing does better if mixed 1 to 2 hours or more before mixing with salad ingredients. This allows the sugar time to dissolve.

FIVE-CUP SALAD

1 can mandarin oranges, drained
1 cup miniature marshmallows
1 cup sour cream
1 small can pineapple tidbits, drained
1 cup flaked coconut
1 cup white grapes
1 cup nut meats (optional)

Mix all ingredients together and refrigerate several hours or overnight. Yield: 6 servings.

MARINATED VEGETABLE SALAD

1 (2 oz.) jar diced pimento, drained
1/2 cup diced celery
1/2 to 1 cup chopped green pepper
1/2 cup chopped onion
1 (17 oz.) can English peas, drained
1 (17 oz.) can white shoe peg corn, drained
1 (15-1/2 oz.) can French style green beans, drained

1/2 tsp. pepper
1 tsp. salt
1/2 cup vegetable oil
3/4 cup vinegar
1 cup sugar

Combine vegetables, toss lightly. Combine remaining ingredients in a medium saucepan; bring to a boil over low heat, stirring occasionally. Pour over vegetables, stirring gently to blend. Cover and chill 24 hours. Yield: 6-8 servings.

FROZEN FRUIT SALAD

1 (3 oz.) pkg. cream cheese
1/4 cup mayonnaise
1 tsp. unflavored gelatin
1 tsp. lemon juice
1 No. 2 can fruit cocktail, drained
1 small bottle cherries, chopped

1/2 cup pecans, chopped
2/3 cup whipping cream
1 small can crushed pineapple
   (optional)
1/2 cup sugar
Pinch of salt

Blend cheese, mayonnaise and salt; soften gelatin in lemon juice; dissolve over hot water. Add to cheese mayonnaise mixture. Whip cream until stiff; add sugar and mix; add pineapple. Pour into wax lined freezer trays or other pan and place in freezer.

MACARONI SALAD

1 (8 oz.) pkg. shell macaroni	1 Tbs. mustard
3/4 cup chopped celery	1-3/4 tsp. salt
1/2 cup chopped bell pepper	1/4 tsp. pepper
1/2 cup mayonnaise	Snipped parsley
1 Tbs. lemon juice	

Cook macaroni according to package directions. Rinse in cold water and drain. Combine macaroni, celery, bell pepper and pimento in a large bowl. Blend remaining ingredients and add to macaroni. Chill before serving. Yield: 4 servings.

PEACH SEAFOAM SALAD

1 large can peach slices, drained and mashed (save 1 cup juice)
1 large box peach gelatin
1 (8 oz.) pkg. cream cheese, softened
1 large carton whipped topping

Heat peach juice to boiling; add gelatin, stir to dissolve. Place gelatin and softened cream cheese in blender container; blend until smooth; add mashed peaches. Refrigerate until cool and thick. Fold in whipped topping. Refrigerate until set. Yield: 6 servings.

POTATO SALAD—I

8 to 10 medium potatoes, sliced and cooked	1 small onion, minced
	2 Tbs. bacon bits
1 (8 oz.) carton sour cream	2 Tbs. cubed pickles
1/4 cup mayonnaise	Salt and pepper to taste
2 Tbs. dry parsley	

Combine all ingredients in large bowl. Yield: 8 servings.

POTATO SALAD—II

6 large potatoes	1 tsp. salt
1 large onion	1 tsp. celery salt
1/2 cup vinegar	1/2 tsp. pepper
3 Tbs. bacon grease	1/2 Tbs. flour

Boil potatoes, peel, chill, slice; finely chop onion; mix. Mix vinegar, bacon grease and seasonings. Heat to boiling and thicken with flour; pour over potatoes and onion, mix and cool. Serve on lettuce leaves; or garnish with sprigs of parsley. Variations: add 2 to 4 hard-cooked eggs, 2 to 4 tablespoons chopped sweet red or green peppers, 1/2 to 1 cup sliced cucumbers, tomatoes, or celery, or combination of any of these. Another variation is to add 4 to 6 cooked, sliced frankfurters or wieners. For Herring Salad, 2 or 3 smoked salt herring, cut in pieces, and 1/2 cup sliced pickled beets.

MEXICAN SLAW

1 head cabbage	1 cup sugar
1 onion	3 tsp. salt (or less)
1 bell pepper	1-1/2 cup vinegar
1/2 carrot	(add a little water)

Shred cabbage; sprinkle with salt and set out at room temperature for 1-1/2 hours. Shred other vegetables. Add sugar and vinegar. Squeeze water out of cabbage with hands. Mix all together and chill. Keeps well in refrigerator.

BEACH BEAN SALAD

8 bacon slices	1 tsp. salt
2 onions, sliced and separated into rings	1 tsp. dry mustard
2 (15 oz.) cans lima beans, undrained	1/2 tsp. garlic powder
2 (15 oz.) cans baked beans, undrained	1/4 cup white vinegar
1 (15 oz.) can kidney beans, undrained	1/4 cup ketchup
3/4 cup firmly packed brown sugar	

Cook bacon in large Dutch oven until crisp remove bacon, reserving 2 tablespoons drippings in skillet. Crumble bacon. Add onion to drippings, and sauté until tender. Stir in bacon, beans, and remaining ingredients; spoon into a lightly greased 11 x 7-inch baking dish. Bake at 350 degrees for 1 hour or until bubbly. Yield: 8 servings.

7-Up Jell-O

2 small pkg. lemon Jell-O
1 large can crushed pineapple,
   drained (save juice)
2 large bananas

1 cup miniature
   marshmallows
2 cups boiling water
2 cups 7-Up

TOPPING:
1 cup pineapple juice
2 Tbs. flour
1/2 pint Cool Whip

2 Tbs. butter
1 beaten egg
1 cup sugar

Dissolve Jell-O with water. Add 7-Up and fruit. Put in refrigerator. Mix juice, flour, butter, egg and sugar. Cook until thickened and then cool. Fold in softened Cool Whip and pour over Jell-O. Refrigerate until set.

CRACKER SALAD

1 stack saltine crackers
1 cup chopped sweet pickles (drained)
1 small jar chopped pimentos (drained)
1 cup chopped onion

1 medium green pepper,
   chopped
5 boiled eggs, chopped
1/2 pint salad dressing or
   mayonnaise

Crush crackers and put in large mixing bowl. Add all ingredients and mix well. This salad is especially good if put in a covered plastic container and chilled for a couple of hours before serving. Do not freeze. Keeps well chilled for several days.

SEVEN-LAYER SALAD

1 head lettuce, shredded
1 cup celery, chopped
1 cup green pepper, chopped
1 large onion, chopped

1 pkg. frozen peas, thawed
1 cup mayonnaise
1/2 cup Parmesan cheese
1/2 cup bacon bits

Place half of lettuce in deep salad bowl. Top with celery, green pepper, onion and peas, in that order. Cover with rest of lettuce. Spread mayonnaise on top and sprinkle with cheese and bacon bits. Cover and refrigerate for 24 hours before serving. Yield: 12 servings.

MACARONI SALAD

1 cup mayonnaise
2 Tbs. vinegar
1 Tbs. prepared mustard
1 tsp. sugar
1 tsp. salt
1/4 tsp. pepper
8 ounces elbow macaroni, cooked, drained
1 cup sliced celery
1 cup chopped green or sweet red pepper

In large bowl, stir together first 6 ingredients until smooth. Add remaining ingredients; toss to coat well. Cover; chill. Yield: 5 cups.

GARLIC SALAD DRESSING

1-1/2 tsp. garlic salt
1/2 tsp. sugar

1/3 cup vinegar
2/3 cup salad oil

In container with stopper or lid, combine all ingredients; blend or shake well. Yield: 1 cup.
Presentation: serve over any mixed green and vegetable salad combination.

HOLIDAY SALAD

1 large can crushed pineapple
1 small container whipped topping
1 pkg. instant pistachio pudding
1 cup miniature marshmallows
1 cup chopped pecans

Blend together above ingredients and serve cold.

WATERGATE SALAD—I

1 large box pistachio Jell-O
1 large container Cool Whip
1 large can crushed pineapple

1 cup miniature marshmallows
1 cup chopped nuts
1 cup coconut

Dissolve Jell-O in pineapple juice. Combine all ingredients and chill.

WATERGATE SALAD—II

1 (11-1/2 oz.) can crushed pineapple with juice
1 pkg. instant pistachio pudding mix
1 (4-1/2 oz.) Cool Whip
1/2 cup chopped pecans
1/2 cup chopped maraschino cherries

Mix pineapple and pudding. Stir until thickened. Fold in Cool Whip, nuts and cherries. Chill before serving.

FRUIT SALAD WITH WHIPPED CREAM

1 No. 2 can peaches, drained
   and diced
1 small can pineapple, drained
3 or 4 bananas, diced

2 cups marshmallows, diced
1/2 pint sweetened whipped cream
1/2 cup nuts, chopped (optional)

Mix all ingredients together and chill for at least 2 hours.

STRAWBERRY SALAD

1-1/2 sticks butter or margarine
3 Tbs. sugar
2 cups pretzels, broken or coarsely chopped

Melt margarine. Stir in sugar and pretzels. Spread in dish and bake 7 minutes at 350 degrees.

1 cup powdered sugar
1 (8 oz.) Cool Whip, thawed
1 (8 oz.) cream cheese, softened

Mix together well and spread on cooled pretzel layer.

1 (6 oz.) strawberry Jell-O
1 box frozen strawberries

Mix Jell-O in 2 cups boiling water. Add frozen strawberries and stir until Jell-O begins to thicken. If necessary, chill a while to slightly jell. Pour over cream cheese layer. Refrigerate to set firmly. Enjoy!

CONGEALED SALAD

1 pkg. lime Jell-O
1 pkg. lemon Jell-O
2-3/4 cups boiling water

1 (3 oz.) pkg. cream cheese
1 cup crushed pineapple
1/2 cup chopped nuts (optional)

Dissolve Jell-O in boiling water. Chill until mixture starts to thicken. Mix remaining ingredients and add to Jell-O mixture. Turn into mold, chill until firm.

CORNBREAD SALAD

Cornbread, crumbled
2 cans pinto beans with onions, drained
1 large onion, chopped
1 can chow chow, drained
Mayonnaise
1 (12 oz.) pkg. shredded sharp Cheddar cheese
Bacon, cooked and crumbled

Layer ingredients in order given, in a 13 x 9 pan. Chill and serve.

SLAW

1 head cabbage, grated
1 small onion, grated
1 bell pepper, chipped
1/2 cup sugar

DRESSING:

1/2 cup vinegar
1/2 cup Wesson oil
1/2 tsp. sugar
1/2 tsp. powdered mustard
1/2 tsp. celery seed

Mix first four ingredients and set aside. Mix dressing in saucepan and boil for about 3 minutes. Pour over cabbage mixture and refrigerate.

BLEU CHEESE DRESSING

1 cup mayonnaise
3/4 cup buttermilk
1/4 tsp. garlic salt
1 tsp. Worcestershire Sauce
2 oz. bleu cheese, crumbled

Combine all ingredients and chill in refrigerator.

TIPS FOR TOSSED SALADS

❖ Always handle salad greens with care.

❖ Wash well, drain and dry greens before storing. Chill well before using.

❖ To core lettuce, strike lettuce head on countertop, stem end down. Then twist the core out.

❖ It is better to tear greens into bite-sized pieces to avoid bruising with knife.

❖ Don't cut up tomatoes for a tossed salad since their juices thin the dressing and wilt the greens. Use them only for garnishing the salad bowl.

❖ Select only firm, hard, green cucumbers. The skin should have a slight sheen, but if it is highly polished, it is probably waxed and should be removed.

❖ Use wild greens such as dandelion, sorrel or winter cress for a different flavor and texture in tossed salads.

ABOUT POTATO SALAD

Potato salad is best made from potatoes cooked in their jackets and peeled and marinated while still warm. Small red waxy potatoes hold their shape when sliced or diced and do not absorb an excessive amount of dressing or become mushy.

SAUCES

BARBECUE SAUCE

1/4 cup vinegar
1/4 cup catsup
1 tsp. brown sugar
1 Tbs. Worcestershire or 1 tsp. chili powder

Add above ingredients to "Quick Tomato Sauce" (below), or use tomato puree instead of tomato soup.

QUICK TOMATO SAUCE—I

1 can tomato soup
2 Tbs. butter
1 onion, chopped (optional)

Heat tomato soup, adding butter and onion. May be thinned with boiling stock or water.

QUICK TOMATO SAUCE—II

1 cup low-sodium stewed tomatoes
1/4 tsp. dried savory leaves or basil leaves
1/4 tsp. onion powder

Process tomatoes and seasoning in food processor or blender until smooth. Pour mixture into small saucepan. Cook over moderate heat until heated through. Yield: 1 cup.

COCKTAIL SAUCE

1 cup chili sauce or ketchup
3 tsp. prepared horseradish
2 tsp. lemon juice
1 tsp. Worcestershire sauce
Dash Tabasco Sauce

TARTAR SAUCE

1 cup reduced-fat mayonnaise
1/4 cup finely chopped dill pickle or dill pickle relish
1 large green onion with top, finely chopped
1 Tbs. drained capers
1 tsp. Dijon mustard
1/2 tsp. dried thyme leaves
Dash of cayenne pepper

Mix all ingredients in medium-size bowl. Cover and refrigerate. Will keep for 1 week. Yield: About 1-1/4 cups (about 10 servings).

TOMATO SAUCE

2 cups or more canned tomatoes,
    or fresh stewed tomatoes
1 slice of onion
2 ribs of celery with leaves (optional)
Parsley (optional)
1 carrot (optional)
1/2 green pepper (optional)
3 Tbs. butter
3 Tbs. flour
1/4 tsp. salt
1/8 tsp. pepper
1/4 tsp. sugar

Cook vegetables for 15 minutes. Strain and season. Melt butter, add flour and when smooth, add strained stock gradually. Stir sauce until smooth and thick. If vegetables other than tomatoes are cut in small pieces, tied in a bag and cooked with tomatoes, they may be taken from bag and replaced in sauce just before it is removed from the fire.

HONEY GLAZE

1/4 cup margarine
1/4 cup plus 2 Tbs. honey
3 Tbs. lemon juice

RED PEPPER CREAM SAUCE

4 Tbs. unsalted butter
1 large red pepper, cored,
    seeded and diced
1/4 cup sliced green onion
1/4 cup all-purpose flour

1/4 tsp. salt
1/4 tsp. white pepper
1-3/4 cups milk
1 Tbs. lemon juice

Melt butter over medium heat in a small saucepan. Add the red pepper and green onion; sauté for 2 minutes. Reduce heat to low and add the flour. Cook for 3 minutes, stirring frequently. Blend in the salt and white pepper. Gradually whisk in milk and lemon juice and cook for 1 minute. Pour the sauce into a blender and puree for 2 minutes, or until the peppers and onions are well-blended. Yield: About 3 cups.

BLAZIN BARBECUE SAUCE

1-1/4 cup catsup
2/3 cup oil
1 cup vinegar
5 Tbs. Worcestershire sauce
1/2 cup brown sugar
1/4 cup water
2 Tbs. dry mustard

3 tsp. freshly grated ginger
1 clove garlic, minced
1 lemon, thinly sliced
3 Tbs. butter
Heavy dash hot sauce
Salt and pepper to taste

Mix all ingredients and simmer until done. Serve over cooked meat.

RED BELL PEPPER SPREAD

1/4 cup pine nuts
3 medium (about 1 lb.)
    red bell peppers
4 medium cloves garlic, peeled

1/4 cup grated Parmesan cheese
2 Tbs. olive oil
1/4 tsp. salt

Place pine nuts on a plate and microwave, uncovered, on high 3 minutes or until lightly toasted. Set aside to cool. Place peppers in a dish large enough to hold them without touching each other. Cover and microwave on high 15 minutes, or until skins loosen. Remove and let stand at least 5 minutes. Longer is okay. Peel off skins, then remove stems and seeds. Pure peppers with nuts, garlic, cheese, oil and salt in a food processor. Use right away. Refrigerate up to 5 days or freeze. Yield: About 1-1/2 cups.

WHITE SAUCE, OR CREAM SAUCE

2 Tbs. butter
1-1/2 Tbs. flour
1/4 tsp. salt
1/8 tsp. paprika
1 cup hot milk

Melt butter and add flour. Stir until ingredients are smooth. Add seasoning and gradually add the hot milk. Use a wire whisk to stir sauce and boil it for 2 minutes. This will make a thin sauce. For a heavier sauce, increase flour to 2 or 3 tablespoons and use an equal amount of butter. Cream may be substituted for milk. Nutmeg, lemon juice, etc. may be added for flavor.

HOLLANDAISE SAUCE

1/2 cup butter   **1 Tbs. lemon juice**
2 egg yolks   **1/4 tsp. salt**
1/3 cup boiling water (optional)

Beat yolks in small saucepan, using wire whisk. Add half the butter and all the lemon juice. Place saucepan over (not in) boiling water. Stir sauce until it thickens, then add remaining butter, bit by bit, add the water slowly. Should sauce separate, add to it very slowly 2 tablespoons heavy cram. Serve sauce at once.

The best way to make this sauce is to put it into a small earthenware bowl that fits tightly into the opening of a tea kettle partly filled with boiling water. If you wish to keep sauce hot, place it over hot but not boiling water and cover it. Reheat by stirring over boiling water.

MOCK HOLLANDAISE SAUCE

1 Tbs. butter   **1/2 tsp. lemon juice**
3 egg yolks   **1 cup boiling water**
1 tsp. cornstarch   **1/4 tsp. salt**

Soften butter; add egg yolks and beat well. Add cornstarch and lemon juice. Just before serving, add 1 cup boiling water very, very slowly. Use bowl and teakettle of boiling water as described above. Stir sauce over steam until it thickens.

MUSHROOM SAUCE

Dilute canned mushroom soup or sauté 1/2 cup sliced fresh mushrooms with butter for white sauce. Canned mushrooms may be added when sauce is done. Use liquid in place of part milk.

CHEESE SAUCE

Soft cheese may be melted in double boiler and thinned with a little milk, or grated cheese may be added to white sauce and stirred over low heat until melted. Use 3/4 cup or less diced or grated cheese. Season sauce with red pepper and mustard (optional).

CARAMEL SAUCE—I

2 Tbs. butter
1 cup dark brown sugar
1/4 cup water
1/4 cup evaporated milk
1/2 tsp. vanilla

Place butter, sugar, and water in a small heavy saucepan. Bring to a boil over medium to medium-high heat. Boil gently 8 to 10 minutes until mixture just reaches the firm ball stage. Remove pan from heat; stir approximately 1 minute to cool down slightly. Slowly drizzle in evaporated milk and vanilla, stirring constantly. Serve either warm or cold. If the sauce is not used immediately, it may be refrigerated, then reheated.

CARAMEL SAUCE—II

1-1/3 heavy cream
1 cup granulated sugar
3 Tbs. water
2 Tbs. unsalted butter, cut into 4 pieces

In a small heavy saucepan, bring cream to simmer. Set aside. In a heavy medium saucepan, combine sugar and water. Stir over medium heat until sugar dissolves. Increase heat to high and boil, without stirring, until caramel is deep amber color, brushing down sides of pan with wet pastry brush if crystals form. Occasionally swirl pan to dissolve crystals, if necessary. Remove from heat and slowly add cream. Return sauce to low heat and stir until smooth. Remove from heat and mix with butter. Serve warm. Yield: 2 cups.

FUDGE SAUCE

2/3 cup corn syrup
2/3 cup water
1/2 cup cocoa
1-1/2 cups granulated sugar
2 oz. unsweetened chocolate, chopped

6 Tbs. unsalted butter
1/2 cup heavy cream
Pinch salt
2 tsp. vanilla extract

Pour corn syrup into a small saucepan over high heat and boil about 2 minutes or until heavy strands form when dropped from a spoon. Remove from heat. Add water. Stir to mix. Set aside. Mix together cocoa and sugar. Whisk into corn syrup. Simmer, stirring, until sugar dissolves completely. Add chocolate, stirring until melted. Blend in butter and cream. Bring to a boil; let boil 15 seconds. Remove from heat. Blend in salt and vanilla extract. Serve warm. Refrigerate in covered jar. Place jar in simmering water to reheat.

SPAGHETTI SAUCE

1 pound ground beef, browned, drained
1 medium onion, chopped
1 medium green bell pepper, chopped
1 (8 oz.) can tomato paste
1 small jar sliced mushrooms
1 tsp. Worcestershire sauce

1 quart tomato juice
2 tsp. brown sugar
1 tsp. basil leaves
1 tsp. garlic
Salt and pepper to taste

Combine all ingredients and simmer for one hour.

EASY SPAGHETTI SAUCE

1 (30 oz.) jar prepared spaghetti sauce, or garden variety sauce
1 lb. ground beef or ground turkey, divided in half
1 small can mushrooms, drained and rinsed (optional)
Dash of sugar (optional)
Dash of Italian seasoning (optional)
Pasta

Crumble half of meat and brown in microwave; drain. Make meatballs with other half of meat and brown in microwave; drain. Put sauce in 2-1/2 quart microwaveable dish. Add dash of sugar and Italian seasoning (optional). Add meat, meatballs and mushrooms. Stir well. Cover and cook on high 5 minutes, stir well. Cover and cook on high 5 minutes longer, stir well. Serve over pasta. Note: Ground turkey makes more tender and less fatty meatballs.

SOUPS

CHEESE BACON SOUP

5 slices bacon
4 cups chicken or beef broth
1/2 cup grated carrot
1/2 cup finely chopped celery
1/2 cup finely chopped onion
1/2 cup finely chopped green
    pepper
1/4 cup all-purpose flour

3 cups shredded sharp process
    cheese loaf
2 cups milk
2 Tbs. dry sherry
1 cup pimento-stuffed olives,
    rinsed and sliced
1/4 tsp. coarsely ground pepper
Chopped fresh parsley

Cook bacon in Dutch oven until crisp; remove bacon, reserving 1 tablespoon drippings in Dutch oven. Crumble bacon; set aside. Cook carrot, celery, onion and green pepper in drippings over low heat, stirring constantly, about 3 minutes or until tender, but not browned. Add flour, stirring to blend; cook 1 minute, stirring constantly. Gradually add broth, stirring constantly. Bring to a boil over medium heat; reduce heat, and simmer about 8 minutes or until thickened. Add cheese, stirring until melted. Stir in milk, sherry, olives, and pepper; cook over medium heat until thoroughly heated. Sprinkle with bacon. Garnish with parsley, if desired. Yield: 9 cups.

VEGETABLE SOUP

1 pound ground beef
Pieces of streak of lean
1 small onion, chopped
2 (1 lb.) cans tomatoes
1 (10 oz.) pkg. frozen butter beans
2 carrots, peeled and sliced
2 stalks celery, sliced
6 small potatoes, cubed
3-4 cups water
1-1/2 Tbs. celery salt

1 (16 oz.) can whole kernel corn,
    drained
1 (16 oz.) can English peas,
    drained
1 (16 oz.) can green beans,
    drained
1 tsp. hot pepper sauce
1 cup catsup
Salt and pepper to taste

In a large pot, brown ground beef and streak of lean with onion. Using a fork, mash tomatoes in pot. Add remaining ingredients, cover and bring to a boil. Simmer for 1 hour or until vegetables are tender.

MID-SUMMER SOUP

Make blended stock from liquids in which vegetables and starches have been boiled; peas, beans, tomatoes, spinach, cauliflower, cabbage, and macaroni, spaghetti, noodles, rice.

Put in pot with an onion and some parsley. Cook until onion is done. Season to taste, and add lightly beaten egg, or add flour or cornstarch to suitably thicken; serve.

STOUP   A cross between STew and sOUP!

1 pound ground round
    (or lean ground beef)
1 (10-3/4 oz.) can tomato soup
1 (14-1/2 oz.) can whole tomatoes,
    chopped
1 (8 oz.) can tomato sauce

1-1/2 cups diced new potatoes
1-1/2 cups diced onion
3 cups mixed vegetables
Salt and pepper to taste
1-2 cups water

In a large pot, brown the ground round. Drain well. Add tomato soup, chopped tomatoes, and tomato sauce; stir well. Add potatoes, onions and mixed vegetables. Stir. Season with salt and pepper to taste. Add enough water to cover the ingredients. Cover and simmer, stirring as needed for approximately 3-4 hours or until potatoes are very soft. Yield: 10 (1-cup) servings. Serve with cornbread, crackers or toast. Double the recipe for some to freeze!

BUSY DAY SOUP

6 cups water
1 pound ground beef
1 pkg. frozen mixed vegetables
1 quart tomatoes
1 pkg. onion soup mix
1/2 cup macaroni
4 bouillon cubes, beef

Put water and beef into pan and bring to boil, skim off fat if needed; add remaining ingredients and simmer for 1 hour (freezes well).

VEGETABLE SOUP—with chopped ham or ham hocks (sugar cured preferred)

1 pound ham, chopped
  or 1 pound ham hocks
1 quart water
2 cups chopped okra

1 large or 2 small chopped onion
6 medium tomatoes, or 1 can
2 cups tender corn, fresh or frozen

Let ham boil in water and add the okra, onions, tomatoes. Cook mixture slow for 1-1/2 hours. Add corn and stir well. Cook slow for another 30 minutes. Salt and pepper to taste. Water may be added to thin as desired.

POTATO SOUP

2 cups sliced onions
1/4 cup butter
5 cups fresh tomatoes
  or 3 cups canned tomatoes
2 tsp. sugar
1 tsp. salt

1/8 tsp. pepper
2 cups sliced potatoes
6 cups boiling water
1 cup cream
2 Tbs. chopped parsley

Cook onions gently in butter for about 1 hour. Cover and add tomatoes and seasoning. Simmer, covered, for 20 minutes. Add potatoes and water and simmer, covered, until the potatoes are very tender. Put soup through strainer. Scald and stir in cream. Add parsley.

VEGETABLE SOUP

1/4 cup carrots
1/4 cup turnips
1/4 cup celery
1/2 cup potatoes
1/4 cup onion
3 cups water

3 Tbs. butter
1/2 Tbs. flour
3/4 tsp. salt
1 beef bouillon cube
3 Tbs. parsley

Dice vegetables. Melt 3 tablespoons butter, add carrots, turnips and celery and cook for 10 minutes. Add potatoes and cook for 2 minutes. Add onion and water, and simmer soup for 1 hour. Melt butter, add flour and a little of soup. Return soup to kettle and cook 1 hour longer. Add beef cube. Beat soup with a fork to break up vegetables, add parsley and serve.

CHEESE SOUP

1/4 cup butter
2 Tbs. chopped onion
3 Tbs. flour
1 tsp. salt
1/8 tsp. pepper

2 cups milk
2 cups chicken broth
1/2 pound grated Cheddar cheese
1 cup chopped asparagus
Dash hot sauce

Melt butter in large saucepan over low heat. Sauté onion until tender. Blend in flour salt and pepper. Gradually add milk stirring until thickened. Add remaining ingredients, stirring occasionally. Heat until cheese is melted, approximately 30-45 minutes. Serve with a dollop of sour cream on top. Yield: 4 servings.

QUICK CHEESE SOUP

1 can cream of celery soup
1 Tbs. chopped onion
1-1/4 cups milk
1/4 tsp. Worcestershire sauce
1/2 cup shredded Cheddar cheese
1 can beef consommé

Combine first 4 ingredients in large saucepan. Add onion and Worcestershire Sauce. Cook over low heat. Do not let soup boil. Yield: 4 servings.

VEGETABLE SOUP

1 pound beef or ground turkey, browned
2 cans mixed vegetables
1 can tomatoes
1 can tomato sauce
1 medium onion, diced

1/2 bag egg noodles
2 tsp. salt
1/2 tsp. pepper
1 tsp. sugar

Combine all ingredients and put into crock pot. Add enough water to fill pot. Cook as little as two hours or cook all day. Yield: 6-8 servings.

TOMATO SOUP

1 No. 2 can tomatoes
1 small onion
3 ribs celery with leaves
2 Tbs. butter
2 Tbs. flour
3 Tbs. chopped parsley

2 cups stock,
   or 2 cups water and 2 beef
   bouillon cubes
1/2 tsp. sugar
1/8 tsp. paprika
Salt

Boil tomatoes with onion and celery for 10 minutes. Strain. Melt butter, add four and when smooth add stock and strained tomato. Boil for 1 minute. Add seasoning and chopped parley and serve.

HEARTY POTATO SOUP

6 potatoes, peeled and cut into
   1/2-inch cubes (2-1/2 pounds)
2 medium onions, diced
2 carrots, thinly sliced
2 celery ribs, thinly sliced
2 (14-1/2 oz.) cans low-sodium
   fat-free chicken broth

1 tsp. dried basil
1 tsp. salt
1/2 tsp. pepper
1/4 cup all-purpose flour
1-1/2 cups fat-free half-and-half
Italian Bread Bowls
Garnish: fresh celery leaves

Combine first 8 ingredients in a 4-1/2 quart slow cooker. Cook, covered, on high for 3 hours or until vegetables are tender. Stir together flour and half-and-half; stir into soup. Cover and cook 30 minutes or until thoroughly heated. Serve in Italian Bread Bowls, and garnish, if desired. Yield: 8-1/2 cups.

ONION SOUP

1-1/2 cups thinly sliced onions
3/4 cup water
4 Tbs. butter
1 Tbs. flour
6 cups stock or substitute

1 tsp. Worcestershire Sauce
Salt
Pepper
Toast
Grated Cheese

Cook onions in water until it is absorbed. Brown onions in butter. Stir in flour, stock and Worcestershire sauce. Simmer covered for 1 hour. Season soup. Place in oven-proof dishes. Cover top with toast sprinkled with cheese. Put in hot oven until cheese is melted. Serve at once.

STEWS

VEGETABLE BEEF STEW

1-1/2 lbs. ground chuck
1 (15 oz) can whole tomatoes,
    chopped
(16 oz.) can tomato sauce
1 to 1-1/2 cups water
2 large potatoes, peeled and
    cut in large chunks

1 can pinto beans, drained and rinsed
1 can whole kernel corn, drained
1 onion, chopped (or green onions
    with tops)
1/4 tsp. garlic powder
Coarse ground black pepper
Thinly sliced cabbage

Coat skillet and crock pot with vegetable oil spray. Brown meat, leaving it in chunks, and drain. Add all ingredients to crock pot. Cook on high for 1 hour, then reduce to low for 2 hours, or cook on low for several hours, until potatoes are tender. (Salt may be reduced by substituting no-salt tomatoes, one 8 ounce can no-salt tomato sauce, one 8 ounce can regular tomato sauce, and no-salt corn.) Yield: Approximately 3 quarts.

BRUNSWICK STEW

1 pound ground beef
2 small onions (or 1 large onion)
2 cups tomatoes
2 cups corn, fresh or frozen

1/2 cup green pepper
Salt and pepper to taste
Dash of cayenne pepper (optional)

Brown ground beef and onions together, add tomatoes and green peppers. Cover and cook slowly for 30 minutes. Add corn and seasoning and stir well; cook slowly for another 30 minutes. Stir often; water may be added if too thick.

EASY BRUNSWICK STEW

1 (24 oz.) can Brunswick stew
1 (12 oz.) can barbecue pork
1 (12 oz.) can barbecue beef
1 (17 oz.) can creamed style corn

1/4 cup barbecue sauce
Juice of 2 lemons
1 Tbs. Worcestershire sauce

Combine all ingredients in a large saucepan; heat until bubbling, stirring occasionally to prevent sticking. Yield: 5 servings.

RANCH STEW

1 Tbs. fat	2 cups whole kernel corn
1 pound ground beef	2 cups kidney beans
1 medium onion, chopped	2 cups canned tomatoes
1 green pepper, diced	1 tsp. chili powder
3/4 tsp. salt	Pepper to taste (optional)

Put fat in heavy kettle, add beef, onion, and green pepper. Cook, stirring occasionally, until meat is browned and onion and pepper are tender. Drain corn, beans and tomatoes. Add liquids to meat and cook until liquid is reduced to about half. Add corn, beans and tomatoes, chili powder and salt. Mix together and heat thoroughly, stirring occasionally to prevent sticking. Serve at once. Yield: 6 servings.

MEATBALL STEW

1 pound ground beef	2 Tbs. flour
1 egg, beaten	3 cups water
1 cup bread crumbs	1 cup red wine (may use 1 cup
1/2 tsp. salt	water instead)
1/4 tsp. pepper	6 carrots, peeled and cut in 1 inch
1/3 cup oil	pieces
	6 potatoes, peeled and quartered
	1 onion, quartered

Combine beef, egg, crumbs, salt and pepper. Form into 1-inch balls. Brown in oil. Remove from oil and stir in flour until brown. Add water and wine, stir until thickened. Add vegetables approximately 20 minutes before placing meatballs back in stew. Simmer for 20-30 minutes or until vegetables are tender. May need to add more water as stew cooks. Yield: 5 or 6 servings.

BEEF STEW

Carrots, sliced thin	Cajun seasoning, or garlic and chili spice
Potatoes, sliced thick	Whole kernel corn
Onion	Tomatoes
Salt and pepper	Celery

Use the amount that fits your needs.

TEXAS RANGER STEW

1-1/2 pounds lean ground beef	2 Tbs. Worcestershire sauce
1 small onion, chopped	1-1/2 tsp. salt
1 (28 oz.) can peeled whole tomatoes	1/2 tsp. dried thyme
1 (10-3/4 oz.) can beef broth	1/8 tsp. pepper
1 soup can water	2 (6 oz.) cans sliced mushrooms
1/4 cup ketchup	1 cup instant rice

In a large skillet on medium high heat, brown ground beef and onion; drain fat. Add tomatoes, broth, water, ketchup, Worcestershire sauce, salt, thyme, pepper and mushrooms. Bring to a boil. Reduce heat and simmer, uncovered, for 5 minutes. Stir in rice, cover and set aside for 5 minutes. Wonderful with corn bread. Yield: 6 servings.

BEEF & WINTER VEGETABLE STEW

2 pounds beef for stew, cut into 1-inch pieces	1 cup dark beer or nonalcoholic beer
2 Tbs. vegetable oil	1 pound small red potatoes, quartered
2 cups chopped onions	3 medium carrots, cut into 1/2 inch pieces
1/2 tsp. salt	2 Tbs. cornstarch, dissolved in 3 Tbs.
1/4 tsp. pepper	water
1 (13-3/4 to 14-1/2 oz.) can ready-to-serve beef broth	Chopped fresh parsley (optional)

Heat oil in Dutch oven over medium heat until hot. Cook and stir beef and onions in two batches; brown evenly. Pour off drippings. Return beef and onions to pan. Season with salt and pepper.

Stir in broth and beer. Bring to a boil; reduce heat to low. Cover tightly and simmer gently 1-1/4 hours.

Add vegetables. Bring to a boil; reduce heat to low. Cover tightly and continue simmering 20-30 minutes or until beef and vegetables are tender.

Stir in cornstarch mixture. Bring to a boil; cook and stir one minute or until thickened.

STEW BEEF

2 pounds stew beef
1 can cream of mushroom soup
1 pkg. Lipton onion soup mix
1/2 soup can of water

Mix all ingredients and cook in crock pot all day. Serve over rice or creamed potatoes.

HELPFUL HINTS

SOUPS/SAUCES/STEWS

Frozen gravies or sauces may be a little thicker after thawing than when they were freshly made. Adding a little appropriate liquid—milk, broth, bouillon or wine—will thin them to the desired consistency.

Canned cream soups make excellent sauces for vegetables, fish, etc. Serve celery soup with lobster, black bean or onion soup with cauliflower, and tomato soup with lamb chops.

If soup tastes very salty, a raw piece of potato placed in the pot will absorb the salt.

Do not despair if you have over salted the gravy. Stir in some instant mashed potatoes and you will repair the damage. Just add a little more liquid to offset the thickening.

An excellent thickener for soups is a little oatmeal. It will add flavor and richness to almost any soup.

If sweet cream is just starting to sour, restore the sweetness with a pinch of baking soda.

To prevent scorching when scalding milk, first rinse pan in hot water.

Instant potatoes are a good thickener for stews.

If you have over-salted soup or vegetables, add cut raw potatoes and discard once they have cooked and absorbed the salt.

A teaspoon each of cider vinegar and sugar added to salty soup or vegetables will also remedy the situation.

If you have over-sweetened a dish, add salt.

Drop a lettuce leaf into a pot of homemade soup to absorb excess grease from the top.

If time allows, the best method of removing fat is refrigeration until the fat hardens. If you put a piece of waxed paper over the top of the soup, etc. it can be peeled right off, along with the hardened fat.

Ice cubes will also eliminate the fat from soup and stew. Just drop a few into the pot and stir; the fat will cling to the cubes; discard the cubes before they melt. Or, wrap ice cubes in paper towel or cheesecloth and skim over the top.

A leaf of lettuce dropped into the pot absorbs the grease from the top of the soup. Remove the lettuce and throw it away as soon as it has served its purpose.

One tablespoon unflavored gelatin will thicken 2 cups liquid.

SALADS

Lemon gelatine dissolved in 2 cups of hot apricot nectar with 1 teaspoon of grated lemon added for zip makes a perfect base for jellied fruit salad.

Pour water into mold and then drain before pouring in mixture to be chilled. Mixture will come out of mold easier.

Lettuce will not "rust" in the refrigerator if it is wrapped in paper toweling.

If fresh vegetables are wilted or blemished, pick off the brown edges, sprinkle with cool water, wrap in paper towel and refrigerate for an hour or so.

Perk up soggy lettuce by adding lemon juice to a bowl of cold water and soak for an hour in the refrigerator.

Lettuce and celery keep longer if you store them in paper bags instead of cellophane.

To remove the core from a head of lettuce, hit the core end once against the counter sharply. The core will loosen and pull out easily.

Lettuce: To separate a tight head, hold under running water or pour water from a pitcher over it.

Sour cream added to mayonnaise for any kind of salad mixing provides that special "umph" that so many salads lack. If you are not "sourminded" use plain whipping cream.

GRAVY

Pale gravy may be browned by adding a bit of instant coffee straight from the jar...no bitter taste, either.

If you will brown the flour well before adding to the liquid when making gravy, you will avoid pale or lumpy gravy.

A different way of browning flour is to put it in a custard cup placed beside meat in the oven. Once the meat is done, the flour will be nice and brown.

Thin gravy can be thickened by adding a mixture of flour or cornstarch and water, which has been mixed to a smooth paste, added gradually, stirring constantly, while bringing to a boil.

Lumpless gravy can be your triumph if you add a pinch of salt to the flour before mixing it with water.

A small amount of baking soda added to gravy will eliminate excess grease.

If gravy is too greasy, a bit of baking soda can be added without affecting the taste of the gravy.

Pour pan drippings into a tall jar. The grease will rise to the top in minutes and can be removed for grease free gravy.

Soup Accompaniments

Clear Soups:	crisp crackers, cheese pastry, cheese-spread toast strips.
Cream Soups:	popcorn, seeded crackers, pretzels, pickles and olives.
Chowders and Meat Soups:	melba toast, sour pickles, oyster crackers, bread sticks, Relishes, toasted garlic bread.

MEATS, EGGS, ETC.—
HELPFUL HINTS

MEATS

When preparing sauces and marinades for red meats, use little oil. Fat from the meat will render out during cooking and will provide plenty of flavor. Certain meats, like ribs, pot roast, sausage and others, can be par boiled before grilling to reduce the fat content.

When shopping for red meats, buy the leanest cuts you can find. Fat will show up as an opaque white coating, and it can also run though the meat fibers themselves, as marbling. Although much outer fat (the white coating) can be trimmed away, there is not much to be done about the marbling. Stay away from well marbled cuts of meat.

Home from work late with no time for marinating meat? Pound meat lightly with a mallet or rolling pin. Pierce with a fork and sprinkle lightly with meat tenderizer and add marinade. Refrigerate for about 20 minutes and you will have succulent, tender meat.

Marinating is a cinch if you use a plastic ziplock bag. The meat stays in the marinade and it is easy to turn and rearrange. Cleanup is easy. Just toss the bag.

Meat may slice more thinly if it is partially frozen.

Tomatoes added to roasts will help tenderize them naturally. Tomatoes contain an acid that works well to break down meats.

Always cut meats across the grain when possible; they will be easier to eat and have a better appearance.

When frying meat, try sprinkling paprika over it and it will turn golden brown.

Thaw all meats in the refrigerator for maximum safety.

Refrigerate poultry promptly after purchasing. Keep it in the coldest section of your refrigerator for up to 2 days. For longer storage, freeze the poultry. Never leave poultry at room temperature for more than 2 hours.

If you are microwaving skinned chicken, be sure to cover the baking dish with vented clear plastic wrap to keep the chicken moist.

Lemon juice rubbed on fish before cooking will enhance the flavor and help maintain a good color.

To make scaling a fish easier, try rubbing vinegar on the scales first.

For extra juicy, extra nutritious hamburgers add 1/4 cup evaporated milk per pound of meat before shaping.

To reheat roast, wrap in aluminum foil and heat in a slow oven.

To remove fish odor from hands, utensils and dishcloths, use one teaspoon baking soda to quart of water.

TENDERIZING METHODS

Boiled Meat   Add one tablespoon of vinegar to the cooking water.

Tough Meat   Make a marinade of equal parts cooking vinegar and heated bouillon. Marinade for 2 hours.

Steak   Rub a mixture of cooking vinegar and oil. Allow too stand for 2 hours.

WHAT TO SERVE WITH FISH

Cod, Creamed Salt	Boiled Potatoes, Cole Slaw, Toast and Green Salad
Codfish Cakes	Baked Beans, Bacon, Green Salad
Fillets, Broiled	Baked Potatoes, Scalloped Tomatoes
Fish, Fried	French Fried Potatoes, Tossed Salad
Halibut, Broiled	Broccoli, Corn Fired in Butter
Lobster	Steamed Clams, Baked Potato
Lobster Newburg	French Fried Onions, Watermelon Pickle
Oysters, Scalloped	Hashed Brown Potatoes, Broccoli
Salmon, Baked	Baked Potato, Tossed Salad, Greens
Salmon, Broiled	Hollandaise Sauce, Mashed Potatoes, Peas
Shrimp, Fried	Mixed Vegetable, Tomato and Onion Salad

Snapper, Baked	Broccoli with Hollandaise Sauce, Mashed Potatoes, Tossed Salad
Sole, Filet	Cole Slaw or Dill Pickles, Tartar Sauce
Trout	Potatoes Diced in Cream, Asparagus, Pickle

WHAT TO SERVE WITH CHICKEN

Chicken, Fricassee	Dumplings, Corn on the Cob
Chicken, Fried	Lima Beans, Mashed Potatoes, Corn on the Cob and Biscuits
Chicken, Roast	Candied Sweet Potatoes, Cauliflower
Chicken Pie	Green Peas, Tossed Salad
Chicken Salad	Potato Chips, Celery, Pickles, and Peas

WHAT TO SERVE WITH MEATS

Bacon	Corn Fritters, Maple Syrup
Chipped Beef	Baked Potato, Green Salad
Corn Beef Hash	Poached Eggs, Green Salad
Frankfurter	Sauerkraut, Baked Beans
Ham, Cold	Baked Beans, Relish, Egg Rolls, Potato Salad, Dill Pickles
Ham, Baked	Sweet Potatoes, Spinach, Rice, Fried Pineapple Rings, Parsley Potatoes, Asparagus
Meat Loaf	Baked Potato, Canned Tomatoes, French Fried Potatoes, Asparagus
Pork, Roast	Brown Potatoes, Applesauce or Fruit Salad, Sweet Potatoes, Sauerkraut, Mashed Potatoes, Celery or Apple Salad
Hamburger	Toasted Buns, Sweet Onion Rings, Potato Salad, Carrots

Ham Steak	Buttered Rice, Glazed Pineapple, Fried Eggs, Hash Brown Potatoes, Hominy, Corn Muffins, Fried Bananas
Lamb Chops	Buttered Parsley Potatoes, Succotash, Browned Potatoes, Spinach, Peas
Lamb, Roast	Mashed Potatoes, Currant Jelly
Lamb Stew	Dumplings, Green Salad
Liver	Bacon, Corn Bread
Pork Chops	Scalloped Potatoes, Fried Apple Rings, Mashed Potatoes, Cabbage Salad
Sausage	Fried Apples, Corn Bread, Mashed Potatoes, Pickled Peaches
Tongue, Boiled	Buttered Noodles, Spinach
Veal Cutlet	Baked Potato, Tossed Salad

<u>Cooking Tips</u>

After stewing a chicken for diced meat for casseroles, etc., let cool in broth before cutting into chunks; it will have twice the flavor.

To slice meat into thin strips, as for Chinese dishes, partially freeze and it will slice more easily.

A roast with the bone in will cook faster than a boneless roast. The bone carries the heat to the inside of the roast quicker.

Never cook a roast cold. Let stand for at least an hour at room temperature. Brush with oil before and during roasting; the oil will seal in the juices.

For a juicier hamburger, add cold water to the beef before grilling (1-2 cup to 1 pound of meat).

To freeze meatballs, place them on a cookie sheet until frozen. Place in plastic bags and they will stay separated so that you may remove as many as you want.

Start hamburger in a salted pan, without oil. Brown as usual. Salt will pull the grease from the hamburger so it can easily be drained off.

Fish

Dip into scalding water for a minute to scale easily.

Thaw fish or wild game in milk. It will remove the strong odor and taste.

Make sure that gills are bright red, eyes bright and full and flesh firm and springy when selecting fish.

A teaspoon of vinegar added to water in which white fish is boiled improves flavor and makes flesh firmer.

Meat, Fish and Poultry Notes

Baking fish on a bed of celery and onions will add to the taste as well as keep the fish from sticking.

Coating will adhere to chicken better if it has been chilled for an hour before cooking.

Sprinkle salt in the frying pan before adding mean and there will be less grease splattered.

For a juicier burger rub both sides with cold water before grilling.

Place cold water and cornstarch or flour in a jar with tight lid. Shake the jar until liquid is well mixed and lumps are gone. Then slowly add this mixture to pan drippings and stir while bringing gravy to a boil.

Always roast poultry breast side down so the white meat will not dry out. Turn the bird for the last portion of cooking so that it will brown well.

Rubbing poultry with salt and lemon juice will lessen any unpleasant odor.

Unwaxed dental floss is good for trussing poultry because it will not burn.

Meat loaf will not crack when baking if it is rubbed with cold water before going in the oven.

Adding cold water to the bottom of the broiling pan before cooking meat helps absorb smoke and grease and makes clean up easier.

To speed up hamburger cooking, poke a hole in their centers when shaping. This causes the center to cook quickly and the holes are gone when the hamburgers are finished cooking.

A large roast can be carved more easily after it stands for about 30 minutes.

Meat or chicken may be floured easily by placing in a bag with flour and shaking well.

Add a little lemon juice to water while boiling to make fish firm and white.

To avoid odors while cooking fish, cover with browned butter and lemon juice.

To prevent splashing when frying meat, sprinkle a little salt into the pan before putting the fat in.

The odor from baking or boiling salmon may be eliminated by squeezing lemon juice on both sides of each salmon steak or on the cut surface of the salmon and letting it stand in the refrigerator for 1 hour or longer before cooking.

When frying fish, boil vinegar in a pan of water to help kill fish odor.

CHEESE

Save leftover piece of cheese and place in a jar with a little wine until you have enough to serve. Very nice flavor.

Wrap cheese in a rag which has been dampened with vinegar. This will retard mold. Place a lump of sugar in with cheese when wrapping. This will absorb moisture and prevent mold.

To keep fresh, cover with cloth moistened in vinegar.

Chill cheese to grate it more easily.

Wrap cheese in cloth soaked in vinegar to keep from hardening.

Cheese will not dry out if it is wrapped in a cloth dampened with vinegar.

Cheeses should be served at room temperature (approximately 70 degrees).

Chunks of cheese will keep longer if covered with a vegetable cooking spray and stored in the refrigerator.

MILK

Never put a cover on anything that is cooked in milk unless you want to spend hours cleaning up the stove when it boils over.

Cream will whip faster and better if you will first chill the cream, bowl, and beaters well.

Soupy whipped cream can be saved by adding an egg white, then chilling thoroughly. Reheat for a fluffy surprise!

A few drops of lemon juice added to whipping cream helps it whip faster and better.

Cream whipped ahead of time will not separate if you add 1/4 teaspoon unflavored gelatin per cup of cream.

A dampened and folded dishtowel placed under the bowl in which you are whipping cream will keep the bowl from dancing all over the counter top.

Rinse a pan in cold water before scalding milk to prevent sticking.

If the whipping cream looks as though it is not going to whip, add 3 or 4 drops of lemon juice or a bit of plain gelatin powder to it and it probably will.

Rinse pan in cold water before scalding milk to prevent sticking.

Remove the burnt taste from scorched milk by putting the pan in cold water and adding a pinch of salt to the milk.

Sour milk may be used in baking instead of sweet milk by adding 1/4 to 1/2 teaspoon baking soda for each cup milk, to recipe, depending upon acidity of sour milk. Sift baking soda with flour rather than with sour milk. One-cup thin sour cream may be substituted for 3 tablespoons butter and 3/4 cup sour milk in any sour milk recipe.

EGGS

Eggs that have been warmed to room termperature will beat better than chilled eggs.

Eggs should be refrigerated immediately to retain freshness.

To store leftover egg yolks cover with water before refrigerating.

Beaten egg white: Add 1 tablespoon cold water to increase its bulk.

To seal eggs that crack while boiling, add 1 Tablespoon vinegar or 1 teaspoon salt.

Hard-boiled eggs: Place in warm water for a minute, if chilled, before putting in boiling water. Cook only 10-12 minutes in steady boiling water. Plunge immediately in cold water.

Poach leftover egg whites & yolks, drain and cool then sieve or grate to use in salads or sandwiches.

In making custard with only egg yolks, substitute 2 yolks for 1 whole egg.

Hard-boiled eggs will peel easily when cracked and placed in cold water immediately after taking out of the hot water.

When recipe calls for adding raw eggs to hot mixture, always begin by adding a small amount of hot mixture to the beaten eggs slowly to avoid curdling, then add all back to mixture.

To divide an egg, beat it and measure in measuring cup.

A little vinegar added to water will keep white from boiling out of cracked eggs.

A speck of egg yolk in the whites may be most easily removed with the edge of an eggshell.

Dip the knife in water to cut hard-cooked eggs in smooth slices.

Some of the eggs may be left out of a custard recipe by substituting 1/2 tablespoon Cornstarch for each egg omitted.

Cracked eggs should only be used in dishes that are thoroughly cooked; they may contain bacteria.

The freshness of eggs can be tested by placing them in a large bowl of cold water; if they float, do not use them.

To preserve leftover egg yolks for future use, place them into a small bowl and add two tablespoons of salad oil. Then put into refrigerator. The egg yolks will remain soft and fresh, and egg yolks kept in this way can be used in many ways.

You may determine the age of an egg by placing it in the bottom of a bowl of cold water. If it lies on its side, it is strictly fresh. If it stands at an angle, it is at least three days old and ten days old if it stands on end.

To keep egg yolks from crumbling when slicing hard-cooked eggs, wet the knife before each cut.

Breadcrumbs added to scrambled eggs will improve the flavor and make larger helpings possible.

A tablespoon of vinegar added to the water when poaching eggs will help set the whites so they will not spread.

When cooking eggs it helps prevent cracking if you wet the shells in cold water before placing them in boiling water.

Add a little vinegar to the water when an egg cracks during boiling. It will help seal the egg.

When you cook eggs in the shell, put a big teaspoon of salt in the water. Then the shell will not crack.

Set eggs in pan of warm water before using as this releases all white from shells.

Egg whites for meringue should be set out to room temperature before beating, then they can be beaten to greater volume.

Eggshells can be removed easily from hot hard-boiled eggs if they are quickly rinsed in cold water.

To determine if an egg is fresh without breaking the shell: Immerse the egg in a pan of salted, cool water; it if sinks to the bottom, it is fresh, if it rises to the surface, throw it away.

RICE/PASTA

Add a teaspoon of lemon juice to each quart of water to cook rice. The grains will stay white and separated.

After purchasing, store dried pasta, rice (except brown rice), and whole grains in tightly covered containers in a cool, dry place. Refrigerate brown rice. Refrigerate or freeze grains if they will not be used within 5 months.

A tablespoon of cooking oil in water when cooking spaghetti or macaroni will prevent sticking together.

Start any pasta in cold water. Bring to a full boil, cover and remove from heat. Let stand until pasta is desired consistency. Drain and add a small amount of oil to keep it from sticking and becoming sticky.

To cook fool proof rice, use three times as much water as called for in a large pot. Wash rice thoroughly before cooking. Add rice slowly. When water comes to a boil, do not stir. Drain and rinse when done. Rice will usually float to top when done. Do not salt while cooking.

FRUITS/NUTS

Grate lemons and oranges before cutting. Freeze grated rind and use with bottle or frozen juice in recipes.

Place lemons and oranges in hot water before squeezing. This will render more juice.

To soften candied fruit, soak overnight in fruit juice.

To peel coconut: Make 2 holes, drain juice (milk) and place in oven and heat until hot to the touch. Remove and tap all over, especially the ends, with a hammer. Give it a good hard knock and the shell will crack open. Lift off shell and peel brown skin covering the meat. Cool before grating.

To grate coconut: Break meat in small pieces. Place milk from coconut in blender and if there is not enough to cover cutting blades, add sweet milk. Start blender (be sure top is on) and add small pieces of coconut through the small opening. Grate only a small amount at a time. Pour meat and juice through a strainer, being sure to save this juice to use in grating another batch.

To keep limes fresh: Place in a closed fruit jar and refrigerate.

A simple way to flame fruit garnish or desserts for any festive occasion, place sugar cubes, moistened with lemon Extract and light just as serving.

Fruits: When dried fruits for cakes are washed they should be thoroughly dried before adding to batter to avoid heavy texture. Juices of spiced and pickled fruits are good for basting meats, especially ham or tongue. Sliced bananas and freshly sliced apples and peaches will not turn dark if coated with lemon juice.

Pineapple: Never use the raw fruit in gelatin desserts; it contains an enzyme which prevents jellying. Cook well first or use canned.

Almonds: Add a few drops of green vegetable coloring to chopped blanched almonds for mock pistachio nuts.

If it is important to you to get walnut meats out whole, soak the nuts overnight in salt water before you crack them.

Seeds and nuts, both shelled and unshelled, keep best and longest when stored in the freezer. Nuts in the shell crack more easily when frozen. Nuts and seeds can be used directly from the freezer.

Marshmallows: To cut easily use damp scissors—also fine for dates and figs.

Nuts: To blanch easily, pour over boiling water, let stand a few minutes until skins loosen and plunge nuts into cold water. Rub off brown skins between towels. Salt nuts in oven instead of skillet to prevent scorching. Meats of many nuts are more easily removed if nuts are boiled in water 15 minutes, then cooled and cracked. Pecan kernels come out whole with no injury to flavor.

Popcorn: To make every grain pop, cover bottom of wire popper with corn, drench with water and shake out just before placing over heat.

Raisins: To separate seeded raisins wash whole package in cold water.

Lemon-Aid:

Look what a lemon will do …

The ordinary lemon can be used for a quick, easy, and inexpensive beauty treatment. Here are just a few ideas of what the lemon can do for you.

1. A few drops of lemon in a favorite shampoo leaves the hair shiny and squeaky.

2. A fresh lemon squeezed into warm water is a great rinse for soap dulled hair.

3. The lemon is a good astringent for your face. Squeeze a fresh lemon into the rinse water for a tingling splash. Rinse with clear water.

4. Keep a lemon half near the sink to rub over your hands to help remove stains and food odors.

5. Rub rough elbows with lemon halves to get rid of dry, scaly skin and help whiten skin. If lemons are at room temperature, they will be juicier and more comfortable.

SEASONINGS

Brown sugar will not harden if an apple slice is placed in the container.

If your brown sugar is brick-hard, put your cheese-grater to work and grate the amount you need.

It is important when and how you add salt in cooking. To blend with soups and sauces, put it in early, but add it to meats jut before taking from the stove. In cake ingredients, salt can be mixed with the eggs. When cooking vegetables always salt the water in which they are cooked. Put salt in the pan when frying fish.

For quick and handy seasoning while cooking, keep on hand a large shaker containing 6 parts of salt and 1 of pepper.

When food is too salty add a cut raw potato, and then discard the potato once it is boiled.

If the dish is too sweet, add salt. On a main dish you can add a teaspoon of vinegar.

If the food is too sharp, a teaspoon of sugar will soften the taste.

If a main dish or vegetable is too sweet add a teaspoon or two of vinegar.

Sugar (Brown): To prevent hardening, place in tightly closed container.

SEASONED SALT

26 oz. box of salt
1-1/2 oz. ground black pepper
2 oz. ground red pepper
1 oz. garlic powder
1 oz. chili powder
1 oz. Accent

Mix well. Good to season all meats. Also good on baked potatoes instead of regular salt and pepper.

BREADS

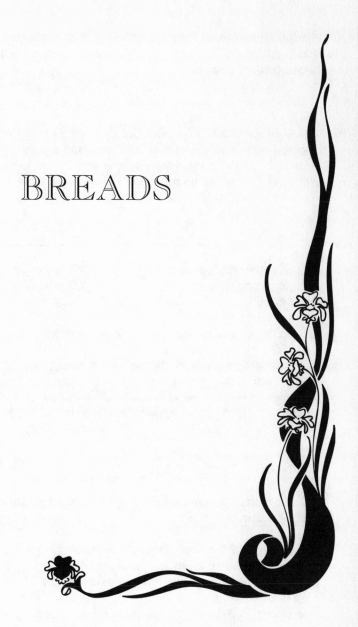

ANGEL BISCUITS—I

5 cups all-purpose flour	1 cup shortening
1 tsp. soda	2 cups buttermilk
3 tsp. baking powder	1 pkg. yeast
1-1/2 tsp. salt	2 Tbs. warm water
2 Tbs. sugar	

Sift dry ingredients together. Cut in shortening. Dissolve yeast in 2 table-spoons warm water. Add milk and yeast mixture to dry ingredients. Mix well. Brush top with melted butter. Refrigerate until ready to use. Shape as for biscuits. Let rise (about 45 minutes). Bake at 400 degrees for 12-15 minutes.

ANGEL BISCUITS—II

1 pkg. active dry yeast	1 Tbs. sugar
1/2 cup warm water	2/3 cup shortening
4-1/2 cups self-rising flour	1 cup milk or 1-1/4 cups buttermilk

Grease three 8-inch round layer pans. Dissolve yeast in warm water and set aside. Stir in yeast water and milk until dough begins to pull away from bowl. Turn out onto floured surface and knead gently 10-12 times. Roll 1/2-inch thick and cut with a 2-inch cutter. Place 8-10 biscuits in each prepared pan. Cover with wax paper. Set aside in warm place to rise for 1 hour. Heat oven to 400 degrees. Bake 20-25 minutes or until brown. Yield: 2 to 2 -1/2 dozen biscuits.

QUICK BUTTERMILK BISCUITS

1/2 cup butter or margarine	3/4 cup buttermilk
2 cups self-rising flour	Butter or margarine, melted

Cut 1/2 cup butter into flour with a pastry blender until mixture resembles course meal. Add buttermilk, stirring until dry ingredients are moistened. Turn dough out onto a lightly floured surface, and knead lightly 3 or 4 times.

Roll dough to 3/4-inch thickness; cut with a 2-inch biscuit cutter. Place on a lightly greased baking sheet. Bake at 425 degrees for 13 to 15 minutes. Brush with melted butter. Yield: 1 dozen.

CHEDDAR BISCUITS

2-1/4 cups all-purpose flour	1/2 cup butter
1 Tbs. baking powder	1 egg
1/2 Tbs. salt	1 cup buttermilk
1/8 cup granulated sugar	1 cup cheddar cheese, grated

Preheat oven to 375 degrees. In a large mixing bowl, combine flour, baking powder, salt and sugar. Cut butter into small pieces and add to flour mixture. Using a pastry blender, cut in the butter until it is the size of small peas. Stir in egg, buttermilk and cheese; mix until the dough just comes together. Roll out on a lightly floured board to 1-inch thickness. Cut into 3-inch round biscuits and bake on a lightly greased baking sheet at 375 degrees for 20 minutes.

MOM'S BUTTERMILK BISCUITS

2 cups all-purpose flour	1/2 tsp. salt
2 tsp. baking powder	1/4 cup shortening
1/2 tsp. baking soda	3/4 cup buttermilk

In a bowl, combine the flour, baking powder, baking soda and salt; cut in shortening until the mixture resembles coarse crumbs. Stir in buttermilk; knead dough gently. Roll out to 1/2-inch thickness. Cut with a 2-1/2-inch biscuit cutter and place on a lightly grease baking sheet. Bake at 450 degrees for 10-15 minutes or until golden brown. Yield: 10 biscuits.

ICE BOX ROLLS

1/3 cup shortening	1/4 cup warm water
1/3 cup sugar	1 pkg. dry yeast
1/2 cup boiling water	1 egg
1/2 cup cold water	3-1/2 cups plain flour

Cream shortening, add sugar and salt; add boiling water and stir until dissolved. Add cold water; mix well. Dissolve yeast in warm water, add to shortening mixture. Add eggs and flour, mix well. Refrigerate overnight. Turn out on floured board 2 hours before time to bake and shape into rolls. Bake in 450 degrees oven for 10 or 15 minutes.

CINNAMON BISCUITS

5 cups self-rising flour	2 cups buttermilk
1/3 cup sugar	5 Tbs. yeast dissolved in 1-1/4 cup
1 cup Crisco	lukewarm water)
1 tsp. soda	Raisins (optional)

Combine dry ingredients. Cut in shortening. Add yeast and buttermilk, and raisins if desired. Roll and cut. Bake at 450 degrees about 10-15 minutes. This is better made the day before baking. Dough will last about 5 days, covered and refrigerated. Mix four tablespoons of cinnamon with sugar and sprinkle in between the biscuits and over the top.

Glaze:
Confectioner's sugar, Butter the size of an egg, and cinnamon (to taste)

CINNAMON ROLLS

2-1/2 cups warm water	4-1/2 cups flour, plain
2 pkgs. yeast	1 box yellow cake mix with pudding
Brown sugar	Cinnamon

Dissolve yeast in warm water. Add cake mix and flour. Kneed dough. Place back in bowl and cover with towel. Let rise till double in warm place (about 15-20 minutes). Roll out half of the dough at a time. Roll into rectangle. Sprinkle with brown sugar and cinnamon. Roll up and slice. Place close together on greased cookie sheet. Let rise till double. Bake at 350 degrees for 15-20 minutes. Frost with powdered sugar and milk icing (optional).

NITE OWL SWEET ROLLS

1 cup pecan pieces	1 sm. pkg. reg. butterscotch pudding
1 pkg. (25 oz.) frozen	1/3 cup butter, cut in small pieces
white dinner rolls	2/3 cup brown sugar, packed

Spread nuts in bottom of greased 9 x 13-inch baking dish. Arrange frozen rolls over nuts. Sprinkle with brown sugar, then dry pudding mix. Place butter pieces over top. Cover and thaw overnight. Bake uncovered at 350 degrees for 30 minutes or until rolls are baked. Turn immediately out into a serving dish.

INSTANT MIRACLE ROLLS

3 pkgs. dry yeast
1/2 cup warm water
5 cups self-rising flour (unsifted)
1/4 cup sugar

1 tsp. soda
1 cup shortening
2 cups lukewarm buttermilk

Dissolve yeast in warm water and set aside. Mix flour, sugar and soda. Cut in shortening. Add buttermilk and yeast, and mix. Place desired amount of dough on floured cloth, pat out; cut with biscuit cutter. Let warm to room temperature before baking in 350 degrees oven, 10-15 minutes. (May be mixed, rolled, cut and placed in oven immediately, if desired; or may be taken from refrigerator and placed immediately in oven, without being allowed to rise.)

Mixture can be stored in covered bowl in refrigerator and used as needed. Keeps several weeks.

NO-KNEAD REFRIGERATOR ROLLS

1-1/2 quarts (6 cups) water
1 oz. active dry yeast
5 pounds White Lily self-rising flour

7 oz. (1 cup) sugar
3/4 lb. (2 cups) all-purpose
   shortening

Dissolve yeast in 1 cup very warm (105-115 degrees) water. Stir flour and sugar together in large bowl. Cut in shortening. Add yeast water and 5 cups cold water. Stir until well blended and elastic strands form. Place in greased bowl. Cover tightly and refrigerate until ready to use (up to 3 days).

About two hours before baking remove from refrigerator. *Turn out onto floured surface and roll out 1/2-inch thick. Cut with 2-inch biscuit cutter. Shape each piece into a ball and place on greased baking pan. Cover with wax paper and let proof in a warm place (84 degrees) until double in size. (This may take as long as 1 to 2 hours, depending on age and temperature of dough)

* About 15 ounces of dough for a dozen rolls.

To bake immediately: Substitute warm water for cold and do not refrigerate the dough. Let dough rise in bowl about 30 minutes. Cut, roll, and shape as above. Let proof until doubled. Bake as above.

YEAST ROLLS—I

4 cups self-rising flour	1 egg
1 pkg. yeast (mix into flour)	2 cups lukewarm water
3/4 cup Crisco (work into flour)	1/4 cup sugar

Mix into batter and put in refrigerator. Fill muffin cups 1/2 full and bake at 425 degrees for 10-12 minutes. Will keep up to two weeks.

YEAST ROLLS —II

1/2 cup Crisco	2 eggs, beaten
1/3 cup sugar	2 small pkgs. yeast dissolved in
1 cup sweet milk, scalded	3 Tbs. warm water
1 cup HOT water	6 cups self-rising flour

Combine milk, water, Crisco and sugar until dissolved and cool. Add eggs, yeast and blend. Then add flour. Let sit overnight in covered container. Take out early in the morning and roll out on flour covered board. Let rise at room temperature and then brush top with melted butter. Bake at 450 degrees until brown.

QUICK ROLLS

1/2 cup margarine, melted
1 cup sour cream or lowfat plain yogurt
2 cups biscuit baking mix

Combine all ingredients; stir until moistened. Drop 1 tablespoon of mixture into regular muffin tins or 1-2 teaspoons if using mini muffin tins.

Bake in preheated 400 degrees oven for 15 minutes or until lightly browned. Yield: Approximately 20 rolls or 35 mini rolls if using regular muffin tins

PECAN BREAD

1 egg
1 cup sugar
1-1/2 cups milk
4 cups flour

4 tsp. baking powder
1 cup pecans
2 Tbs. butter or shortening

Beat egg in large bowl. Add sugar, then alternately milk and flour sifted with baking powder. Mix well, add pecans. Pour in greased pan. Let stand 20 minutes. Bake 1 hour in slow oven.

ONION DILL BREAD

1 (1/4 oz.) pkg. active dry yeast
3-1/2 cups bread flour
1/4 tsp. salt
1 unbeaten egg, room temperature
1/4 cup water
3/4 cup cream-style cottage cheese

3/4 cup sour cream
3 Tbs. sugar
3 Tbs. minced dried onion
2 Tbs. dill seed
1-1/2 Tbs. butter or margarine

In bread machine pan, place first four ingredients in order given. In a saucepan, combine remaining ingredients and heat just until warm (do not boil). Pour into bread pan. Select "white bread" setting. Bake according to bread machine directions. Yield: 1 loaf 1-1/2 pounds.

HOMEMADE WHITE BREAD

2 pkg. granular yeast
1/4 cup lukewarm water
1 tsp. sugar
3 tsp. salt

4 Tbs. shortening
4 Tbs. sugar
4 cups milk, scalded
12 cups flour (approximate)

Add yeast to lukewarm water and 1 teaspoon sugar. Let stand 5 minutes. Add salt, shortening and remaining sugar to milk and cool to lukewarm. Add yeast mixture and 6 cups flour. Beat well. Add enough more flour to make a soft dough. Place remaining flour on board, turn out dough on floured board and knead until smooth and elastic. Place in greased bowl. Turn over so that greased side is up. Cover with cloth and let rise until double in bulk. Punch down and let rise a second time. Cut dough into 4 equal parts; knead into loaves and place in greased bread pans. Grease tops, cover with cloth and let rise until doubled in bulk. Bake in hot oven (400 degrees) 10 minutes, reduce temperature to 350 degrees and bake 35 or 40 minutes longer. Yield: 4 one-pound loaves.

Variations: If one desires, raisins may be added to the scalded milk, which makes delicious raisin bread. Also, this same dough makes wonderful cinnamon rolls. Also, if desirable, one can use whole wheat flour instead of white and use molasses instead of sugar, which makes real delicious whole wheat bread.

BANANA BREAD

1/2 cup butter or other shortening
1 cup sugar
3 large or 4 small bananas, mashed
2 eggs well beaten
2-1/2 cups plain flour

1 tsp. soda
1 tsp. salt
1 tsp. vanilla
1 cup chopped nuts if desired

Cream butter and sugar; add mashed bananas and eggs. Sift dry ingredients and combine. Add nuts and vanilla. Bake in greased loaf pan 45 minutes at 350 degrees.

CORNBREAD DRESSING

3 eggs, boiled and chopped
2 cups crumbled cornbread
2 cups yeast bread crumbs
4 cups chicken broth

1/2 cup butter or other shortening, unless broth is fatty
1 onion, finely diced
Salt and pepper to taste

Combine all ingredients and mix well. Bake for 30 minutes at 450 degrees.

MONKEY BREAD—I

4 (10-each) cans biscuit
1 cup sugar
2 Tbs. cinnamon
1 stick margarine, melted

Grease a tube cake pan with solid shortening. Mix sugar and cinnamon in covered bowl or Ziploc bag. Doing one can at a time, cut biscuits into quarters. Put quarters into bowl or bag; shake well to coat pieces with cinnamon and sugar. Layer in pan and drizzle with margarine. Repeat with rest of biscuits. Bake at 300 degrees until golden brown. Turn out onto serving plate.

MONKEY BREAD—II

4 cans biscuits (40 biscuits)
1-1/2 Tbs. cinnamon
1/2 cup butter or margarine
1 cup white sugar
1 cup brown sugar
1/2 cup pecans, raisins and coconut if desired

Cut each biscuit into 4 pieces; place sugar and cinnamon in plastic bag. Add biscuit pieces a few at a time and shake to coat; place pieces in a greased tube pan until all are used. Sprinkle layers with pecans, coconut. Bring brown sugar and margarine to a boil in saucepan. Pour over top of biscuits. Bake at 350 for 45 minutes. Cool and turn upside down.

GRITS CORNBREAD

1/2 cup cooked grits
1-1/2 cup self-rising meal mix
1 egg, beaten
1 cup buttermilk
1/2 cup butter, melted

Combine above ingredients and pour into a hot, greased 8-inch baking pan or iron skillet. Bake at 425 degrees for 30-35 minutes.

GOLDEN CORN LOAF

2 (1 lb.) cans whole kernel corn, drained
1 (6 oz.) can evaporated milk
1 egg, beaten
2 Tbs. finely chopped onion
1/2 tsp. salt
1/2 cup soft bread crumbs

Dash pepper
2 slices bacon, crisp & crumbled
1 cup process Swiss cheese, shred
1 Tbs. butter or margarine, melted

Combine corn, milk, egg, onion, salt, pepper and 3/4 cup of the cheese. Turn into 5 x 9-inch deep loaf dish. Toss bread crumbs with melted butter and remaining 1/4 cup cheese. Sprinkle over corn mixture. Bake in a preheated 350-degrees oven 25 to 30 minutes. Garnish with green pepper rings and pimento. Yield: 4 to 6 servings.

CARROT CORNBREAD

1 cup yellow cornmeal
1 cup grated carrots
1 Tbs. brown sugar
1 tsp. salt
2 Tbs. salad oil

3/4 cup boiling water
2 egg yolks
2 Tbs. water
2 egg whites, beaten stiff

Combine cornmeal, carrots, sugar, salt and oil. Mix well, add boiling water, mix well; beat egg yolks, add 2 tablespoons water, then add to cornmeal mixture. Fold in stiffly beaten egg whites. Bake at 450 degrees for 20-25 minutes.

GINGERBREAD

2 eggs, lightly beaten
3/4 cup dark brown sugar
3/4 cup dark molasses
3/4 cup melted shortening
2-1/2 cups plain flour
1/2 tsp. baking powder
1/2 tsp. salt

2 tsp. soda
2 tsp. ginger
1-1/2 tsp. cinnamon
1/2 tsp. cloves
1/2 tsp. nutmeg
1 cup boiling water

Mix sugar, molasses and shortening together. Add beaten eggs and mix well. Add sifted dry ingredients and beat until well blended. Then add boiling water and beat until smooth. The batter will be thin. Pour into greased and floured 9 x 14 oblong pan. Bake at 350 degrees for 30 to 40 minutes.

OATMEAL BREAD

1 (1/4 oz.) pkg. active dry yeast
1 cup quick-cooking oats
3 cups bread flour
1 tsp. salt
1/2 cup molasses
1 Tbs. vegetable oil
1 1/4 cups plus 1 Tbs. warm water

In bread machine pan, place ingredients in order given. Select "white bread" setting. Bake according to bread machine directions. Yield: 1 loaf (1-1/2 pounds)

QUICK SOURDOUGH BREAD

2 cups sourdough starter
1 tsp. dry yeast
3 Tbs. warm water (110 degrees)
3 Tbs. sugar

1-1/2 tsp. salt
3 Tbs. powdered milk
2 Tbs. melted shortening
or cooking oil

Measure out sourdough starter. In a small separate bowl, dissolve yeast in warm water. Add to sourdough starter along with sugar, salt, powdered milk and shortening or cooking oil. Mix well. Slowly add the flour until the dough pulls away from the sides of the bowl. Turn out onto a floured surface and knead until smooth and elastic, adding more flour if necessary. Shape the dough and place in a well-greased loaf pan. Cover with a cloth. Set in a warm place free from drafts and let rise until doubled in size. Bake at 350 degrees for 50 minutes or until done. Yield: 1 loaf.

QUICK, OVERNIGHT SOURDOUGH STARTER

(This gives a mild sourdough flavor in a hurry!)

1 pkg. plus 1 Tbs. dry yeast
4 cups lukewarm water
4 cups all-purpose flour

Dissolve yeast in a small amount of lukewarm water. Stir flour into remaining water and add yeast mixture. Mix well and cover. Let mixture stand in a draft-free area that is near 85 degrees for at least 6 hours or overnight. Starter is now ready to be mixed with other ingredients for your favorite sourdough recipe.

Use and replenish your starter once a week and it will live indefinitely, gaining flavor and tang, as it grows older. To replenish your starter, measure out the correct amount of sourdough starter for your recipe from your starter pot. Then add equal portions of flour and lukewarm water.

Cover with a towel or plastic wrap and set in a warm place (80 to 85 degrees) overnight. Next morning before adding any other ingredients to the mixture, return at least 1/2 of the mixture to your starter pot and store the starter pot in the refrigerator. Never add anything to your starter except flour and water and a sprinkle of dry yeast when needed to liven up the mixture. If you are not going to use it for a while, pop it in the freezer for periods up to three months. When you take it out again, let it thaw slowly, stir in a small amount of flour with an equal amount of lukewarm water and let it sit overnight in a warm place. In the morning it should greet you with that appetizing sourdough aroma.

APRICOT BANANA BREAD

1/3 cup butter or margarine, softened
2/3 cup sugar
2 eggs
1 cup mashed ripe bananas
(2 or 3 medium)
1/4 cup buttermilk
1-1/4 cups all-purpose flour

1 tsp. baking powder
1/2 tsp. baking soda
1/2 tsp. salt
1 cup 100% bran cereal
(not flakes)
3/4 cup chopped dried
apricots
1/2 cup chopped walnuts

In a mixing bowl, cream butter and sugar. Add eggs; mix well. Combine bananas and buttermilk. Combine the flour, baking powder, baking soda and salt; add to creamed mixture alternately with banana mixture. Stir in bran, apricots and nuts. Pour into a greased 9 x 5 x 3 loaf pan. Bake at 350 degrees for 55 to 60 minutes or until bread tests done. Cool 10 minutes before removing from pan to a wire rack. Yield: 1 loaf.

CRACKLING BREAD

2 cups cornmeal
1-1/2 cups milk or water
1-1/2 cups finely broken cracklings
1 egg
1-1/2 tsp. salt

Mix all ingredients thoroughly and pour into greased pan. Bake for 1 hour at 325 degrees. The top of the bread should also be greased before baking.

CORN FRITTERS

2-1/2 cups flour
2-1/2 tsp. baking soda
2 tsp. salt
1 egg
1 cup milk

2 Tbs. cornmeal
1 Tbs. water
1 (12 oz.) can whole kernel corn, drained
Vegetable oil
Maple syrup

Sift flour with baking soda and salt. Beat egg into milk and add to flour with cornmeal, water and corn; stir well. Drop by tablespoon into hot oil; fry until brown, turning once. Serve with maple syrup.

CORN PUDDING

2 cups corn (fresh or frozen)	2 Tbs. flour
1 cup sweet milk	1 Tbs. sugar
1 Tbs. butter	3 eggs
2 tsp. salt	Dash black pepper

To the corn add flour, melted butter, salt sugar and pepper. Beat eggs until light and add to the corn mixture. Bake in greased dish 1 hour or until firm at 325 degrees.

CORN BREAD

1/2 cup flour	2 eggs
1-1/2 cups cornmeal	1 cup milk
4 tsp. baking powder	1/4 cup shortening
1 tsp. salt	1 Tbs. sugar

Combine flour, meal, sugar, salt and baking powder. Add eggs, milk and shortening. Mix until smooth. Bake in 425 degrees oven for 20 or 25 minutes.

CORN MUFFINS

1 cup cornmeal	2 Tbs. melted shortening
2/3 cup flour	1 cup milk or water
1 tsp. salt	1 egg
2 tsp. baking powder	1 Tbs. sugar

Combine meal, flour, salt and baking powder. Beat egg with milk and stir into mixture. Add melted shortening and stir. Fill greased muffin tins 2/3 full. Bake at 425 degrees for 20 to 25 minutes. Yield: 12 muffins.

OKRA BREAD

1/2 cup hush puppy mix	Dash of pepper
1/2 cup milk	3 Tbs. vegetable oil
1 egg, beaten	2 cups thinly sliced okra
1 tsp. salt	

Combine first six ingredients, stir in okra. If batter is too moist, add a bit more hush puppy mix. Pour into greased and floured 8-inch pan. Bake at 350 degrees for one hour or until golden. Cut into squares.

HUSH PUPPIES—I

2 cups cornmeal
1 Tbs. flour
1/2 tsp. soda
1 tsp. baking powder

1 tsp. salt
1 small onion, chopped
1 cup buttermilk
1 egg

Mix dry ingredients together. Add onion, then buttermilk and finally a beaten egg. Drop by spoonfuls into the pan in which fish has been fried. Fry to a golden brown and drain on absorbent paper.

HUSH PUPPIES—II

1/2 cup cornmeal
1/2 cup flour
1 egg
1 Tbs. sugar

1 tsp. baking powder
1 small onion, chopped fine
1/2 tsp. salt
Beer, as required

Mix meal, flour, sugar, baking powder and salt together. Add onion mixed with eggs. Mix with enough beer to make a thick paste. Fry in deep fat by dropping with teaspoon. Fry until brown.

FARMHOUSE BARBECUE MUFFINS

1 tube (10 oz) refrigerated buttermilk biscuits
1 pound ground beef
1/2 cup ketchup
3 Tbs. brown sugar
1 Tbs. cider vinegar
1/2 tsp. chili powder
1 cup (4 oz.) shredded cheddar cheese

Separate dough into 10 biscuits; flatten into 5-inch circles. Press each into the bottom and up the sides of a greased muffin cup; set aside. In a skillet, brown ground beef; drain. In a small bowl, mix ketchup, brown sugar, vinegar and chili powder; stir until smooth. Add to meat and mix well. Divide the meat mixture among biscuit-lined muffin cups, using about 1/4 cup for each. Sprinkle with cheese. Bake at 375 degrees for 18-20 minutes or until golden brown. Cool for 5 minutes before removing from tin and serving. Yield: 10 servings.

QUICK PIZZA DOUGH

**3 cups all-purpose white flour
1 pkg. quick-rising yeast
1 tsp. salt
1/2 tsp. sugar
1 tsp. olive oil**

In a food processor, pulse to mix flour, yeast, salt and sugar. In a small saucepan or in a glass measuring cup in the microwave, heat oil mixed with 3/4 cup water to between 120 and 130 degrees. With the processor on, gradually pour the warm liquid through the feed tube. (If the mixture is too dry, add 1 or 2 tablespoons warm water.) Process until the dough forms a ball, then process for 1 minute to knead. Transfer the dough to a lightly floured surface. Cover with plastic wrap and let rest for 10 to 15 minutes.

The dough can be made ahead, enclosed in a plastic bag and stored in the refrigerator overnight. Bring to room temperature before using.

DOUGHNUTS

**4 pkg. dry yeast
1 cup warm water
2 cups sweet milk
1-1/2 cup sugar
1 tsp. salt
3/4 cup Crisco
8 cups plain flour**

Mix together the yeast and water, and set aside. Combine other ingredients, then add yeast mixture. Roll 1/2-inch thick.

Deep fry to a golden brown.

GLAZE:
2/3 cups boiling water and 1 pkg. powdered sugar.

STARTER

2 pkgs. dry yeast
1/2 cup warm water, 105 to 115 degrees
2 cups warm water, divided
1-1/3 cups sugar, divided
6 Tbs. potato flakes, divided

Dissolve yeast in the 1/2 cup warm water. Then feed it 1 cup warm water, 2/3 cup sugar and 3 tablespoons potato flakes. Let mixture sit out all day, then refrigerate for two to five days. Take it out and feed again with remaining 1 cup water, 2/3 cup sugar and 3 tablespoons potato flakes and let sit out all day or overnight. Now you are ready to use 1 cup of starter to make your first batch of bread. The rest goes back in the refrigerator.

BREAD

1 cup starter (above)
1-1/2 cups warm water
1/2 cup vegetable oil
1 Tbs. salt
2/3 cup sugar
4 generous cups unsifted all-purpose flour

Mix all ingredients together with a wooden spoon. Knead for about 8 minutes or until satiny. Turn dough into a greased bowl, cover and let rise until doubled. Punch down dough; shape into loaves and place in lightly greased loaf pans. Or form into rolls and arrange on lightly greased baking sheets. Let rise again until doubled. Bake at 350 degrees for 18 minutes for rolls and 30 to 49 minutes for loaves. Yield: 2 loaves.

HELPFUL HINTS

Rolls and biscuits: For crisp crust, brush tops with milk, cream, egg yolks with a little water add to egg white.

Fresh bread will slice better if knife is run though a flame to heat.

Reheat leftover rolls: Place inside a paper bag which has been moistened with water. Twist top to close and place in hot oven until heated though.

Yeast: Add a pinch of sugar to yeast when softening in water. Will start it to working.

Cut very fresh bread with heated sharp knife.

When bread is baking, a small dish of water in the oven will help to keep the crust from getting too hard or brown.

Use shortening, not oleo or oil to grease pans, as oleo and oil absorb more readily into the dough or batter and do nothing to release baked goods from pan (especially bread).

Use a metal ice tray divider to cut biscuits in a hurry. Press into dough and biscuits will separate at dividing lines when baked.

Self-rising flour: 4 cups flour, 2 teaspoons salt and 2 tablespoons baking powder. Mix well and store in a tightly covered container.

Hot water kills yeast. One way to tell the correct temperature is to pour the water over your forearm, and if you cannot feel wither hot or cold, the temperature is just right.

When in doubt, always sift flour before measuring.

When milk is used in making bread, you get a finer texture. Water makes coarser bread.

If your biscuits are dry, it could be from too much handling, or the oven temperature may have not been hot enough.

Nut breads are better if stored 24 hours before using.

Small amounts of leftover corn may be added to pancake batter for variety.

To make bread crumbs, use fine cutter of the food grinder and tie a large paper bag over the spout to prevent flying crumbs.

When bread is baking, a small dish of water in the oven will help to keep the crust from getting hard.

Use the divider from an ice tray to cut biscuits in a hurry. Shape dough to conform with size of divider and cut. After baking biscuits will separate at dividing lines.

KITCHEN
HELPFUL HINTS

GETTING THE MOST FROM CONVENIENCE FOODS

❖ Perk up frozen, quick-cooking, or store-bought dishes by adding vegetables, cheese, and other foods. You can get nearly the same texture, flavor, and nutritional quality as home-cooked meals.

❖ Add fresh mushrooms, onions, and peppers to bottled or canned spaghetti sauce.

❖ Top frozen pizza with fresh tomatoes, peppers, and onions.

❖ Add a single-serving can of tuna to a pasta salad from a salad bar.

❖ Thin mayonnaise dressing on coleslaw with low-fat yogurt.

❖ Spice up frozen or canned corn with lemon juice and salsa.

❖ Add fresh onions, peppers, beans, chicken bouillon or tomato sauce to quick-cooking rice.

❖ Add steamed zucchini, mushrooms, and a bit of grated cheese to a microwave "baked" potato.

❖ Mix slices yellow squash, broccoli florets, or green peas into a flavored rice-and-noodle casserole.

❖ Add diced mushrooms, celery, carrots, and onions to prepared poultry-stuffing mixes.

❖ Increase the calcium in instant mashed potatoes. Follow package directions but reverse the quantities of milk (use skim) and water called for in the directions.

HINTS FOR EASE

Fresh lemon juice will remove onion scent from hands.

To measure shortening: Subtract the amount needed from one cup. Put water in a measuring cup the amount of the remainder. Add enough shortening to bring the water level up to one cup. Drain off water. Example: If a recipe calls for 1/4 cup shortening, put 3/4 cup of water in a cup.

Too salty? While cooking, add 1 teaspoon each of vinegar and sugar. For soups, add a few slices of raw potato.

If you don not own a wire whisk, invest in one. They are great for taking lumps out of gravy and all blending.

Screw-top jars hard to open? Place lid down in 3 inches of boiling water. Try again.

To remove scum from jelly, preserves, soups, etc., use a vegetable brush to gather it. Rinse the skim again.

Sealing jelly jars with paraffin: Place a piece of string across top, long enough to extend beyond each edge, before covering with wax. It will lift off easily when ready to use.

Always give jams and jellies a second coat of paraffin.

To clean a burnt or gravy pan: Quickly place 1 inch of water in pan and add 1 teaspoon or more of soda and heat to boiling.

To remove vegetables stains from fingers: Try rubbing with a slice of raw potato.

To remove odors from jars and bottles: Pour in a solution of water and dry mustard or diluted chlorine solution. Let stand for several hours. Rinse with hot water.

Keep oil or shortening clean or cooked particles when used in a deep fryer by straining though a piece of old nylon stocking. Raw potato cooked in it will fresh taste.

To keep out weevils: Store flour, meal, cereals and dried foods in glass jars with a tight fitting lid. Cut out label and place in jar.

Shortening: To cream it easily, pour a little boiling water in mixing bowl; let stand until heated through; drain and dry before adding shortening. Measure easily by submerging in water—thus for 1/3 cup, fill cup 2/3 full of water and add shortening until water reaches 1 cup mark. Pour off water and remove shortening without sticking.

KITCHEN HELP

A pair of scissors (not the fowl kind—they are heavy and awkward to handle) fine for slivering celery, onion, meats, and cheese.

To clean aluminum pots when they are stained dark, merely boil with a little cream of tartar, vinegar or acid foods.
Baking powder will remove tea or coffee stains from china pots or cups.

Learn where your fuse box and master cut-off switch is located. If you know where the lever is to pull you can always cut the current off until a service man can come.

Slip your hand inside a waxed sandwich bag and you have perfect mitt for greasing your baking pans and casserole dishes.

To keep steady when mixing, place bowl on wet, folded cloth.

To keep from slipping off ice, place a rubbed fruit ring underneath bowl.

Remember that every time you open the oven door the temperature drops about 25 degrees.

The coldest part of any refrigerator is the top back shelf.

Never freeze more than 4 pounds of fresh food per cubic foot of freezer capacity at one time.

For highest refrigerator efficiency, air should circulate around each container.

Dripping faucets can be quieted by tying a string to it that reaches into the sink. The water will slide down the string quietly.

Try loosening rusty screws by putting a drop of ammonia on it.

Keeping a piece of charcoal in the tool drawer will keep the moisture out and preventing rust.

Rusty bolts can usually be loosened by pouring club soda on them.

When cooking in glass pans, reduce oven temperature by 25 degrees.

To keep hot oil from spattering, sprinkle a little salt or flour in the pan before frying.

Spray your grill with vegetable oil to prevent sticking.

Use the type can opener that leaves a smooth edge and remove both ends from a flat can (the size can that tuna is usually packed in) and you have a perfect mold for poaching eggs.

A teaspoon of ground mustard dissolved in dishwater will remove odor of fish or garlic on dishes.

To eliminate a lot of mess when whipping cream with an electric beater, try this: Cut 2 small holes in the middle of a piece of waxed paper, then slip the stems of the beaters through the holes and attach the beaters to the machine. Simply place paper and beaters over the bowl and whip away.

Stocking your pantry and refrigerator: When you have the ingredients within easy reach, preparing meals with balance and variety will not be hard. As a rule, use fresh herbs and spices rather than dried or powdered versions.

Glazed pottery, earthenware, glass, metal…take your pick. All can be used for casseroles. Many of these casserole containers come in bright colors and pleasing designs to contrast or complement your kitchen décor or tableware. The type of container you use makes very little difference, as long as it is heat-proof. Some of the earliest casseroles were made of earthenware and were glazed inside. They had covers and were similar to those that are still used today.

Food Chopper: To fasten it securely, place piece of sandpaper on table, rough side down, before fastening screws. To sharpen it, run a piece of sand soap or cake cleanser though—also polishes blades and removes grease. Place bowl underneath to catch juice when grinding fresh fruits.

Lids: Tea or coffeepot lids should always be left open when not in use to avoid musty pots.

Paper Bags: Save small paper bags from grocery store to use in flouring chicken, chops, etc., or coating doughnuts with powdered sugar. Just shake food vigorously in closed bag and it will be evenly coated. Also tie jars of preserved foods in bags to keep clean. Contents may be noted on bag.

Sandwiches: To keep fresh wrap in clean cloth wrung out of cold water.

SUBSTITUTE ONE INGREDIENT FOR ANOTHER

1 whole egg, *for thickening or baking*	2 egg yolks. *OR* 2 tablespoons dried whole egg plus 2-1/2 tablespoons water.
1 cup butter or margarine *for shortening*	7/8 cup lard, or rendered fat, with 1/2 teaspoon salt. *OR* 1 cup hydrogenated fat (cooking fat sold under brand name) with 1/2 tea spoon salt.
1 square (ounce) chocolate	3 or 4 tablespoons cocoa plus 1/2 tablespoon fat.
1 teaspoon double acting *baking powder*	1-1/2 teaspoons phosphate baking powder. *OR* 2 teaspoons tartrate baking powder.
Sweet milk and baking powder, *for baking*	Equal amount of sour milk plus 1/2 teaspoon soda per cup. (Each half teaspoon soda with 1 cup sour milk takes the place of 2 teaspoon. baking powder and 1 cup sweet milk.)
1 cup sour milk, for baking	1 cup sweet milk mixed with one of the following: 1 Tablespoon vinegar. *OR* 1 tablespoon lemon juice. *OR* 1-3/4 teaspoons cream of tartar.
1 cup skim milk	4 tablespoons nonfat dry milk plus 1 cup water.
1 tablespoon flour, *for thickening*	1/2 tablespoon cornstarch, potato starch, rice starch, or arrowroot starch. *OR* 1 tablespoon granulated tapioca.
1 cup cake flour, for baking	7/8 cup all-purpose flour.
1 cup all-purpose flour, *for baking breads*	Up to 1/2 cup bran, whole-wheat flour, or corn meal plus enough all- purpose flour to fill cup.

VEGETABLES

BAKED BEANS

1 large can pork and beans
1/2 cup firmly packed brown sugar
1 Tbs. mustard
1/4 cup catsup
Sliced bacon
Hot sauce

Mix and cover with sliced bacon. Sprinkle with hot sauce to suit taste. Cook at 350 degrees for 30 minutes.

RANCH STYLE BAKED BEANS

1 pound ground beef
1 envelope onion soup mix
1/2 cup water
1 cup ketchup
2 Tbs. mustard
2 tsp. cider vinegar
2 one pound cans pork and beans
1 one pound can kidney beans, drained

In a large skillet brown meat. Add remaining ingredients and mix well. Pour into a quart baking dish and bake at 400 degrees for 30 minutes. Yield: 8 servings.

HARVARD BEETS

3 cups cooked beets
1/2 cup sugar
1-1/2 Tbs. cornstarch
1/2 cup water
1/2 cup cider vinegar
2 Tbs. butter

In a saucepan combine sugar, cornstarch, water and vinegar. Bring to a boil and boil 5 minutes. Stir beets into mixture, cooking slowly and stirring occasionally until heated through. Add butter and continue cooking until butter has melted. Serve.

CABBAGE CASSEROLE

1 small cabbage or 1/2 large cabbage
1 medium vidalia onion
1/2 stick (1/4 cup) margarine
1/4 cup mayonnaise
1 10.75 oz. can cream of mushroom or cream of chicken soup
 (salt and pepper to taste)

TOPPING:

1 stick (1/2 cup) margarine
1 cup grated sharp Cheddar cheese
1 stack round butter crackers, crushed

Coarsely chop cabbage and place in 2-to-3 quart casserole dish. Chop onion and place on top of cabbage. Melt 1/2 stick margarine and pour over cabbage. Sprinkle with salt and pepper to taste. In small bowl, mix soup and mayonnaise together. Spread over top of cabbage mixture.

Preheat oven to 350 degrees. To make topping, melt the remaining stick of margarine. In small bowl, mix melted margarine, grated cheese and crushed crackers. Sprinkle cracker-cheese mixture over top of casserole. Bake for about 45 minutes or until top is browned and inside is bubbly. Yield: 8 servings.

POLISH CABBAGE ROLLS

1 pound ground beef
2 cups quick rice
1/2 cup chopped onion
Salt and pepper to taste
1 head cabbage, cored
1 can (16 ounce) whole tomatoes or tomato sauce

Combine beef, rice, onion, salt and pepper. Steam cabbage whole until leaves pull off easily. (Only a few leaves will pull off at a time, place cabbage back over steam until all are removed.)

Place small leaves in bottom of a 9" x 13" pan. Roll 1-3 tablespoons of beef mixture In each leaf; place seams down in pan. Pour tomato sauce or tomatoes (if using In whole tomatoes, add 1/2 cup water) over cabbage rolls. Cover and bake at 350 degrees for 1 hour or until tender. Keep checking water; do not allow to cook dry. Add water if necessary. Yield: 12-14 rolls. Serves 6-8.

SKILLET FRIED CABBAGE

1 Tbs. oil
3 cups shredded cabbage
1 green pepper, chopped
1 onion chopped
1/2 tsp. salt
dash black pepper

Put all ingredients in skillet with oil, stir well. Cover and cook 5 minutes.

STEWED CABBAGE

3 slices bacon, crumbled
1 small cabbage, sliced
2 tart apples, sliced
3 Tbs. vinegar

Fry bacon crisp in a large skillet; drain. Pour off excess grease. Place crumbled bacon back in pan and add remaining ingredients. Fill pan half full of water. Cover and simmer 20-30 minutes or until cabbage and apples are tender. Yield: 6-8 servings.

MARINATED CARROTS

2 pounds carrots
1 onion
3/4 cup sugar
1 tsp. salt
1 tsp. Worcestershire sauce

1 bell pepper
1 can tomato soup
1/2 cup corn oil
1 tsp. dry mustard
1/4 tsp. pepper

Cut carrots into thin strips or rounds. Parboil until just tender. Drain. Chop bell pepper. Cut onion into thin slices. Place in a large bowl. Set aside. Mix tomato soup, sugar, oil, vinegar, mustard, salt, pepper, Worcestershire sauce in a saucepan. Bring to a boil and cook 10 minutes. Pour over carrot mixture and let cool. Refrigerate overnight. Will keep 2-3 weeks.

BAKED CORN

4 cups cream style corn
2 Tbs. sugar
1 tsp. salt
1/4 cup butter, melted

2 eggs, beaten
2 Tbs. flour or cornstarch
1-1/2 cups milk

Combine all ingredients and place in a greased 9 x 12-inch baking dish. Bake at 350 degrees for 45-60 minutes or until thickened and slightly browned. Yield: 8 servings.

FRIED CORN ON THE COB

1 cup all-purpose flour
1 Tbs. salt
1/2 tsp. paprika
(Black pepper to taste)
1 12-ounce can beer
2 to 3 quarts cooking oil
(canola, safflower or peanut)
6 ears of corn

In a medium bowl, combine the flour, salt, paprika and pepper. Slowly whisk in the beer until smooth. Chill the batter for a couple of hours. Heat the cooking oil to 350 degrees. Dip the ears of corn in the beer batter (keep the batter as chilled as possible). Drop the corn, a couple of ears at a time, into the hot oil and fry 3 to 5 minutes.

CORN-N-PEA CASSEROLE

1 can (15 oz.)   LeSeur peas
1 can (15 oz.) shoepeg corn
1 can cream of mushroom soup
1 dozen ritz crackers
1 cup grated cheddar cheese
1 Tbs. butter

Drain veggies and mix with soup in a casserole dish. Cover top with cheese. Top with crumbled ritz crackers and dot with butter. Bake at 350 degrees until bubbly (20 to 30 minutes).

SHOE PEG CORN CASSEROLE

2 cans shoepeg corn
1 can french cut green beans
1 can cream of celery soup
1/2 cup grated cheddar cheese
1/2 cup chopped onion

1/2 cup sour cream
1/2 cup slivered almonds (or water
    chestnuts)
1 pack ritz-type crackers
1 stick margarine, melted

Drain beans and corn. Mix all ingredients except crackers and margarine. Put in greased casserole dish. Crush crackers and sprinkle over casserole. Drizzle melted margarine over crackers. Bake at 350 degrees for 30-40 minutes.

SANTA FE SPICY CORN AND CHEESE BAKE

2 eggs
1 can (15-1/4 oz.) whole kernel golden sweet corn, drained
1/4 cup milk
1/2 cup sour cream
1 jar (2 oz.) chopped pimento, reserving
1/4 cup creamy cottage cheese
1 tsp. for topping
1 tsp. salt
1/4 cup chopped onion
1 Tbs. sugar
2 Tbs. chopped green chillies
1/8 tsp. cayenne pepper or to taste
1-1/2 Tbs. butter, melted
3 Tbs. flour
 1 cup crushed corn chips
1 cup (4 oz.) shredded cheddar cheese
red and green pepper and parsley sprigs (optional for garnish)

Preheat oven to 350 degrees. Beat eggs in large bowl and add milk, sour cream, cottage cheese, salt, sugar and cayenne pepper. Mix well. Combine flour and cheddar cheese and stir in to cottage cheese mixture. Stir in corn, pimento, red and green pepper, onion, chillies and butter. Pour in to buttered 1-1/2 quart casserole. Sprinkle with reserved pimento.

Bake 30-35 minutes or until almost set. Remove from oven and spoon corn chips around edge of casserole. Cook about 5 minutes longer or until knife inserted in center comes out clean. Garnish with peppers if desired. Yield: 6 servings.

PINEAPPLE AND CHEESE CASSEROLE

1 (20 oz.) can pineapple chunks
1 cup grated cheese
1/2 cup sugar
3 Tbs. flour
3 Tbs. pineapple juice
1/2 cup ritz crackers
1/4 cup melted margarine

Mix pineapples and cheese and pour into casserole dish. Mix sugar, flour and pineapple juice together, pour into dish. Crumble crackers and melted margarine; add to top of mix. Bake at 350 degrees for 20-30 minutes.

OKRA PATTIES

1 pound fresh okra
1 bag (18 oz.) frozen cut okra
1/2 cup chopped onion
1 tsp. salt
1/4 tsp. pepper
1 egg

1/2 cup water
1 tsp. baking powder
pinch of garlic powder (optional)
1/2 cup flour
1/2 cup corn meal
oil (1/2-inch)

Combine cut okra, onion, salt, pepper, water and egg. Mix well. Combine flour, baking powder, corn meal and garlic powder. Add to okra mixture, stirring well. Spoon into about 1/2 inch hot oil. Fry over medium heat until well browned on both sides. Drain on paper towels.

OKRA AND TOMATOES

4 bacon slices
1 (16 oz.) pkg. frozen sliced okra, thawed
2 Tbs. all-purpose flour
1 large onion, chopped
4 plum tomatoes, seeded and chopped

2 tsp. sugar
1/2 tsp. salt
1/2 tsp. pepper

COOK bacon in a large skillet over medium heat until crisp; drain and crumble, reserving 2 tablespoons drippings in skillet. Set bacon aside.
DREDGE okra in flour.
SAUTE' onion in reserved drippings until tender. Add okra; cook, stirring occasionally, 5 minutes or until lightly browned. Stir in tomato and sugar; cook over low heat, stirring occasionally, 6 to 8 minutes. Stir in salt and pepper. Sprinkle with bacon. Yield: 4 servings.

OKRA WITH CORN AND TOMATOES

1 pkg. (10 oz.) frozen whole kernel corn
2 cups fresh or frozen okra pods
2 medium-size tomatoes, cut up
1 medium-size yellow onion, chopped
1/4 tsp. ground red pepper (cayenne)
1/4 cup chopped cooked lower-sodium ham (optional)

1/4 cup water
1 tsp. dried oregano leaves
1 stalk celery, thinly sliced
1/4 tsp. salt

In a 10-inch skillet, combine the corn, fresh or frozen okra, tomatoes, onion, celery, ham (if using), water oregano, salt, and red pepper. Bring mixture to a boil over high heat. Lower the heat and simmer, covered, for 10 minutes or until vegetables are tender, stirring occasionally. Simmer, uncovered, for 5 minutes more or until most of the liquid has evaporated. Yield: 6 servings.

STUFFED GREEN PEPPERS

1 10-ounce pkg. frozen corn
1 15-ounce can red kidney beans,
  drained and rinsed
1 28-ounce can crushed tomatoes
1/4 cup chopped onion
1-1/2 cups cooked rice
1 tsp. Worcestershire sauce
4 small green peppers, tops removedand seeded

1/4 tsp. salt
1/2 tsp. pepper
2 cups shredded cheddar cheese
 (1/4 cup reserved)

Combine all ingredients except reserved cheese and green peppers. Stuff peppers to top. Put in crockpot. (Place 3 peppers in bottom and 1 on top.) Cover; cook on Low (6 to 8) hours or on High (3 to 4 hours). Sprinkle with 1/4 cup cheese in last 30 minutes. Yield: 4 servings.

POTATO CHOWDER

Peel and cut into dice shape, 6 medium-sized potatoes (about 3 cups) and 1/4 pound of bacon or salt pork, cubed. Add 1 tablespoon finely chopped onion; put pork cubes into hot frying pan, saute' until light brown. Put layer of potatoes into saucepan; sprinkle on layer of pork. Add onion, salt and pepper to taste, and a little finely chopped parsley. Build layers alternately until all ingredients are used. Add 2 cups water or stock, cover and let simmer 20 minutes; then add 2 cups milk and 1 tablespoon each flour and melted butter worked together. Stir with fork to avoid breaking up potato cubes, until chowder boils. Serve with crackers.

CORN CHOWDER

Follow Potato Chowder recipe, and add 2 cups fresh green corn with potatoes; or, add 2 cups cooked or canned corn with milk. Peas may be substituted for corn.

VEGETABLE CHOWDER

Follow Potato Chowder recipe and add 2 cups of one or more vegetables finely chopped, in addition to potatoes.

FISH CHOWDER

Follow Potato Chowder recipe, and add 1 to 2 cups flaked fish (depending upon strength) with potatoes.

If salt fish, such as cod, is used, flake or shred and soak out salt in lukewarm water before adding. If canned fish, use the liquid, adding only enough water to make the 2 cups required. Use all milk instead of part water if desired; or 1 cup may be sweet cream.

Broken crackers, softened in a little milk, may be added just before last boiling.

BROWN RICE

1 can beef consommé soup	**1 stick margarine**
1 can french onion soup	**1 small jar mushrooms**
1 cup uncooked white rice	

Melt butter in casserole dish. Pour in cup uncooked white rice. Pour in other ingredients. Do not stir. Cook 1/2 hour at 350 degrees, then stir and cook 20-30 minutes longer.

QUICK CHEESE SOUP

1 can cream of celery soup	**1/2 cup shredded cheddar cheese**
1 can beef consommé	**1 Tbs. chopped onion**
1-1/4 cups milk	**1/4 tsp. Worcestershire sauce**

Combine first 4 ingredients in large saucepan. Add onion and Worcestershire Sauce. Cook over low heat; do not let soup boil. Yield: 4 servings.

SWEET AND SOUR CABBAGE SOUP

3 pounds lean beef for stewing,
2 (8 oz.) cans tomato sauce
1 soup bone
1 cup firmly packed brown sugar
1-1/2 tsp. pepper
1 (16 oz.) can sauerkraut, undrained
2 (10 oz.) cans stewed tomatoes, undrained cut into 1-inch cubes

1 large cabbage, shredded
3 large onions sliced thinly
1-1/2 tsp. salt
3 quarts water
1/2 cup vinegar

Combine beef, soup bone, and water in a large stock pot. Bring to a boil, reduce heat. Cover and simmer 1-1/2 hours. Add remaining ingredients and simmer, uncovered for 1 hour, stirring occasionally. Remove and discard soup bone. Yield: 2 gallons.

NOTE: Short ribs may be substituted for soup bone or may leave out all together.

QUICK POTATO-CHEESE SOUP

3 cups instant mashed potatoes
1 medium onion, chopped
1/4 cup bacon bits
2 Tbs. butter
1/4 tsp. dry mustard

1/4 tsp. pepper
1 tsp. celery salt
6 cups milk
2 cups grated cheddar cheese
2 tsp. parsley flakes

Prepare mashed potatoes according to package directions. Sauté' onion and bacon bits in butter until tender. In a large saucepan add remaining ingredients. Cook over low heat, stirring frequently, until thoroughly heated and cheese is melted. Do not boil. Yield: 6 servings.

SQUASH DELIGHT

1 pound yellow squash, cooked,
  mashed, and drained
2 cup chopped onion
1/2 cup grated cheese
1/2 cup chopped nuts
1 egg, beaten

1/2 cup chopped green peppers
2 Tbs. chopped pimiento
1/2 cup mayonnaise
Bread crumbs

Combine all but the last ingredient. Place in a buttered 2-quart casserole. Top with bread crumbs. Bake at 325 degrees for 30 minutes or until firm. Yield: 6 servings.

SQUASH FRITTERS

2 cups grated squash
1/4 tsp. grated onion
2 tsp. sugar
1 tsp. salt

Pepper to taste
6 Tbs. flour
2 eggs
2 tsp. melted oleo

Grate squash. Mix first 5 ingredients. Beat eggs and add to mixture, then add oleo. Stir to blend. Heat small amount of oil in large skillet. Drop batter on hot skillet and cook until crisp and brown on both sides.

SQUASH PATTIES

2 cups squash, cooked and drained
1 egg
3 Tbs. flour
1/3 cup chopped onion
salt and pepper to taste

Mix all ingredients and beat well. Spoon patties into hot cooking oil in skillet.

SWEET POTATO CASSEROLE

3 cups mashed sweet potatoes
1/8 cup orange juice
1 cup sugar
2 eggs
1 stick margarine
1 tsp. salt
1 tsp. vanilla

TOPPING:
1 cup pecans
1 cup brown sugar
1 stick butter
1 cup self-rising flour

Mix ingredients with sweet potatoes; mix well. Pour in baking dish. Mix topping ingredients well; sprinkle on potatoes and bake 45 minutes at 345 degrees.

SWEET POTATO SOUFFLÉ CRUNCH

3 cups cooked, mashed sweet potatoes
1 cup sugar
1/2 tsp. salt
2 eggs. Slightly beaten
2-1/2 Tbs. melted butter
1/2 cup milk
1 tsp. vanilla

Mix all ingredients together and pour into a greased baking dish. Cover with crunch topping. Bake at 350 degrees for 35 minutes.

Crunch Topping:
Melt 2-1/2 tablespoons of margarine. Add 1 cup brown sugar, 1/3 cup all-purpose flour and 1 cup chopped pecans. Yield: 6-8 servings.

JIMMY CARTER'S YUMMY YAMS

5 cups shredded raw yams or sweet potatoes
1/2 stick (4 ounces) butter
1 cup white corn syrup
3/4 cup sugar
1 cup pineapple juice

Cover shredded yams with cold water to retain color. Melt 2 tablespoons butter in a 2-quart baking dish. Cook corn syrup, sugar and pineapple juice until sugar melts. Drain yams. Pour syrup over yams and dot with remaining butter. Bake at 350 degrees for 35 to 40 minutes or up to an hour, depending on oven.

SWEET POTATO BALLS

Roll mashed sweet potato around a marshmallow to form a small ball. Dip balls in 1 egg diluted with 2 tablespoons water, then in seasoned bread crumbs. Fry balls in deep fat, or bake. Bake at 350 degrees for 10 to 15 minutes.

SENATOR'S RUSSELL'S SWEET POTATOES

3 cups cooked and mashed sweet potatoes
1 cup sugar
2 eggs
1/2 cup butter

TOPPING:
1 cup brown sugar
1/2 cup flour
1/2 butter
1 cup chopped pecans

Mix first set of ingredients until thoroughly blended. Combine topping ingredients and crumble over all. Bake 30 minutes at 350 degrees.

SCALLOPED TOMATOES

6 medium sized tomatoes
4 strips bacon
2 hard cooked eggs, sliced thin
2 cups cracker crumbs
1/2 cup hot water

bacon drippings
salt and pepper
1/2 cup grated cheese

Fry bacon crisp, saving drippings for seasoning. Peel and slice tomatoes. In a one quart casserole, place a layer of tomatoes, part of crumbled bacon, and sliced egg. Add salt and pepper, then a layer of crushed crackers. Repeat layers ending with tomatoes. Add some bacon drippings to hot water and pour over tomatoes. Top with cheese, bake at 325 degrees for 30 minutes. Yield: 6 servings.

FRIED TOMATOES & CREAMY GRAVY

Bacon fried crisp; reserve drippings
1/4 tsp. pepper
1/2 cup cornmeal
4 large tomatoes, sliced 1/2-inch thick
3 Tbs. all-purpose flour
1 cup half and half
2 tsp. sugar
1/2 tsp. salt
2 tsp. salt
English muffins, toasted

Combine cornmeal, flour, sugar, salt and pepper. Coat tomato slices with mixture. Fry until golden brown in bacon drippings, turning once. Remove slices from pan and place on platter to keep warm. Over medium to low heat, heat cream and salt, adding 1-2 tablespoons of cornmeal mixture as needed, stirring until thick. Place bacon, tomato slices and gravy over English muffins. Yield: 6 servings.

TOMATO CHEESE PIE

Crust:
3/4 cup all-purpose flour
3/4 cup instant mashed potato flakes
1/4 cup grated Parmesan cheese
1/4 tsp. salt
1/3 cup butter, softened
1/4 cup water

Combine dry ingredients; cut in butter until crumbly. Add water and stir well until dough holds together. Press into an ungreased 9-10-inch pie plate. Pierce bottom with a fork. Bake at 350 degrees for 10 minutes.

FILLING:
1-1/2 cups shredded cheddar cheese
1/4 cup instant mashed potato flakes
1 medium tomato, chopped
5 eggs, beaten
1/4 cup sour cream
1 tsp chopped chives
3/4 tsp. salt

Spread 1 cup of cheese in bottom of baked piecrust. Sprinkle potato flakes over cheese, spoon tomato onto flakes and top with remaining 1/2 cup cheese. Combine remaining ingredients and pour into pie shell. Bake at 350 degrees for 25-30 minutes or until a knife inserted in center comes out clean. Allow to set for 5 minutes before serving. Yield: 5 servings.

FRIED CABBAGE

Bacon grease
6 bacon strips
Accent

1 cabbage
Soy sauce

Cut your cabbage into pieces 1-inch wide. Get 4-6 strips bacon and lay horizontally on cutting surface and cut vertically about 1-inch wide. Get skillet hot and add bacon and stir fry for 3-4 minutes on medium heat. Pour bacon and grease into separate bowl. Put 4 tablespoons bacon grease into pan. Turn stove to high heat, put cabbage in and cook, stirring occasionally, for 8-10 minutes. Add Accent. Add bacon to cabbage and mix it. Add soy sauce; simmer for 5 minutes with cover on skillet.

CORN MEDLEY

Mix together:
2 cans yellow corn, drained
2 cans white corn, drained
1 jar (4 oz.) pimientos
1 large onion, chopped
1 green pepper, chopped

Bring to a boil:
1-1/2 cup sugar
1 cup oil
1 cup vinegar
2 tsp. salt
1 tsp. pepper

Pour over vegetable mixture. Refrigerate at least 4 hours. Overnight is better. Drain before serving.

CORN AND BACON

Fry 6 or 8 slices of bacon crisp. Remove from drippings and let cool and crumble. Pour up drippings except about 2 Tbs. Add 1 cup water. To boiling mixture add 2 cups fresh or frozen corn. Stir often and cook slow for 30 minutes. Salt and pepper to taste and add crumbled bacon. More water may be added if needed to thin mixture.

GEORGIA GUMBO

Combine the following ingredients:

2-1/2 cups chopped ripe tomatoes
1/2 cup diced celery
1/4 cup diced onion
1-1/2 cup cut okra
1 Tbs. salt

1/4 tsp. pepper
1 Tbs. vinegar
1 Tbs. sugar
2 Tbs. butter

Cook in open pan on low heat about 45 minutes.

ONION-ROASTED POTATOES

1 envelope Lipton Recipe Secrets Onion or
  Onion-Mushroom Soup Mix
2 pounds all-purpose potatoes,
  cut into large chunks
1/3 cup olive or vegetable oil

Preheat oven to 450 degrees. In large plastic bag or bowl, add all ingredients. Close bag and shake, or toss in bowl, until potatoes are evenly coated. Empty potatoes into 13 x 9-inch baking or roasting pan; discard bag. Bake uncovered, stirring occasionally, 40 minutes or until potatoes are tender an golden brown. Garnish, if desired, with chopped fresh parsley. Yield: About 4 servings.

SCALLOPED POTATOES

6 medium sized potatoes peeled and sliced thin
1-1/2 or 2 cups whole milk or light cream
Salt and pepper to taste
2 medium onions chopped
1 can pimiento, cut in trips (optional)
1 stick butter or oleo
2 cups bread crumbs

Into greased casserole dish place a layer of sliced potatoes, sprinkle with salt and pepper, add a few strips of pimiento and over this spread a layer of bread crumbs and a portion of the melted butter or oleo. Repeat until all ingredients are used. Over the dish pour enough milk or cream to cover potatoes completely. Top with bread crumbs and butter. Bake at 375 degrees about 1-1/2 hours. Heating the milk or cream will lessen cooking time.

SWEET POTATO PUDDING

3 cups sweet potatoes, grated   1 stick butter, melted
1-1/2 cups sugar   1 cup nuts, chopped
3/4 cup buttermilk   1/2 tsp. salt
1/2 cup sweet milk   2 eggs, well beaten
1/2 tsp. cinnamon   Grated orange rind
1/2 tsp. cloves

Mix ingredients in order. Bake for 1 hour at 300 degrees. Yield: 10-12 servings.

SWEET POTATO PONE

3 cups grated raw sweet potato
1/2 cup brown sugar
1 cup cane syrup
3 eggs
2 cups sweet milk
1/2 cup melted butter

Combine all ingredients, add 1/2 tsp. each of cinnamon, allspice and a dash of salt. Place mixture in greased baking dish and bake in 350 degree oven for about 1-1/2 hours.

SWEET POTATO SOUFFLÉ

4 medium potatoes or about 3 cups
  canned potatoes
1 tsp. vanilla
1 cup sugar
1 egg
1/4 cup milk

3 Tbs. flour
1/2 cup butter or oleo
1 tsp. cinnamon

Cook and mash potatoes, add sugar, butter, flour, well beaten egg, milk, vanilla and cinnamon and mix thoroughly. Put into greased baking dish and cook for 45 minutes at 350 degrees. Marshmallows may be placed on top when done and browned slightly.

ORANGE RICE

3 Tbs. butter
2/3 cup sliced celery
2 Tbs. chopped onions
1-1/2 cups water
1 cup orange juice

2 Tbs. grated orange peel
1-1/4 tsp. salt
1 cup uncooked rice

Melt butter in sauce pan with cover, add celery and onions and cook until tender and light brown. Stir in water, orange peel, juice. Add salt. Bring to boil and add rice. Cover and steam on very low heat 25 to 30 minutes or until rice is tender. Use with ham or poultry. Yield: 6 servings.

TOMATO PUDDING

1 10-oz. can of tomato puree
3/4 cup boiling water
1 cup brown sugar
1/2 tsp. salt
1 quart bread cubes with crust removed
1/2 cup melted butter

Add sugar, water, and salt to puree. Boil 5 minutes. Place bread cubes in casserole and pour melted butter over cubes. Add hot tomato mixture and place cover on casserole. Bake at 350 degrees for 30 minutes.

BAKED CHEESE GRITS

6 cups water
2-1/2 tsp. salt
1-1/2 cups uncooked regular grits
1/2 cup butter or margarine
4 cups (1 pound) shredded Cheddar cheese
3 eggs, beaten
1 tsp. garlic

Combine water and salt; bring to a boil. Stir in grits; cook until done, following package directions. Remove from heat. Add butter and 3-3/4 cups cheese; stir until completely melted. Add a small amount of hot grits to eggs, stirring well; stir egg mixture into remaining grits. Pour grits into a lightly greased 2-1/2 quart baking dish; sprinkle with remaining 1/4 cup cheese. Bake at 350 degrees for 1 hour and 15 minutes. Yield: 6 to 8 servings.

CUP OF GOLD

1/4 cup margarine, melted
1/4 cup shredded Cheddar cheese
2 Tbs. Parmesan cheese

3 cups corn flakes
6 eggs

(The night before) combine corn flakes, Cheddar cheese and margarine, toss-ing lightly. Press mixture into 6 greased custard cups. Place on cookie sheet and refrigerate overnight. (In the morning) remove custard cups from refriger-ator and break an egg into each cup. Sprinkle with Parmesan cheese. Bake in 350 degree oven for 20 minutes. Bake in 350 degree oven for 20 minutes. Serve immediately. Yield: 6 servings.

BROCCOLI AND RICE

2 cups cooked rice
2 cups broccoli flowerets
1 cup water
1-1/2 Tbs. reduced calorie margarine
1-1/2 Tbs. flour
2 oz. reduced fat Cheddar cheese
Salt and pepper to taste

In medium saucepan, combine broccoli and water. Simmer, covered about 10 minutes. Drain and reserve liquid, adding water if necessary to make 1 cup. In small saucepan, melt margarine. Blend in flour to form a smooth paste. Slowly add the cup of reserved liquid. Cook over medium heat, stirring until thickened. Add cheese and stir until melted. Season as desired. Combine sauce with broccoli and rice. Serve as a side dish. Yield: 4 servings; each serving contains 171 calories (30% from fat).

SHERRY'S BROCCOLI AND CHEESE

1-1/2 lb. Fresh broccoli (can substitute 10 oz. frozen spears)
6 oz. process American cheese, sliced
1/3 cup milk
1/4 tsp. onion salt
1 drop red pepper sauce (optional)

Trim off large leaves. Remove tough ends of lower stems. Wash. Make lengthwise gashes in them. In covered microwaveable dish, put 1/4 cup water. Cook on High for 5 minutes; stir. Cover again and cook until stems are tender, about 4 to 6 minutes longer. Let stand 1 minute and drain. Heat remaining ingredients over medium heat, stirring frequently, until cheese is melted and mixture is smooth (6 to 8 minutes). Pour over broccoli. Can also be served on baked potatoes.

SAUER KRAUT

Chop a dish pan of cabbage; add one cup white vinegar; 3/4 cup canning salt; 1 gallon water-mix and set aside for about 15 minutes. Pack in cans using some liquid to fill cans. Put lids on; set in a cool dark place for about 2 weeks. Wash off cans and store. Before eating, rinse in colander.

TOMATOES

To peel: Dip ripe tomatoes in boiling hot water for 3 minutes; and thin outer skin can then be peeled or stripped off with ease.

Stewed: Remove skins, slice tomatoes into stewpan. Place over fire and let stew in their own juice about 20 minutes; add a little butter, season with salt and pepper, and continue stewing for another 15 minutes. They may be thickened with soft bread crumbs, or sweetened with a little sugar. A chopped onion may be added, or the tomatoes may be mixed with green corn or other vegetables.

Baked: Wash ripe tomatoes, take slice off stem end; cut out core and remove soft seed-pulp; stuff with buttered bread crumbs, seasoned with salt and pepper; sprinkle more crumbs on top with a little butter on each and bake in hot oven about 20 minutes.

Scalloped: Drain stewed tomatoes; cover bottom of greased baking dish with some of pulp, adding a little butter dotted over them; season with a sprinkle of salt, pepper and brown sugar and a generous layer of bread crumbs; repeat until dish is nearly filled; moisten with tomato juice; cover with another layer of crumbs, lightly buttered; bake in moderate oven 20 minutes.

Grilled: Wipe ripe tomatoes with damp cloth and brush each with melted cooking fat; place on a grill-pan before a clear fire and cook 8 to 10 minutes.
Fried Green: Slice solid green tomatoes; season and dip in egg or in fritter batter. Fry in deep fat or sauté' in drippings in a frying pan.

Broiled: Slice tomatoes into thick crosswise slices. Season with salt, paprika and brown sugar. Place in a pan, sprinkle with bread crumbs, chopped onion and grated cheese (or dot with butter). Broil in moderate hot oven or bake in moderate oven until done.

Stuffed: Cut hollows into firm unpeeled tomatoes. Salt and invert to drain. Fill hollows with cooked food; cover tops with bread crumbs, dot with butter or sprinkle with cheese. Place tomatoes in pan with very little water. Bake in moderate oven about 15 minutes. Tomatoes, peppers, cucumbers, acorn squash, turnips, onions, etc. make good cases for hot food. Much the same stuffing or filling may be used for all of them and they are all good served with sauce (cheese, onion, etc.).

Left-over food (hash, fish, vegetables) may be combined in some palatable way and used as filling. Thicken it with bread crumbs or egg. Use stuffed olives, mashed potatoes, creamed ham or fish, shrimp, crabmeat, onions, rice, mushrooms, corn peas, baked beans, macaroni, etc.

HELPFUL HINTS

To ripen green pears, just place 2 or 3 in a brown bag, loosely closed, and store at room temperature out of direct sunlight.

Anything that grows under the ground start off in cold water—potatoes, beets, carrots, etc. Anything that grows above ground, start off in boiling water—English peas, greens, beans, etc.

To keep cauliflower white while cooking, add a little milk to the water.

When boiling corn, add sugar to the water instead of salt. Salt will toughen the corn.

To ripen tomatoes, put them in a brown paper bag in a dark pantry and they will ripen overnight.

Do not use soda to keep vegetables green. It destroys Vitamin C.

When cooking cabbage, place a small tin cup or can half full of vinegar on the stove near the cabbage. It will absorb the odor.

Potatoes soaked in salt water for 20 minutes before baking will bake more rapidly.

Let raw potatoes stand in cold water for at least half an hour before frying to improve the crispness of French-fired potatoes. Dry potatoes thoroughly before adding to oil.

Use greased muffin tins as molds when baking stuffed green peppers.

A few drops of lemon juice in the water will whiten boiled potatoes.

Buy mushrooms before they "open." When stems and caps are attached snugly, mushrooms are truly fresh.

Do not use metal bowls when mixing salads; use wooden, glass or china.

Lettuce keeps better if you store it in the refrigerator without washing it so that the leaves are dry. Wash lettuce the day you are going to use it.

To keep celery crisp, stand it up in a pitcher of cold, salted water and refrigerate.

All fruits, especially berries, should be spread on a platter and lightly covered with cellophane or waxed paper for storing in refrigerator or other cold place.

Strong flavored fruits and vegetables like cantaloupe and onions should be wrapped in waxed paper when stored with other foods like butter that absorb flavors easily.

To save money and vitamins: Pour all leftover vegetables and water they are cooked in, into a freezer container. When full, add tomato juice, and seasoning to have "free" soup for lunch.

Three large stalks of cut-up celery added to about two cups of beans (navy, brown, pinto, etc.) will make them more easily digested, as will a bit of soda.

When cooking vegetables that grow above ground, remember to boil them without a cover.

Allow 1/4 teaspoon salt to each cup of water for cooking vegetables.

A lump of sugar added to water when cooking greens helps vegetables retain their fresh color.

Never soak vegetables after slicing; you will lose much of their nutritional value.

Fresh vegetables require little seasoning or cooking. If the vegetable is old, dress it up with sauces or seasoning.

To bake potatoes quickly, place them in boiling water for 10-15 minutes. Pierce skin with a fork and then bake in a preheated oven.

To cut down on odors when cooking cabbage, cauliflower, etc., add a little vinegar to the cooking water.

To avoid tears when cutting onions, try cutting them under running cold water or placing them in the freezer briefly before cutting.

A little vinegar or lemon juice added to potatoes before draining will make them extra white when mashed.

To avoid toughening beans or corn, add salt when cooking is halfway through.

To dress up buttered, cooked vegetables, sprinkle them with toasted sesame seed, toasted chopped nuts, crumbled cooked bacon, cannon french-fried onions, or slightly crushed seasoned croutons.

When you are grilling your main dish, try grilling your vegetables, too, for an easy no-mess side dish.

Give mashed potatoes a beautiful whipped cream look by adding hot milk to them before you start mashing.

Do not add sugar to stewed fruits until they have boiled for 10 minutes. They need less sugar then.

Potatoes will take on a golden taste and appearance if sprinkled lightly with flour before frying.

Bananas that have darkened can be peeled and frozen in a plastic container until it is time to bake bread or cake.

A teaspoon of cider vinegar will take care of too-sweet vegetable or main dishes.

One lemon yields about 1/4 cut juice; one orange yields about 1/3 cup juice. This is helpful in making fresh orange juice or lemonade!

Cottage cheese and small amount of grated onion blended in mixer or blender makes a delicious mix for hot baked potatoes.

Potatoes soaked in salt water for 20 minutes before baking will bake more rapidly.

Sweet potatoes will not turn dark if put in salted water (5 teaspoons to 1 quarter of water) immediately after peeling.

Let raw potatoes stand in cold water for at least half an hour before frying to improve the crispness of French fried potatoes.

Use a strawberry huller to peel potatoes, which have been boiled in their "jackets."

Use greased muffing tins as molds when baking stuffed green peppers.

A few drops of lemon juice in the water will whiten boiled potatoes.

The skins will remain tender if you wrap potatoes in aluminum foil to bake them. They are attractively served in the foil, too.

If you add a little milk to water in which cauliflower is cooking, the cauliflower will remain attractively white.

When cooking cabbage, place a small tin cup or can half full of vinegar on the stove near the cabbage, and it will absorb all odor from it.

It is easy to remove the white membrane from oranges—for fancy desserts or salads—by soaking them in boiling water for 5 minutes before you peel them.

You can get more juice from a dried up lemon if you heat it for 5 minutes in boiling water before you squeeze it.

Dip your bananas in lemon juice right after they are peeled. They will not turn dark and the faint flavor of lemon really adds quite a bit. The same may be done with apples.

No tears in your eyes when you peel onions if you hold them under running cold water as you peel them.

To get the corn silk off of corn on the cob, brush downward with a paper towel.

If onions are peeled under water they will not make you cry. To extract onion juice, remove slice from bottom and grate over small saucer.

To bake potatoes quickly boil in water 10 minutes and then put in hot oven. For crisp edible skins, scrub well, dry and rub with bacon fat before putting in oven.

HOUSEHOLD
HELPFUL HINTS

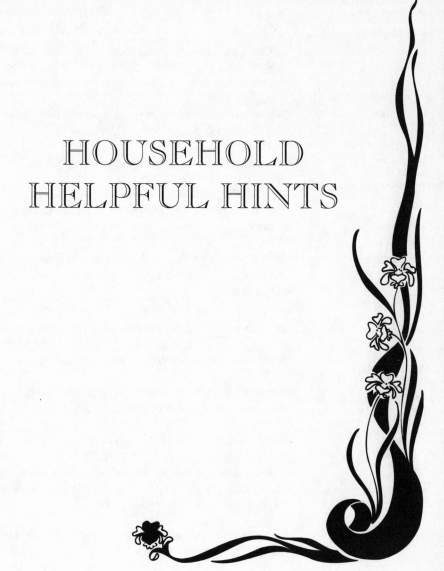

TO REMOVE *STAINS*

Cod Liver Oil   Rub a fresh stain promptly with a little dry cleaning solvent such as carbon tetrachloride; wash in lukewarm suds.

Old dark stains must be bleached; chlorine for cotton or linen; fresh peroxide for white silk or wool. As soon as stain has disappeared wash in lukewarm suds and rinse.

Coffee   Stains are removed from silk by putting between clean damp cloths and pressing with a hot iron.

Fruit   If fresh boiling water does not remove fruit stains, apply lemon juice and bleach in sun.

Grass   If stains cannot be removed with soap and water, use alcohol.

Grease   To remove stains from silk or wool, put a piece of clean white blotting paper on each side of the fabric and iron with a warm iron.

For coarse materials, cover with corn meal or salt, brushing it off as it absorbs the grease. When dirt is mixed with the grease, chloroform, benzol, naphtha or gasoline may be necessary but should be used with care.

Iodine   Remove stains with a weak solution of baking soda, sal soda or borax (1 tablespoon to a pint of water).

Ink   If stains will not wash out, rub with corn meal, salt, French chalk or talcum powder, brushing off as ink is absorbed and repeating. If this is not successful soak stains in milk for one or two days, or rub with a cut lemon, squeezing on some of the juice and rinsing frequently.

Iron   Remove iron rust by rubbing with lemon juice and a little salt and bleaching in sun.

Mildew   Remove by moistening stains with lemon juice, or soaking overnight in sour milk, and bleaching in sun without rinsing.

For very heavy stains, dissolve 1 pound sal soda in 1 quart cold water, add 1/4 pound calcium hypochlorite. Apply with a medicine dropper and as soon as stains have disappeared wash with a solution of oxalic acid which neutralizes the harmful effects of the first mixture and rinse.

Paint   Stains are most easily removed with acetone and need not be washed afterwards or use turpentine or benzol and wash with warm soap and water.

Tar   Turpentine, chloroform or benzol is successful in removing tar; asphalt or road oil stains, followed by thorough washing in soap and hot water.

Tea   Stains that will not wash out may be removed by soaking stains with lemon juice while bleaching in sun.

Varnish   Stains may be removed by rubbing with alcohol or ether, followed by washing in soap and warm water.

To Remove STAINS FROM *Washables*

Alcoholic Beverages   Pre-soak or sponge fresh stains immediately with cold water, then with cold water and glycerin. Rinse with vinegar for a few seconds if stains remain. These stains may turn brown with age.

If wine stain remains, rub with concentrated detergent; wait 15 minutes; rinse. Repeat if necessary. Wash with detergent in hottest water safe for fabric.

Blood   Pre-soak in cold or warm water at least 30 minutes. If stain remains, soak in lukewarm ammonia water (3 table spoons ammonia per gallon water). Rinse. If stain remains, work in detergent, and wash, using bleach safe for fabric.

Candle Wax   Use a dull knife to scrape off as much wax as possible. Place fabric between two blotters or facial tissues and press with warm iron.

Remove color stain with non-flammable dry cleaning solvent. Wash with detergent in the hottest water safe for fabric.

Chewing Gum   Rub area with ice, then scrape off with dull blade. Sponge with dry cleaning solvent; allow to air dry. Wash in detergent and hottest water safe for fabric.

Chocolate and Cocoa   Pre-soak stain in cold or warm water. Wash in hot water with detergent. Remove any grease stains with dry cleaning solvent. If color remains, sponge with hydrogen peroxide, wash again.

Coffee   Sponge or soak with cold water as soon as possible. Wash, using detergent and bleach safe for fabric.

Remove cream grease stains with non-flammable dry cleaning solvent. Wash again.

Crayon   Scrape with dull blade. Wash in hottest water safe for fabric, with detergent and 1-2 cups of baking soda.

NOTE: If full load is crayon stained, take to cleaners or coin-op dry cleaning machines.

Deodorants   Sponge area with white vinegar. If stain remains, soak with denatured alcohol. Wash with detergent in hottest water safe for fabric.

Dye   If dye transfers from a non-colorfast item during washing, immediately bleach discolored items. Repeat as necessary BEFORE drying.

Use color remover on whites.

CAUTION: Do not use color remover in washer or around washer and dryer as it may damage the finish.

Egg   Scrape with dull blade. Pre-soak in cold or water for at least 30 minutes. Remove grease with dry cleaning solvent. Wash in hottest water safe for fabric, with detergent.

Fruit and Fruit Juices   Sponge with cold water. Pre-soak in cold or warm water for at least 30 minutes. Wash with detergent and bleach safe for fabric.

Grass	Pre-soak in cold water for at least 30 minutes. Rinse. Pre-treat with detergent. Wash, using detergent, hot water, and bleach safe for fabric.
	On acetate and colored fabrics, use 1 part of alcohol to 2 parts water.
Grease, Oil, Tar	Method 1: Use powder or chalk absorbents to remove as much grease as possible. Pretreat with detergent or non-flammable dry cleaning solvent, or liquid shampoo. Wash in hottest water safe for fabric, using plenty of detergent.
	Method 2: Rub spot with lard and sponge with a non-flam mable dry cleaning solvent. Wash in hottest water and detergent safe for fabric.
Ink (Ball point pen)	Pour denatured alcohol through stain. Rub in petroleum jelly. Sponge with nonflammable dry cleaning solvent. Soak in detergent solution. Wash with detergent and bleach safe for fabric.
Ink (Fountain pen)	Run cold water through stain until no more color will come out. Rub in lemon juice and detergent. Let stand 5 minutes. Wash.
	If a yellow stain remains, use a commercial rust remover or oxalic acid, as for rust stains.
	CAUTION: HANDLE POISONOUS RUST REMOVERS CAREFULLY. KEEP OUT OF REACH OF CHILDREN. NEVER USE OXALIC ACID OR ANY RUST REMOVER AROUND WASHER AND DRYER AS IT CAN DAMAGE THE FINISH. SUCH CHEMICALS MAY ALSO REMOVE PERMANENT PRESS FABRIC FINISHES.
Lipstick	Loosen stain with a non-flammable dry cleaning solvent. Rub detergent in until stain outline is gone. Wash in hottest water and detergent safe for fabric.
Meat Juices	Scrape with dull blade. Pre-soak in cold or warm water for 30 minutes. Wash with detergent and bleach safe for fabric.
Mildew	Pre-treat as soon as possible with detergent. Wash. If any stain remains, sponge with lemon juice and salt. Dry in sun. Wash, using hottest water, detergent and bleach safe for fabric.

NOTE: Mildew if very hard to remove, treat promptly.

Milk, Cream, Ice Cream
Pre-soak in cold or warm water for 30 minutes. Wash. Sponge any grease spots with non-flammable dry cleaning solvent. Wash again.

Nail Polish
Sponge with polish remover or banana oil. Wash. If stain remains, sponge with denatured alcohol to which a few drops of ammonia have been added. Wash again.

Do not use polish remover on acetate or triacetate fabrics.

Paint (Oil Base)
Sponge stains with turpentine, cleaning fluid or pain remover. Pre-treat and wash in hot water.

For old stains, sponge with banana oil and then with non-flammable dry cleaning solvent. Wash again.

Paint (Water Base)
Scrape off paint with dull blade. Wash with detergent in water as hot as is safe for fabric.

Perspiration
Sponge fresh stain with ammonia; old stain with vinegar. Pre-soak in cold or warm water. Rinse. Wash in hottest water safe for fabric.

If fabric is yellowed, use bleach. If stain still remains, dampen and sprinkle with meat tenderizer, or pepsin. Let stand 1 hour. Brush off and wash.

For persistent odor, sponge with colorless mouthwash.

Rust
Soak in lemon juice and salt or oxalic acid solution (3 tablespoons oxalic acid to 1-pint warm water). A commercial rust remover may be used.

CAUTION: HANDLE POISONOUS RUST REMOVERS CAREFULLY. KEEP OUT OF REACH OF CHILDREN. NEVER USE OXALIC ACID OR ANY RUST REMOVER AROUND WASHER AND DRYER AS IT CAN DAMAGE THE FINISH. SUCH CHEMICALS MAY ALSO REMOVE PERMANENT PRESS FABRIC FINISHES.

Scorch
Wash with detergent and bleach safe for fabric. On heavier scorching, cover stain with cloth dampened with hydrogen peroxide. Cover this with dry cloth and press with hot iron. Rinse well.

CAUTION: Sever scorching cannot be removed because

of fabric damage.

Soft Drinks   Sponge immediately with cold water and alcohol. Heat and detergent may set stain.

Tea   Sponge or soak with cold water as soon as possible. Wash using detergent and bleach safe for fabric.

HOUSEHOLD HINTS

BATHROOM:
For quick clean up in the bathroom, rubbing alcohol is effective and quite sanitary.

A GOOD TREATMENT FOR SICK PLANTS:
Put several empty egg shells in a milk bottle filled with water and let stand for a day. Then water the plants with this mixture.

WINDOW AND MIRROR CLEANING SOLUTION:
Mix 1 quart water, 1/2 cup clear ammonia and 1/8 cup white vinegar. Apply and polish with newspapers.

BRASS AND COPPER:
Apply vinegar and salt to piece that needs cleaning. It works like a charm and requires no elbow work. It can be applied in any manner you prefer. The piece can be wet with vinegar and the salt sprinkled on or you can mix the two ingredients together and apply with sponge or brush. It is marvelous! If it seems dull after the tarnish is removed, go over it with steel wool soap pad.

A weak solution of ammonia will remove the greenish deposit of copper.

BRASS POLISH:
Make a thin paste with 1 teaspoon ammonia and Comet.

REMOVE RUST FROM STAINLESS STEEL SINKS:
Use a little lighter fluid.

CLEANING TOILET BOWLS:
Lower the water level by pouring a bucket of water in commode…just enough for it to flush. Clean with a good scouring powder. Apply bleach and let stand. If stains still persist, use the finest sandpaper—the black kind called wet and dry.

OYSTER SHELLS IN THE TANK OR A CLEAN BRICK:
If you place oyster shells in the tank or a clean brick, the chemicals will adhere to this, and keep chemicals from forming in toilet bowls.

COFFEE STAINS IN PLASTIC CUPS:
Apply baking soda and let soak.

FORMICA:
Clean with rubbing alcohol. Use liquid bleach on stains powdered cleaners dull the finish.

MAYONNAISE:
Use it to remove white watermarks from furniture. Use mayonnaise for an oil treatment for the hair. It can also be used for hot oil treatment. It does not matter if the mayonnaise is old; it will work just as well.

MINERAL OIL:
Use it to seal cutting boards and wooden bowls. It also can be used to polish furniture and stainless steel. Remove excess.

REMOVE FILM FROM DISHWASHER, PLATES AND GLASSES:
Load dishwasher but do not have anything with metal on it in the machine. Place a bowl with one cup of bleach, in the bottom rack. Run the machine through the wash cycle but do not dry. Do not forget this! Fill the same bowl now with a cup of vinegar and run the machine through the complete cycle this time.

TILE SHOWERS:
To remove white film, wipe while dry with dry piece of steel wool. It will loosen like powder. Wash it away. Wipe walls with rag dipped in kerosene once a week to keep it off.

REFINISH ANTIQUES OR REVITALIZE WOOD:
Use equal parts of linseed oil, white vinegar, and turpentine. Rub into furniture (or wood) with soft cloth and lots of elbow grease.

ANTS:
Stalk the ants in your pantry and seal off cracks where they are entering with putty or petroleum jelly. Try sprinkling red pepper on floors and counter tops.

SLIDING EASE:
rub wax along sliding doors, windows and wooden drawers that stick.

IRON CLEANER:
Baking soda on a damp sponge will remove starch deposits. Make sure the iron is cold and unplugged.

STALE ODORS:
Can be removed in the wash by adding baking soda.

TEFLON:
Combine 1 cup water, 2 tablespoons baking soda, 1/2 cup liquid bleach and boil in stained pan for 5-10 minutes or until stain disappears. Wash, rinse and dry and condition with salad oil before using pan again.

CORNINGWARE COOKWARE can be cleaned by filling them with water and dropping in two denture cleaning tablets. Let stand for 30-45 minutes.

INSTANT COFFEE will work wonders on your furniture. Just make a thick paste of your favorite instant and a little water, and rub it into the nicks and scratches on your dark wood furniture. You will be overjoyed at how new and beautiful those pieces will look.

CLOGGED SHOWERHEAD, try boiling it in 1/2 cup vinegar and 1 quart water for 15 minutes.

SPICY AROMA, toss dried orange and lemon rinds into your fireplace.

TIN COFFEE CANS make excellent freezer containers for cookies.

SALT SHAKER: Add raw rice to the salt shaker to keep the salt free flowing.

ICE CUBES will help sharpen the garbage disposal blades.

VINEGAR WILL REMOVE RUST and mildew stains from most chrome.

WHITE APPLIANCES: Mix together 1/2 cup bleach, 1/4 cup baking soda and 4 cups warm water. Apply with sponge and let set for 10 minutes. Rinse and dry thoroughly. Instead of commercial cleaners shine with rubbing alcohol.

QUICK CLEAN UPS: rub equal parts of household ammonia and water on dirty areas. Or, try club soda, it cleans and shines at the same time.

GREASE: Save all grease left from cooking to make soap.

BROKEN GLASS: A safe easy way to gather up small pieces of broken glass is to pat them up with dampened absorbent cotton.

WAX FLOOR:
Before using a cloth to wax the floor, soak it in cold water and wring it out. You will find that the cloth will not, in this way, absorb the wax and that you will save a good deal of wax that would have otherwise been wasted.

BRIGHTEN RUG:
To brighten a rug, sprinkle salt over it before using vacuum cleaner. Sweeps out the spot.

BATHROOM:
A solution of soda and water applied with a whisk broom kept for the purpose will remove the brown streaks in bathroom bowls made by sediment in the dripping water; if the spots do not come off readily, let the solution stand a few minutes before rubbing.

BROOM:
Bore a hole though the broom handle and slip a string though it so you can hang it up.

CLOTHES WRINGER:
Clean the rollers of the clothes wringer with gasoline and wipe off all superfluous oil from cogs and crank to prevent spotting clothes.

DISHWASHING:
To clean the frying pan after frying, pour off the hot lard and wipe the pan with clean paper until all sediment is removed. It can then be easily washed. A few stalks of rhubarb cut up and boiled in a tea kettle full of water will soften the deposit of lime so that it may be all scraped away.

MIXING PAN:
The mixing pan can be quickly cleaned if a little boiling water is poured into it for a few minutes and a close cover put over it. The steam softens the dried dough so that it sill readily wash off.

TINWARE:
May quickly be cleaned by rubbing it with a damp cloth, dipped in soda. Rub briskly and wipe dry. Do not put pans and kettles partly filled with water on the stove to soak, as it only makes them more difficult to clean. Fill them with cold water and soak away from the heat. Discolored china baking dishes can be made as clean as new by rubbing them with whiting.

GLASS: To wash a glass, from which milk has been poured, plunge first into cold water before putting it into warm. The same rule holds well with egg cups or spoons from which eggs have been eaten.

FLOORS: Sour or skim milk added to the water with which linoleum is washed, gives it a luster like new. To remove grease from wood floors, sand is much better than soap. If the floor is dirty mix a little chloride of lime with the sand and use plenty of warm water.

FURNITURE: An equal mixture of turpentine and linseed wool will remove the white marks from furniture caused by water or heat. Cane-seated chair bottoms that have sagged may be made as tight as ever by washing them with hot water and leaving to dry in the open air. Salt water used in washing wicker furniture keeps it from turning yellow and is also good for cleaning straw mats. Equal parts of water and skimmed milk, warm, will remove fly-specks from varnished woodwork or furniture, and make it look fresh.

PIANO KEYS: Clean the keys of the piano with a soft cloth dampened with alcohol, and wipe quickly with a clean, dry cloth.

KEROSENE: Will remove the gummy spots on the sewing machine.

JELLY CUPBOARD: A panful of lime kept in the cupboard with your jams and preserves will help prevent molding.

KNIFE HANDLES: Loose knife handles are easily mended. Take the handle off, mix together three parts resin and one of brick dust. Nearly fill the handle with this, heat the steel beyond the blade till nearly red hot, insert in the handle, and press down into place. It will be as firm as when new.

OILCLOTH: A double layer of brown paper on the pantry shelf and kitchen table covered with oilcloth will enable the oilcloth to last longer.

PICTURE FRAMES: By mixing enough flowers of sulfur with a pint of water to give a golden tinge, and in this boiling three bruised onions, you can renovate your gilt picture frames.

REFRIGERATOR: In an emergency when no refrigerator is at hand, a block of ice may be best kept by placing it in a stone crock of sufficient size. After wrapping the ice in wet newspapers; the jar should then be thoroughly surrounded with feather pillows; it will keep in this manner several days. When 2 trays of ice cream are to be stored in your mechanical refrigerator, you may still have an ample supply of ice cubes if you place the cubes in the defrosting tray, or even in a bowl directly under the shelf which holds this tray.

SCREENS: Wipe screens with kerosene after removing all dust. They will look new and keep away mosquitoes as long as the smell remains.

SILVER: To clean a large amount of silver quickly, immerse it in a gallon of hot water, in which 1 table- spoon salt and 1 teaspoon baking soda have been dis-solved, in either an aluminum pan or dish pan containing an old aluminum lid. Let soak 10 minutes. Wash silver in fresh hot water and soap, rinse and dry. Since the tarnish is transferred to the aluminum keep an old pot or lid just for this purpose. If a small piece of camphor is placed in a silver chest the silver will not become discolored.

WALLPAPER: Greasy spots on wallpaper may be removed or improved by holding a piece of blotting paper over them and pressing on it with a hot iron.

MORE HINTS

An easy, economical way to clean copper is to dip half a lemon in salt and rub the object. Rinse in hot water and polish with a soft cloth.

Clean your candles with a cloth dampened in alcohol.

You will prevent the inside of your metal salt shaker top from rusting if you paint it with ordinary nail polish. When the lacquer is dry, use a darning nee-dle to open the holes from the inside out.

Baked-on stains in the oven? Leave a shallow dish of ammonia in the closed oven one night. Stain will soften and be easy to remove.

Sharpen scissors by cutting a piece of sandpaper, once or twice, with them.

A soap sock for the kids: Keep a small white sock in your bathroom and put all small pieces of soap into it. Tie a knot at the open end of the sock and use this at bathtime for the kiddies. Very handy and they love it—something different!

When you defrost your refrigerator, dry the freezer compartment inside with a towel and put shortening (solidified, not oil) on a paper napkin, and wipe the metal parts inside the freezer compartment. And the next time you defrost the ice will fall off like magic.

To remove paint odor in a room cut a large onion in half and put pieces in a pan of water—leave overnight.

Epsom salts mixed in a water solution is an effective spray for powdery mildew on plants.

Use paper cups as handy containers for your "drippings" in the refrigerator as they take up little room and can be thrown away when empty.

To remove burned-on starch from your iron, sprinkle salt on a sheet of waxed paper and slide iron back and forth several times. Then polish it with silver polish until roughness or stain is removed.

Spray garbage sacks with ammonia to prevent dogs from tearing the bags before picked up.

You can clean darkened aluminum pans easily by boiling them in two teaspoons of cream of tartar mixed in a quart of water. Ten minutes will do it.

To dry drip-dry garments faster and fewer wrinkles, hang garment over the top of a dry cleaner's plastic bag.

To pick up slivers of glass, it helps to use a dampened paper towel.

If zippers stick, just run some bar soap over the zipper and the zipper will work fine.

To draw a straighter line, use a knife instead of a pencil.

To remove your child's crayon marks from linoleum or tile, use silver polish.

Most of time very hot water will revive your wilted flowers.

Your new white tennis shoes will last longer if sprayed heavily with starch when you first get them.

CAKES
&
DESSERTS

CAKES

BIBLE CAKE

1 cup butter (Judges 5:25)
2 cups sugar (Jeremiah 6:20)
6 eggs (Isaiah 10:15)
3-1/2 cups plain flour (I Kings 4:22)
1/2 tsp. salt (Leviticus 2:13)
2 tsp. baking powder
(I Corinthians 5:6)

1/4 tsp. each spice (I Kings)
1 cup water (Genesis 24:11)
1 Tbs. water (Exodus 16:31)
2 cups figs or raisins (I Samuel
25:18)
1 cup chopped nuts (Genesis
43:11)

Mix well and bake until done in greased tube pan. Bake at 375 degrees. This is a good Christmas or Easter cake.

QUICK LUSCIOUS COCONUT CAKE

1 pkg. yellow cake mix
2 eggs

1-1/2 cups buttermilk
1/2 tsp. soda

Bake in two layers until done. Split with thread into four layers. Fill and frost with icing (recipe follows).

ICING:

2 (6 oz.) pkg. frozen coconut
1-1/2 cup sugar

1 cup sour cream
1 small pkg. Cool Whip

Whip sour cream until double in bulk. Add sugar and whip thoroughly until dissolved. Fold in Cool Whip. Fold in 1-1/2 packages thawed coconut. Fill and stack layers and frost sides and top. Sprinkle top with remaining 1/2 package coconut.

EASY LEMON CAKE

1 lemon cake mix
1 carton lemon pie filling

1 carton prepared lemon icing
1 (3 oz.) pkg. cream cheese

Prepare cake mix as directed, baking in 3 layers. Cool completely. Spread pie filling between layers. Beat together icing and cream cheese. Ice sides and tops.

FOUR-DAY COCONUT CAKE

1 box white or yellow cake mix	1 cup sugar
14 oz. shredded coconut	1 pt commercial sour cream
1 tsp. vanilla	

Prepare and bake cake according to directions, using two 9-inch cake pans or one 13 x 9 x 2-inch pan. Let cool. Split layers. Mix coconut, sugar, sour cream and vanilla together. Cover layers, split side up, with filling. Sprinkle top with extra coconut. Refrigerate for 4 days before serving.

MILKY WAY CAKE

8 Milky Way bars	1/2 cup ground nuts
2 sticks margarine, divided	1 cup buttermilk
2 cups sugar	1/2 tsp. soda
4 eggs	1 Tbs. vanilla
2-1/2 cups cake flour	Icing (recipe follows)

Melt together Milky Way bars and 1 stick margarine. Let cool. Cream 1 stick margarine, sugar and eggs (one at a time). Add flour and nuts. Add alternately with buttermilk, soda and vanilla. Fold in Milky Way mixture. Bake 1 hour in broiler pan in 375 degrees oven.

ICING:

4 Milky Way bars	3 Tbs. sweet milk
1 stick margarine	1 tsp. vanilla
Powdered sugar	

Mix together Milky Way bars, margarine, sweet milk and vanilla. Add enough powdered sugar for spreading consistency (about 1 cup).

BAKELESS FRUIT CAKE

1/2 lb. graham crackers, crushed	1/2 lb. marshmallows, cut fine
1/2 lb. dates, cut fine	2 cups nuts, chopped
1 cup cream	10 cherries, chopped

Mix thoroughly all the ingredients. Press firmly in loaf pan which has been lined with oiled paper. Let stand overnight.

AN EASY APPLE CAKE

1 box yellow cake mix
1 tsp. cinnamon
2 cups fresh apples, chopped

Mix cake as directed on package. Add cinnamon and apples. Bake as directed.

CARMEL FILLING:
1 cup light brown sugar
1 stick butter
1/4 cup evaporated milk

Cook mixture for two minutes; let cool; spread on cake.

COCONUT CREAM CHEESE POUND CAKE

1/2 cup butter or margarine
1/2 cup shortening
1 (8 oz.) pkg. cream cheese
3 cups sugar
6 eggs
3 cups all-purpose flour

1/4 tsp. baking powder
1/4 tsp. salt
1 (6 oz.) pkg. frozen coconut
(thawed)
1 tsp. vanilla flavoring
1 tsp. coconut flavoring

Cream together butter or margarine, cream cheese and shortening. Gradually add sugar, beating at a medium speed of an electric mixer until light and fluffy. Add eggs one at a time, beating well after each addition. Sift before measuring 3 cups of flour and re-sift with baking powder and salt. Add sifted ingredients to cream mixture at a low speed, mixing only until well-blended. Fold in the coconut and flavorings. Pour batter into a greased and floured 10-inch tube pan and bake in a preheated 350 degrees oven for 1 hour and 15 minutes. Cool for 10-15 minutes before removing from pan then let cool completely.

GRAHAM CRACKER CAKE

1 lb. box graham crackers crushed fine
4 eggs
2 cups sugar
2 cups pecans, chopped

2 cups raisins
1 cup milk
1/2 lb. butter
1 Tbs. vanilla flavoring

Cream butter and sugar. Add milk and flavoring, then add crackers, raisins, and pecans. Mix well. Bake in well-greased cake pan for one hour or until done at 350 degrees F.

ST. LOUIS CAKE

1 yellow cake mix
1 stick butter
2 eggs

8 oz. cream cheese
2 eggs
1 box powdered sugar

Mix first 3 ingredients and press into 9x13-inch pan. Mix last 3 ingredients and pour over crust.
Mix: 3 tablespoons powdered sugar and 1 cup chopped pecans top the cake. Bake at 350 degrees for 35-45 minutes. Very rich. Freezes well.

WHIPPING CREAM POUND CAKE

2-1/2 cups sugar
6 eggs
1 tsp. vanilla flavoring
1 tsp. baking powder

1 cup shortening
1 tsp. lemon flavoring
3 cups sifted all purpose flour
1/2 pint whipping cream

Cream sugar and shortening. Add eggs one at a time, beat well after each addition. Add lemon and vanilla flavorings. Sift dry ingredients. Alternately add flour and whipping cream to sugar and shortening. Mix slowly. Place in a greased and floured tube pan or a 16-1/2 inch x 5-inch x 4-inch pan. Bake 40 minutes at 275 degrees, then move temperature to 325 for 30 minutes without opening oven door or moving pan. Test for doneness by inserting toothpick. Cake may need to cook for 5-10 additional minutes. Do not overcook. Cake should be very moist.

JAM CAKE

5 eggs, beaten
2 cups sugar
1 cup butter
1 tsp. soda
1 tsp. cloves
1 tsp. cinnamon
1 cup chopped pecans

3 cups flour
1 cup buttermilk
1/4 tsp. salt
1 tsp. allspice
1 cup raisins
1 cup jam

Cream butter and sugar until light and fluffy, add eggs. Sift flour before measuring and add spices and salt. Dissolve soda in buttermilk and add alternately with the flour to eggs, sugar and butter mixture. Lightly dredge fruit and nuts with extra flour. Add to mixture. Add jam. Bake in 3 well-oiled and paper-lined 6 x 10 cake pans in 325 degrees oven for 25 or 30 minutes.

SOUR CREAM COFFEE CAKE

1/2 cup butter
1 cup sugar
2 eggs
2 cups sifted flour
1 tsp. baking soda

1-1/2 tsp. baking powder
1/8 tsp. salt
1 cup sour cream
1 tsp. vanilla

FILLING:

1/2 cup sugar
1 tsp. cinnamon
3/4 cup shopped pecans

Cream butter and sugar. Add eggs, one at a time. Beat after each addition. Sift dry ingredients together. Add to creamed mixture alternately with sour cream. Stir in vanilla. Mix filling ingredients. Grease 10-inch tube pan. Pour in half the batter. Sprinkle with half the filling mixture. Repeat last two steps. Bake at 350 degrees F. for 40 minutes.

FRESH APPLE CAKE

1-1/4 cups cooking oil
2 cups sugar
3 large eggs
3 cups flour sifted with
    1 tsp. salt & 1 tsp. soda)

3 cups raw sliced apples
1-1/2 cups pecans or black walnuts
1 tsp. vanilla flavoring

Mix in order given and pour into greased 12 3/4 x 9 x 2 baking dish or pan. Bake at 325 degrees for one hour. Allow cake to remain in baking pan and cover warm cake with following glaze:

1 cup light brown sugar (firmly packed)
1 stick of butter or margarine
1/4 cup cream
1 tsp. vanilla

Combine in small saucepan and cook for 2-1/2 minutes, stirring constantly. Spoon over cake while both are warm. Cake will stay moist for days.

ORANGE SLICE CAKE

2 cups sugar
1 cup shortening
4 eggs
4 cups all purpose flour
1 tsp. baking soda
1 tsp. salt

1/2 cup buttermilk
1 cup chopped pecans
1 8 oz. box chopped dates
1 11 oz. pkg. orange slice candy
   chopped
1/2 cup flour

In a large mixing bowl, cream together sugar and shortening; add eggs, mixing well after each addition. Add flour, soda, salt and buttermilk; mix well. Toss pecans, dates and candy with 1/2 cup flour and fold into batter. Pour into prepared 10-inch tube pan and bake at 250 degrees for 2-2-1/2 hours

BEST CHOCOLATE CAKE

1 box devil's food cake mix
1 small box chocolate pudding mix
1 12 oz. pkg. semi-sweet chocolate morsels
2 eggs
1 3/4 cup sour cream

Mix together all ingredients and pour batter into a well-greased and floured bundt pan or tube pan. Bake 50-55 minutes at 350 degrees until cake springs back when pressed lightly.

DEEP CHOCOLATE CAKE

8 plain Hershey chocolate bars
1 cup butter
2 cups sugar
4 eggs
1 cup chocolate syrup

2 tsp. vanilla
2-1/2 cups all-purpose flour
1/2 tsp. baking soda
1 cup buttermilk
1 cup chopped pecans

Preheat oven to 350 degrees. Melt candy in a double boiler or microwave; cool. Cream butter and sugar. Add eggs one at a time; add candy, syrup and vanilla; beat well. Sift flour with soda and add alternately with buttermilk to chocolate batter. Add nuts. Pour into a lightly greased tube pan and bake for 1-1/2 hours.

PUMPKIN CAKE

3 cups sugar
1 cup oil
4 eggs

2 cups cooked, mashed pumpkin
3-1/2 cups self-rising flour
1 tsp. coconut flavoring

Cream together sugar and oil, add remaining ingredients, mix well. Pour batter into three 9-inch prepared cake pans. Bake at 350 degrees for 30 minutes. Frost cooled cake with cream cheese frosting.

CREAM CHEESE FROSTING

11 oz. cream cheese, softened
1/2 cup butter, softened
1 one lb. box powdered sugar
1 cup chopped pecans

Place all ingredients except pecans, in a medium sized mixing bowl and mix until smooth. Fold in pecans.

FRUIT COCKTAIL CAKE

1-1/2 cups brown sugar
2 cups flour
2 eggs

2 tsp. soda
1/2 cup pecans, chopped
1 can fruit cocktail (do not drain)

Stir all ingredients together and pour into greased 9 x 12 pan. Bake at 350 degrees until done.

ICING:

1/2 cup coconut
1 stick oleo
1/2 cup evaporated milk
1/2 cup brown sugar

Cook until thick and spread over top of cake.

EASY ORANGE POUND CAKE

1 box deluxe yellow cake mix
1 box (5 1/4 oz.) instant vanilla pudding
1/2 cup vegetable oil
4 eggs
3/4 cup orange juice
1 tsp. orange extract (more if desired

Preheat oven to 350 degrees. Combine ingredients and mix. Pour into a pre-pared tube pan. Bake for 40-45 minutes or until done. Top with glaze while still warm.

PEAR AMBROSIA

5 pears, cubed
4 oranges
1 cup flaked coconut
1 16 oz. can crushed pineapple, drained
1 small jar maraschino cherries, halved

Cube pears, cut up oranges and combine remaining ingredients. Chill until serving time. Serves 4-6.

POOR MAN'S CAKE

2 cups all-purpose flour
1 cup sugar
1/2 cup cocoa
2 tsp. baking soda

1/2 tsp. salt
1 cup mayonnaise
1 cup water
1 tsp. vanilla

Sift together first five ingredients. Add remaining ingredients to flour mixture; beat until smooth. Pour into greased and floured 9-inch square baking pan. Bake at 350 degrees for 35-40 minutes or until cake tests done. Frost as desired.

ITALIAN CREAM CAKE

1 stick margarine
1/2 cup vegetable shortening
2 cups sugar
5 egg yolks
2 cups flour
1 tsp. soda

1 cup buttermilk
1 tsp. vanilla extract
1 small can angel flake coconut
1 cup chopped nuts
5 egg whites, stiffly beaten

Cream margarine and shortening; add sugar and beat until mixture is smooth. Add egg yolks and beat well. Combine flour and soda and add to creamed mixture alternately with buttermilk. Stir in vanilla extract. Add coconut and nuts. Fold in egg whites. Pour into three greased and floured 8-inch cakepans. Bake at 350 degrees F. for 25 minutes or until cake tests done; cool. Frost with Creamed Cheese Frosting

Cream Cheese FROSTING:

1 8-oz. pkg. cream cheese, softened
1/2 stick margarine
1 box powdered sugar
1 tsp. vanilla extract
Chopped pecans

Beat cream cheese and margarine until smooth; add sugar and mix well. Add vanilla extract and beat until smooth. Spread on cake. Sprinkle top with pecans.

COCONUT CAKE

1 pkg. yellow cake mix
2 cups sour cream
2 cups confectioner's sugar
1 pkg. (12 oz.) frozen coconut-thawed
1 container (13-1/2 oz.) cool whip

Prepare cake mix according to package directions. Bake in two 9-inch cake pans. Cool—Then split each layer cross-wise. Combine sour cream, confectioner's sugar and coconut and refrigerate while cake is baking. Spread between layers of cake, then spread top and sides of cake with cool whip and sprinkle freely with coconut-top and sides. Place cake in air tight container and refrigerate for three days before serving. Keeps well for several days if kept covered in the fridge.

ANGEL CAKE

1 stick margarine	1/2 cup crisco
2 cups sugar	5 egg yolks
2 cups plain flour	1 tsp. soda
1 cup buttermilk	1 tsp. vanilla
1 small can coconut	1 cup chopped nuts
5 egg whites, beaten	

Combine sugar, margarine, and crisco and beat well. Add egg yolks and beat. Add flour, soda and buttermilk and beat well. Stir in flavoring, nuts, and coconut and fold in egg whites. Bake 350 degrees for 25 minutes. Yield: 3 layers.

FROSTING:

1 8 oz. cream cheese	1 tsp. vanilla
1/2 stick margarine	1/2 cup coconut
One box powdered sugar	1/2 cup nuts

Beat well and ice.

PINEAPPLE-COCONUT CAKE

2 cups flour	1 tsp. vanilla
2 tsp. soda	2 cups sugar
1/4 cup oil	1 large can crushed pineapple (undrained)
2 eggs	1/4 tsp. salt

Mix ingredients and beat 3 minutes; pour into a lightly greased 13 x 9 x 2-inch pan. Bake 30-40 minutes at 350 degrees.

TOPPING:

1 cup evaporated milk	1 tsp. vanilla
1-1/2 cup sugar	1 cup chopped nuts
3/4 stick margarine	1 cup coconut

Place all ingredients except nuts and coconut in a pan and bring to a boil. Add nuts and coconut and cook for 5 minutes. Pour over cake as soon as cake is taken from the oven. Let stand 30 minutes before cutting. Stays moist and fresh for more than a week.

WASHINGTON APPLE CAKE

3 eggs
2 cups sugar
1 cup cooking oil
2 cups all-purpose flour
2 tsp. cinnamon

1 tsp. baking soda
1/2 tsp. salt
1 tsp. vanilla
1 cup chopped nuts (walnuts)
4 cups thinly sliced, pared tart
    apples (5 medium)

Beat eggs with mixer until thick and light. Combine sugar and oil; pour into eggs with mixer on medium speed. Stir together flour, cinnamon, soda and salt; add to egg mixture with vanilla; beat to mix, stir in walnuts. Spread apples in buttered 13 x 9 x 2-inch pan. Pour batter over apples, spreading to cover. Bake 350 degrees for 1 hour. Remove from oven and cool; spread with cream cheese icing.

Cream Cheese ICING:

Soften 2-3 oz. packages of cream cheese; beat until fluffy. Beat in 1/4 cup melted butter, then beat in 2 cups powdered sugar and 1 teaspoon lemon juice. Spread over cooled cake. Refrigerate. Yield: 12-15 servings.

STRAWBERRY CAKE

1 box white cake mix
1 pkg. strawberry gelatin
3/4 cup salad oil
4 eggs 1 cup strawberries

Sift together cake mix and gelatin. Add oil, beat in eggs one at a time. Add berries and mix well. Bake on 350 degrees for 30-35 minutes. Yield: 3 layers.

Strawberry FILLING and ICING:

1 box confectioner's sugar, sifted
Blend with 1 stick oleo, melted
Add 1/2 cup strawberries and mix well

VANILLA WAFER POUND CAKE

1 (12 oz.) box vanilla wafers
2 sticks margarine
2 cups sugar
6 eggs

1/2 cup sweet milk
7 oz. bag coconut
1 cup walnuts

Cream together margarine and sugar. Add eggs, milk, crushed wafers, coconut and nuts. Bake in tube pan 1-1/2 hours at 300 degrees.

BLUEBERRY POUND CAKE

1 cup plus 2 Tbs. butter
2 1/4 cups sugar, divided
4 eggs
1 tsp. vanilla

3 cups all-purpose flour, divided
1 tsp. baking powder
1/2 tsp. salt
2 cups fresh blueberries

Grease a 10-inch tube pan with 2 tablespoons butter. Sprinkle pan with 1/4 cup sugar. Cream remaining butter, gradually add remaining sugar, beating well. Add eggs, one at a time, beating well after each addition. Add vanilla and mix well. Combine 2 3/4 cups flour, baking powder, and salt; gradually add to creamed mixture, beating until well blended. Dredge blueberries into batter. Pour batter into prepared pan. Bake at 325 degrees for one hour 10 minutes. Remove from pan and cool completely.

POUND CAKE

3-1/3 cups sugar
1 lb. butter (2 cups)
10 eggs

4 cups flour
1 tsp. vanilla
1 tsp. salt

Cream butter and sugar. Add eggs one at a time, beating after each addition. Add vanilla and salt. Beat thoroughly. Place in oven 275 degrees and bake for one hour. Turn heat to 300 degrees and bake for another hour or until done.

GINGER CAKES

1/2 cup shortening
1/2 cup sugar
1/2 cup cane syrup
1/4 cup water

1/2 tsp. soda
1/2 tsp. ginger
1/2 tsp. cinnamon
2-1/4 cups plain flour

Blend all ingredients well, adding enough flour to make stiff dough. Roll thin on floured board. Cut in squares or with cookie cutter and place on greased cookie sheet. Bake at 400 degrees for 10 minutes or until brown.

LEMON CHEESE CAKE

1 cup butter
2 cups sugar
4 eggs
1 cup milk

3 cups plain flour
3 tsp. baking powder
1/2 tsp. salt
1 tsp. vanilla

Cream shortening and sugar until light and fluffy. Add eggs one at a time, beating well after each addition. Add sifted dry ingredients alternately with milk, beating after each addition. Add vanilla. Bake in 3 layers 350 degrees for 30 minutes or until done.

SOUR CREAM POUND CAKE

2 cups sugar
3-1/2 cups plain flour
3 tsp. baking powder
1/2 tsp. salt
3/4 cup butter

1 cup sour cream
1/2 tsp. baking soda
1 tsp. vanilla
6 egg whites or
4 eggs separated

Whip egg whites until stiff but not dry. Add 1/8 tsp. salt and put in refrigerator until remainder of cake is mixed. Sift sugar, and cream it with butter until light and creamy. Sift flour, then resift with baking powder, salt and soda. Add dry ingredients in 3 parts to the butter mixture alternately with thirds of the sour cream. Beat batter until smooth after each addition. Beat in flavoring. Fold in egg whites. Bake in moderate oven 325 degrees for one hour or until done.

SMALL POUND CAKE

1 cup butter
1-3/4 cups sugar
5 eggs
1/2 tsp. lemon flavoring (optional)

2 cups plain flour
1 tsp. vanilla
1/2 tsp. salt

Cream butter and sugar well, then add egg one at a time, beating after each addition. Add flour, salt and flavoring. Bake 1 hour at 350 degrees.

POUND CAKE

2 sticks margarine
1/2 cup crisco
(cream the above)

5 eggs (add one at a time, beating well after each addition)
2 tsp. vanilla

Bake 325 degrees for 1 hour, then 350 degrees for 30 minutes.

FROSTING:

1 8 oz. pkg. of cream cheese (softened)
1 box powdered sugar
1 tsp. vanilla

Cream together and spread on cake.

SOUR CREAM POUND CAKE

1 cup butter or margarine
3 cups sugar
6 eggs
1 tsp. vanilla extract

1/2 tsp. lemon extract
1/4 tsp. almond extract
1 cup sour cream
3 cups cake flour, sifted

Cream butter or margarine in large bowl of an electric mixer, slowly add sugar. Add eggs one at a time, beating well after each addition at a medium speed. Add extracts. Add 2 tablespoons of flour, then the sour cream. Add remaining flour gradually until well blended. Pour batter into a greased and floured 9 or 10-inch tube pan. Bake in preheated 325 degrees oven for 1-1/2 hours or until tests done. One sixteenth of the cake contains 370 calories.

3-LAYER QUICK METHOD CAKE

2-1/2 cups plain flour
1-2/3 cups sugar
1 tsp. salt
3-1/2 tsp. baking powder

2/3 cups butter or Crisco
1-1/4 cups milk
3 eggs
1 tsp. vanilla

Combine flour, sugar, salt and baking powder in mixing bowl. Add butter or Crisco and 1/2 of milk. Beat with mixer for 2 minutes. Add eggs, additional milk and vanilla. Beat 2 more minutes. Bake 30 minutes at 350 degrees in 3 layers. Use any filling desired.

CONFECTIONER'S SUGAR POUND CAKE

1 box confectioner's sugar (sifted)
1 box plain flour, sifted
1 cup butter
1 stick oleo

6 eggs
1 tsp. vanilla
1 tsp. salt

Cream sugar, oleo, and butter. Add eggs beating after each addition. Add flour, vanilla and salt. Beat thoroughly. Bake at 325 degrees for 1 hour or until done.

CHOCOLATE POUND CAKE

5 eggs
1 cup butter
1 block oleo
3 cups sugar
3 cups flour
1 tsp. baking powder

2/3 cup cocoa
1 cup milk
pinch salt
1 tsp. vanilla
1 cup nuts (optional)

Cream butter, oleo and sugar. Add cocoa and beat. Add eggs one at a time, beating after each addition. Add milk and dry ingredients alternately and vanilla. 1 cup nuts chopped fine and floured slightly may be added to batter. Bake at 275 degrees for 2-1/2 hours.
Chocolate filling that may be spread on cake if desired:

2 cups confectioner's sugar
2 heaping Tbs. cocoa
2 Tbs. butter or other shortening

2 Tbs. of cream or more
1 tsp. vanilla

Blend mixture well and beat until creamy. If too thick for spreading add more milk or cream. Let cake cool before spreading filling if used.

PINEAPPLE SUPREME POUND CAKE

1 pkg. pineapple cake mix
4 eggs
1 cup water
1/2 cup Crisco Oil
1 pkg. pineapple instant pudding mix
Blend all ingredients in a large bowl, then beat at medium speed for 2 minutes. Bake in a greased and floured 10-inch tube pan at 350 degrees for 45-55 minutes, until center springs back when touched lightly. Cool right side up for about 25 minutes, then remove from pan.

GLAZE:
Blend 1 cup confectioner's sugar with either 2 tablespoons milk or 2 tablespoons liquid from canned pineapple. Drizzle over cake.

When baking recipe at high altitudes: Stir 1/3 cup flour into mix. Mix as directed using 1 package pineapple instant pudding mix, 1/3 cup Crisco Oil, 1-1/4 cups water and 4 eggs. Bake at 375 degrees for about 40-45 minute.

PINEAPPLE POUND CAKE

8 eggs
2 cups vegetable shortening
1 tsp. vanilla
3 cups sugar

3 cups plain flour
dash of salt
1 small can crushed
  pineapple (juice and all)

Cream shortening and sugar. Add eggs, one at a time, beating after each addition. Add flour and salt gradually. Stir in vanilla and crushed pineapple. Bake in floured and greased tube pan for 1 hour or until done at 350 degrees.

GLAZE:
1 box confectioner's sugar
1 stick margarine

(Add orange juice until thin enough to spread)

SUNBELT POUND CAKE

1-1/2 cups butter	4-1/2 cups all-purpose flour
3 cups sugar	1 tsp. salt
6 eggs	3/4 tsp. baking soda
1-1/2 tsp. vanilla	3/4 tsp. baking powder
1-1/2 tsp. lemon extract	1-1/2 cups buttermilk

Cream butter. Gradually add sugar, beating until light and fluffy. Add eggs, all at once, beating well about 2-3 minutes. Blend in flavoring. Combine dry ingredients. Add alternately with buttermilk, beating just until thoroughly combined. Spread evenly in 2 greased 9 x 5 x 3-inch loaf pans or 1 greased 10 x 4-inch tube pan. Bake in preheated oven at 350 degrees for 1 hour and 10 minutes for loaf pan or 1 hour and 20 minutes for tube pan or until cake tester inserted near center comes out clean. Cool in pans on wire racks for 10 minutes. Remove from pans and cool completely.

CHOCOLATE POUND CAKE

1 pkg. cake mix	1 cup water
4 eggs	1/2 cup oil
1 pkg. chocolate instant pudding mix	

Blend all ingredients in a large bowl, then beat at medium speed for 2 minutes. Bake in a greased and floured 10-inch tube pan at 350 degrees for 45-55 minutes, until center springs back when touched lightly. Cool right side up for about 25 minutes, then remove from pan.

Chocolate GLAZE:

2 Tbs. cocoa	1 Tbs. corn syrup
1 Tbs. plus 2 tsp. water	1 cup confectioner's sugar (sift if 1
Tbs. Crisco Oil	lumpy)

In a small saucepan combine all ingredients except sugar. Cook and stir over low heat until mixture is smooth. Remove from heat; beat in sugar. If mixture is too thick to pour easily, add a little more water. Drizzle over cake.

When baking recipe at high altitudes: Stir 1/3 cup flour into mix. Mix as directed using 1 package chocolate instant pudding mix, 1/3 cup Crisco Oil, 1-1/4 cups water and 4 eggs. Bake at 375 degrees for about 40-45 minutes

HOT FUDGE CAKE

1 cup all-purpose flour
3/4 cup sugar
6 Tbs. baking cocoa, divided
2 tsp. baking powder
1/4 tsp. salt
1/2 cup milk

2 Tbs. vegetable oil
1 tsp. vanilla extract
1 cup packed brown sugar
1-3/4 cups hot water
Whipped cream or ice cream
  (optional)

In a medium bowl, combine flour, sugar, 2 tablespoons cocoa, baking powder and salt. Stir in the milk, oil and vanilla until smooth. Spread in an ungreased 9-inch square baking pan. Combine brown sugar and remaining cocoa; sprinkle over batter. Pour hot water over all; do not stir. Bake at 350 degrees for 35-40 minutes. Serve warm. Top with whipped cream or ice cream if desired. Yield: 9 servings.

WALNUT POUND CAKE

3 cups sugar
3 cups plain flour
2/3 cups self-rising flour
1-1/2 cups crisco
1 cup walnuts

1 tsp. walnut or vanilla flavoring
6 eggs & pinch of salt
1-1/2 cups sweet milk

Beat eggs, sugar, crisco, and flavoring. Add dry ingredients with milk, fold in walnuts. Bake at 225 degrees or 250 degrees for 1-1/2 hours or longer.

ICING:

1 box powdered sugar
1 tsp. vanilla
8 oz. cream cheese
1/2 cup chopped walnuts
1 stick oleo

(Add enough milk to spread)

CHOCOLATE CREAM CHEESE POUND CAKE

1-1/2 cups butter	3 cups flour
8 oz. pkg. cream cheese	1 tsp. vanilla
3 cups sugar	1 cup finely chopped pecans
6 eggs Chocolate Frosting	
1/2 cup cocoa	

Cream butter, cream cheese and sugar. Add eggs one at a time mixing well after each one. Sift cocoa with flour and add slowly to egg mixture. Add vanilla and nuts. Pour into a greased tube pan and bake at 325 degrees for 1-1/2 hours or until cake tests done.

Chocolate FROSTING:

1 cup sugar	Dash of salt
1/4 cup cocoa	1/2 tsp. vanilla
1/4 cup milk	1/2 cup finely chopped pecans
1/4 cup butter	

In a saucepan, combine all ingredients except pecans and heat for 1-1/2 minutes. Cool to spreading consistency. (If too stiff, add a small amount of milk). Frost cake and sprinkle sides and top with pecans.

STRAWBERRY TRIFLE

1 medium-size angel food cake
1 small pkg. strawberry gelatin
1 large pkg. frozen strawberries, defrosted
1 small pkg. instant vanilla pudding
1 large banana or 2 small ones
1 small container prepared whipping topping

Tear cake into chunks and place into a large glass bowl. Combine dry gelatin with strawberries and mix well. Pour over cake. Pour prepared pudding on top of the strawberry mixture. Add sliced banana. Then add whipped topping on top. Garnish with fresh sliced strawberries in the spring and summer. Sliced maraschino cherries can be used in the fall and winter.

BUTTERNUT CAKE

1 cup Crisco
1 cup sweet milk
2-1/2 cups plain flour
Dash of salt

2 cups sugar
1/2 cup self rising flour
4 eggs
1 Tbs. butternut flavoring

Bake 1 hour on 325 degrees in tube pan.

ICING:

1 box powdered sugar
1 Tbs. butternut flavoring
Enough milk to mix (can use powdered milk)
1/4 cup Crisco

DO NOTHING CAKE

2 cups all purpose flour
2 eggs, slightly beaten
1/2 tsp. salt
1 20-oz. can crushed pineapple, drained

2 cups sugar
1 tsp. vanilla
1 tsp. baking soda

Combine all ingredients and mix by hand. Do not use an electric mixer. Pour into a greased 9x12-inch pan and bake for 30-35 minutes at 350 degrees. Spread topping over cake while warm. Yield: 12 servings.

TOPPING:

1 5-oz. can milk
1/2 cup butter or margarine
1 cup sugar
1-1/2 cup coconut
1 cup chopped pecans

Mix milk, sugar and margarine together, boil 5 minutes. Add coconut and pecans. Spread over warm cake.

CHEESECAKE

2 pkgs. (8 oz.) cream cheese
1 cup sugar
2 tsps. Lemon juice
1 tsp. vanilla

5 eggs, separated
2 cups sour cream
1 9-inch crust, prebaked

Beat cream cheese with 1/2 cup sugar until smooth. Add lemon juice, rind and vanilla. Beat in egg yolks; add sour cream. Beat egg whites until foamy; gradually add remaining sugar and beat until stiff. Fold egg yolk mixture into egg whites. Pour into prepared graham cracker crust. Bake in a 325 degrees oven 1-1/4 hours. Turn off heat. Cool in oven with door open for 1/2 hour. Cool completely at room temperature. Chill.

CRUST:

1-1/2 cups graham cracker crumbs
1/4 cup melted butter

2 Tbs. sugar
1 tsp. lemon rind, grated

Mix ingredients, press into the bottom and part way up the sides of a 9-inch springform pan. Bake in a 325 degrees oven for 10 minutes. Cool before filling.

CHOCOLATE SYRUP CAKE

1 cup sugar
1/2 cup butter
4 eggs

1 16 oz. can chocolate syrup
1 tsp. vanilla
1 cup self-rising flour

Combine sugar and butter in a large bowl. Add eggs, beating well after each addition. Add remaining ingredients and mix well. Pour into a greased and floured 9 x 13-inch cake pan. Bake at 325 degrees for 35-45 minutes or until done.

ICING:

1-1/2 cups sugar
6 Tbs. butter
1/2 cup cream

8 oz. chocolate chips
1 tsp. vanilla
1 Tbs. marshmallow cream

Place sugar, butter and cream in a medium sized saucepan. Bring to a boil; add remaining ingredients. Stir to prevent sticking. Pour over cooled cake. Serves 8.

LEMON CHEESE CAKE

2 cups sugar
1 cup vegetable shortening
1 cup milk

3 cups flour
3 tsp. baking powder
6 egg whites beaten

Combine sugar and shortening and cream well. Sift together flour and baking powder, and alternate with milk in adding to sugar and shortening mixture. Bake in 3 cake layer pans at 375 degrees F. for 25 minutes or until done.

CARROT CAKE

2 cups plain flour
2 cups sugar
1 tsp. soda
1/2 tsp. salt

1 tsp. cinnamon
1-1/2 cups cooking oil
4 eggs
2-1/2 cups finely grated carrots

Sift together flour, sugar, soda, salt, and cinnamon; place in mixing bowl and add remaining ingredients. Bake well. Cook at 375 degrees until firm in pan. Yield: 3 layers.

FILLING:

1 box powdered sugar
1 stick butter
1 tsp. vanilla

1 8 oz. pkg. cream cheese
1 cup chopped pecans

7-UP CAKE

3 cups sugar
1 stick oleo
1 stick butter (real)
1/2 cupCrisco
5 eggs

3 cups plain flour
1 tsp. vanilla
Dab of orange flavoring
1/2 tsp. coconut flavoring
1 (7 oz.) 7-Up

Cream shortening, then cream in sugar. Add eggs, one at a time. Alternate flour and 7-Up. Bake at 325 degrees for 1-1/2 hours.

JAPANESE FRUIT CAKE

1 cup butter or other shortening
2 cups sugar
4 eggs
3 1/4 cups flour
2 tsp. baking powder
1 tsp. salt

1 cup milk
1 tsp. cinnamon
1 tsp. allspice
1 tsp. vanilla
1 cup raisins chopped fine

Cream butter and sugar. Add eggs one at a time beating after each addition. Add flour, bread , powder and salt that have been sifted together, alternately with milk. Add vanilla. Pour enough batter in one of the cake pans for one layer (about 1/3 of batter). Add to the remaining batter the spices and chopped raisins and mix. Divide this mixture into the other two cake pans. Bake in 350 degrees oven for 30 minutes or until done. Use the layer without spices in center of cake.

Japanese Fruit Cake FILLING:

4 cups coconut
1 cup boiling water
2 cups sugar

3 Tbs. cornstarch
1 cup cold water
Juice of 2 lemons, grated
    rind of one

Mix coconut, sugar with boiling water and let come to boil in heavy pan or boiler. Mix corn starch in cup of cold water, lemon juice and rind and add to first mixture. Cook over low heat and stir until mixture thickens. Let cool before spreading on cake.

APPLE CAKE

3 cups sifted flour
2 cups sugar
3 eggs
1 cup oil
1 tsp. soda
1 tsp. salt

1/2 tsp. ground cloves
1/2 tsp. nutmeg
1/2 tsp. cinnamon
3 cups sliced apples
1 cup nuts (pecans)

Put apples in batter last. Bake at 350 degrees for one hour. Put in brown paper bag for 10 – 15 minutes.

ORANGE SLICE CAKE

1 cup butter
4 eggs
2 cups sugar
1 tsp. soda (dissolved in
   1/2 cup buttermilk)

1 box dates, cut into small pieces
1 bag or can coconut
2 cups chopped nuts
1 lb. bag of orange slice candy
3-1/2 cup plain flour

Cream butter and sugar, add eggs one at a time, add flour alternating with milk roll nuts orange slice candy and dates in flour, add coconut to batter. Bake in tube pan at 250 degrees for 2-2-1/2 hours.

Orange Slice <u>SAUCE</u>:

1 cup orange juice (fresh or frozen)
2 cups powdered sugar

Mix well, pour over cake as soon as taken from oven, let cake stand in pan overnight.

MIRACLE WHIP CHOCOLATE CAKE

1-1/2 cups sugar
1-1/2 tsp. vanilla
3 cups flour
1 cup water

3/4 cup cocoa
1-1/2 tsp. baking soda
1/8 tsp. salt
1-1/2 cups Miracle Whip salad dressing

Combine salad dressing, sugar and vanilla. Add combined dry ingredients alternately with water, mixing well after each addition. Pour into two wax paper-lined 8 or 9-inch layer pans. Bake at 350 degrees, 30 to 35 minutes or until wooden pick inserted in center comes out clean. Cool 10 minutes; remove from pans. Cool. Fill and frost with:

Creamy Cocoa <u>FROSTING</u>:

1 tsp. vanilla
Dash of salt
1/2 cup cocoa

1 8 oz. pkg. cream cheese, softened
5 cups sifted powdered sugar
2 Tbs. milk

Combine cream cheese, vanilla and salt, mixing until well blended. Add combined sugar and cocoa alternately with milk, beating until light and fluffy.
Variation: Substitute wax paper-lined 13 x 9-inch baking pan for 8 or 9-inch layer pans. Bake 35 to 40 minutes.

PEANUT BUTTER CAKE

1/2 cup butter or margarine	1 cup buttermilk
1/2 cup peanut oil	1 cup crunchy peanut butter
2 cups granulated sugar	1 tsp. vanilla
5 egg yolks	1 can (3-1/2 oz.) coconut
2 cups all-purpose flour	5 egg whites
1 tsp. baking soda	

Preheat oven to 350 degrees. Grease three 9-inch round cake pans. Into large bowl, measure all ingredients except egg whites, with mixer at medium speed, beat until well mixed. Whip egg whites until stiff and fold into batter. Pour batter into pans and bake 25 minutes or until toothpick inserted in center comes out clean. Cool layers in pans on wire racks 10 minutes, remove from pans and cool on racks.

FROSTING:

1 pkg. (8 oz.) cream cheese
1/2 cup butter or margarine
1 box (16-oz.) confectioner's sugar
1 tsp. vanilla
1/3 cup chopped roasted peanuts

Whip cream cheese and margarine until fluffy. Gradually add confectioner's sugar and vanilla. Frost cake layers, garnishing top with peanuts.

ICEBOX CAKE

1 8 oz. cream cheese, softened	1 egg
1 stick margarine, softened	1 12 oz. cool whip
1 cup sugar	1 cup chopped nuts
1 15 oz. crushed pineapple, drained	Vanilla wafers

Layer 2 layers wafers in bottom 13x9 pan. Cream together cheese, margarine and sugar. Add egg, beat well. Stir in nuts and cool whip. Top with crushed wafers. Refrigerate overnight.

RED VELVET CAKE

2 cups oil
2 cups sugar
2 eggs
2-1/2 cups flour
1 tsp. baking soda
1 tsp. salt

1 Tbs. cocoa
1 bottle red food coloring
1 cup buttermilk
1 tsp. vinegar
1 tsp. vanilla extract

Cream sugar and oil. Add eggs, beating well after each egg. Sift dry ingredients together in a separate bowl. Add food coloring to cake mixture. Alternately add buttermilk and flour mixture, starting with milk and ending with flour. Add vanilla and vinegar and beat. Pour into three greased and floured cake pans. Bake at 350 degrees for 35 minutes.

FILLING:

1 stick butter, softened
8 oz. cream cheese, softened
1 box 10X sugar
1 cup chopped pecans
Pecan halves

Cream all until smooth. Spread evenly between cooled cake layers. Garnish with pecan halves.

SWEET POTATO CHEESECAKE

8 oz. cream cheese, softened
6 Tbs. sugar
Dash of salt
1 unbaked pie shell
1 cup cooked mashed sweet potatoes

1/2 tsp. nutmeg
1/2 tsp. cinnamon
1 egg

Combine cream cheese and sugar; beat at medium speed until smooth. Blend in sweet potatoes and spices. Add egg and beat well. Pour into unbaked pie shell. Bake at 350 degrees for about one hour. Refrigerate. (Recipe can be doubled).

FRESH APPLE CAKE

Mix together:

1-1/4 cups cooking oil
2 cups sugar
3 eggs-well beaten

1/2 to 1 cup chopped nuts
2 tsp. vanilla
3 cups diced cooking apples

Sift together:

3 cups plain flour
1 tsp. salt
1 tsp. soda

Mix ingredients in order given above. Makes two layers, bake in 8 or 9-inch pans at 325 degrees.

FILLING for Cake:

1 cup light brown sugar
1 stick oleo or butter

1/4 cup evaporated milk or cream

Cook mixture for 2 minutes and let cool. Spread on cake. Any caramel filling may be used.

APPLE DAPPLE CAKE

3 eggs
1-1/2 cups salad oil
2 cups sugar
3 cups all-purpose flour
1 tsp. salt

1 tsp. soda
2 tsp. vanilla extract
3 cups chopped apples
1-1/2 cups chopped pecans
2 Tbs. cinnamon

Mix eggs, salad oil and sugar, and blend well. Sift flour, salt and soda; add to egg mixture. Add vanilla, chopped apples and nuts. Pour into a greased 8 or 9-inch tube pan. Bake at 350 degrees for one hour. While cake is still hot, pour hot Topping over it in the pan and let cool. When completely cool, remove from pan.

TOPPING:

1 cup brown sugar
1/2 cup milk

1 stick margarine

Combine all ingredients and cook 2-1/2 minutes. Pour immediately over cake in pan.

APPLE CAKE

3 cups plain flour	1 tsp. soda
2 cups sugar	1 tsp. salt
1-1/4 cups cooking oil	1 tsp. cinnamon
3 eggs	1 tsp. allspice
3 medium size apples cubed	1 tsp. vanilla
(1 cup nuts chopped fine if desired)	

Place flour, sugar, soda, salt and spices in mixing bowl. Add oil and blend well. Add eggs beating after each addition. Add vanilla, cubed apples and nuts and stir. Place in cold oven and turn heat to 275 degrees for 10 minutes. Then turn to 350 degrees and bake for 1 hour. Remove from oven and let cool before turning out.

FILLING:

Melt one stick of margarine and one cup light brown sugar over medium heat. Add 2/3 cup evaporated milk and stir until it boils, boil a few minutes, cool, spread between the two layers and over top of cake.

BLACK WALNUT CAKE

2-1/2 cups flour (all-purpose)	1 cup milk
1-1/2 cups sugar	2 eggs
3 tsp. baking powder	1-1/2 tsp. vanilla
1 tsp. salt	1-1/2 cups black walnuts
1/2 cup shortening or butter	

Sift together flour, sugar, baking powder and salt until mixed well. Add the walnuts to flour mixture. Put shortening in mixing bowl with eggs, cream well until smooth. Mix alternately with flour mixture and milk. Add vanilla. Makes two layers. Bake at 350 degrees for 25 minutes.

FROSTING:

1-1/2 cups milk
1-1/2 cups sugar
1 tsp. vanilla
1/4 tsp. salt

Mix in a sauce pan. Boil over low heat until thick enough to spread well. Add vanilla when mixture is thick.

OATMEAL CAKE WITH TOPPING

1-1/4 cups boiling water	2 eggs
1 cup quick cooking oats	1-1/2 cups all-purpose flour
1/2 cup butter or margarine	1 tsp. soda
1 cup sugar	1 tsp. cinnamon
1 cup brown sugar	1 tsp. salt

In a large mixing bowl combine water, oats and butter or margarine, cover and let stand 20 minutes. Add remaining ingredients and mix well. Place in a 9 x 13-inch pan. Bake at 350 degrees for 35 minutes. Spread with topping while still warm. Serves 12.

TOPPING:

2 Tbs. butter or margarine	1/2 cup shredded coconut
1/4 cup evaporated milk	1/2 tsp. vanilla
1/2 cup sugar	1/2 cup chopped pecans

Combine all ingredients and spread on cake. Place under broiler until topping begins to bubble, 2-3 minutes.

BLACKBERRY FRUIT CAKE

1-2/3 cup sugar	1 cup blackberries sweetened or
3 eggs (keep out 2 whites for filling)	1 cup blackberry preserves
1 cup shortening	1-1/2 cup dark raisins
1 cup black walnuts	1 cup buttermilk
1 cup other nuts-English walnuts or Brazil nuts	1 tsp. allspice, cinnamon, vanilla, and lemon

Enough flour to make right batter; if it doesn't look black enough, add more blackberries or juice. This will make three layers.

FILLING:

Use milk from 1 coconut, about 2-1/2 cups sugar. Let cook not quite hard. Add grated coconut and 2 egg whites, beaten good and fluffy. Spread between layers.

PEANUTTY APPLE CRUNCH

4 cups fresh apples, sliced
2/3 cup brown sugar
1/2 cup all-purpose flour
1/2 cup oatmeal

3/4 tsp. nutmeg
1/3 cup soft butter
1/2 cup roasted peanuts, crushed
3/4 tsp. cinnamon

Arrange apples in a greased 8 inch square pan or 1-1/2-quart baking dish. Blend remaining ingredients until mixture is crumbly. Spread over apples. Bake at 375 degrees for 30 minutes or until top is golden brown. Serves 6.

BETTER THAN SEX

Yellow cake mix
1 cup sugar
1 large can crushed pineapple
1 box Instant vanilla pudding pecans

1 cup sour cream
8 oz. cool whip
flake coconut

Bake in 13 x 9 inch pan.

COLA CAKE

2 cups all-purpose flour
2 cups sugar
1 cup butter
3 Tbs. cocoa
1 cup coca cola

1/2 cup buttermilk
2 eggs, beaten
1 tsp. baking soda
1 tsp. vanilla
1-1/2 cups miniature
    marshmallows

Combine flour and sugar in a large mixing bowl. Heat butter, cocoa, and cola to boiling, pour over flour mixture. Mix thoroughly and add buttermilk, eggs, soda, vanilla, and marshmallows. Mix well. Place in a greased and floured 9 x 13-inch pan. Bake at 350 degrees for 35 minutes.

ICING:

1/2 cup butter
3 Tbs. cocoa
1 cup broken pecans

6 Tbs. cola
1 one lb. box powdered sugar

Combine margarine, cocoa and cola in a medium saucepan, heat to boiling point. Place powdered sugar in mixing bowl and pour cola mixture over sugar. Beat well and stir in pecans. Pour over cake.

MAYONNAISE CAKE AND FROSTING

1 cup sugar
1/4 tsp. salt
2-1/4 cups all-purpose flour
1 cup cold water
1/4 cup cocoa
1 cup mayonnaise
1-1/2 tsp. baking powder
1 tsp. vanilla
1-1/2 tsp. soda
1/4 tsp. red food coloring

Sift the dry ingredients. Add water, mayonnaise and remaining ingredients. Mix on medium speed for 2 minutes. Pour into two greased, floured, 9-inch square pans. Bake 30 minutes at 325 degrees.

FROSTING:

2 cups sugar
1/2 cup cocoa
1 tsp. vanilla

1/2 cup milk
1 stick margarine

Combine all ingredients, except vanilla. Boil for two minutes. Beat until spreading consistency and add vanilla. Spread on cake. This cake freezes well.

COCONUT CAKE

1 box yellow cake mix
3 eggs
3 Tbs. sugar

1 tsp. vanilla
1/4 cup oil
1-1/3 cups water

Mix all ingredients together and cook in sheet layer pan.

ICING:

2 large packs frozen coconut
2 cups sugar
1 cup sour cream

Pour over cake while hot, put cake in refrigerator over night. Also delicious frozen.

EASY FRUIT CRISP "DUMP" CAKE DESSERT

1 can (21 oz.) cherry pie filling
1 can (8 oz.) crushed pineapple, undrained
1 pkg. yellow cake mix
1/2 cup margarine, butter or spread, melted

Heat oven to 350 degrees. Spread pie filling and pineapple in ungreased rec-
tangular pan, 13 x 9 x 2-inch. Stir together cake mix (dry) and margarine in
large bowl unttl crumbly. Sprinkle evenly over fruit. Bake 35-40 minutes or until
light brown. Serve warm or cool. 16 servings.
*If using spread, use only stick that has more than 65% vegetable oil.
High Altitude (3500-6500 ft): Bake 40-45 minutes.

PUDDING POKE CAKE

1 pkg. (2-layer size) yellow cake
    or pudding-included cake mix
2 pkgs. (4-serving size) Jell-O Chocolate Flavor Cook and Serve Pudding
    and Pie Filling
1 cup powdered sugar
4 cups milk
2 Tbs. margarine or butter

PREPARE and bake cake mix as directed on package for 13 x 9-inch baking
pan. Remove from oven. Immediately poke holes down through cake to pan
with round handle of wooden spoon. (Or poke holes with a plastic drinking
straw, using turning motion to make large holes.) Holes should be a 1-inch
intervals.

MIX pudding mix and sugar in medium saucepan. Gradually stir in milk. Add
margarine. Stirring constantly, cook on medium heat until mixture comes to full
boil. Quickly pour hot pudding evenly over warm cake and into holes to make
stripes.

REFRIGERATE at least 2 hours or until ready to serve. Store cake in refrigerator.

SWISS CHOCOLATE CAKE

1 box Swiss chocolate cake mix	3 eggs
1 small box vanilla instant pudding	3/4 cup oil
1-1/2 cup milk	

Mix all ingredients, Bake at 325 degrees for 25-30 minutes. Yield: 3 layers.

FROSTING:

8 oz. cream cheese	12 oz. cool whip
1 cup powdered sugar	1/2 cup pecans (optional)
1 cup granulated sugar	2 Hershey candy bars
	(shaved or shredded)

Cream granulated sugar and cream cheese. Add powdered sugar, cream together. Add rest of ingredients. Add candy last. (Save some candy for decoration).

"TRIFLE" OR PUNCH BOWL CAKE

2 pkgs. instant vanilla pudding	1/4 tsp. cinnamon
4 cups milk	1 (12 oz.) jar raspberry preserves
Almond, brandy, rum or	2 frozen pound cakes,
cherry flavoring	broken into one inch cubes
16 oz. whipping cream, sweetened	Slivered almonds
1 (161/2 oz.) can dark sweet cherries	1/2 cup sugar

Mix pudding and milk according to package directions, adding 1/4 teaspoon flavoring. Whip cream and add 1/4 teaspoon flavoring. In a saucepan, combine cherries, sugar and cinnamon; boil for five minutes. Cool slightly and add raspberry preserves. In a large decorative glass bowl, layer: cake, cherry mixture, pudding and whipped cream; repeat, ending with whipped cream. Top with slivered almonds. Chill well. Recipe can be cut in half. Serves 10-15.

STRAWBERRY SHORT CAKE

1 box white cake mix	1 cup boiling water
1 pkg. strawberry Jello	Cool Whip

Bake cake as directed. When done, poke holes in cake with fork. Mix strawberry jello with 1 cup boiling water and pour over cake. Then spread strawberry syrup over cake. Refrigerate overnight and serve with a generous amount of Cool Whip. Garnish with fresh strawberries.

DESSERTS

BANANA PUDDING

2 (3 1/4 oz.) vanilla instant pudding mix
1 8 oz. cool whip
1 8 oz. sour cream
6 large bananas
1 box vanilla wafers

Blend pudding mix, sour cream and 1/2 of cool whip. Mix well. Pour over bananas and wafers. Top with cool whip Chill for one hour.

BANANA PUDDING

1 large (6 oz.) pkg. instant vanilla
  pudding mix
1 6 oz. carton sour cream
1 12 oz. carton whipped topping

1 10 oz. box vanilla wafers
4 large bananas
3 cups milk

Put milk in large mixing bowl. Add the pudding mix and mix on low speed until it thickens. Add the sour cream and mix until it is mixed well, about 2 minutes. Fold the whipped topping into this mixture, until it is well blended. Place a layer of vanilla wafers on the bottom of a large deep dish, then a layer of sliced bananas, cover this with half of the pudding mixture. Repeat with another layer. To dress it up, sprinkle some vanilla wafer crumbs on top. Refrigerate until ready to serve. Serves 6-8.

SWEET POTATO PUDDING

3 cups grated sweet potatoes
1-1/2 cups sugar
1/2 cup butter, melted
1 cup milk

2 eggs, beaten
1/2 cup corn meal
1/4 tsp. salt
1 cup grated coconut

Combine all ingredients and pour into casserole dish. Bake at 350 degrees for 45 minutes or until set.

RICE PUDDING

1 cup cooked rice
1 cup milk
3 Tbs. butter or margarine
1/2 cup sugar

1 Tbs. vanilla
1/2 cup seedless raisins
4 eggs, beaten
1 tsp. ground cinnamon

Combine all ingredients, except cinnamon. Turn into a buttered 2-quart casserole dish. Sprinkle with cinnamon. Bake at 350 degrees for about 30 minutes. Yield: 6 servings.

COOKIE PEACH COBBLER

2-1/2 lbs. peaches, peeled and sliced—5 peeled and sliced (5 cups)
1/4 cup sugar
2 Tbs. cornstarch
1/2 tsp. ground cinnamon
1/2 cup light corn syrup
1 pkg. (17 oz.) refrigerator sugar cookie dough

Place peaches in 8 x 8 x 2-inch baking dish. In small bowl, stir together sugar, corn starch and cinnamon. Gradually stir in corn syrup until smooth. Pour over peaches; toss to coat well. Slice cookie dough into 1/4-inch slices. Arrange slices in rows on top of peach mixture. Bake at 350 degrees for 1 hour or until golden brown. Cool. If desired, serve with ice cream. Yield: 8 servings.

GRANDMA'S BLACKBERRY COBBLER

1 cup sugar
1/2 cup water
2 cups blackberries
2 Tbs. butter

1 egg
1 cup self-rising flour
2/3 cup milk

Mix 1/2 cup sugar and water; bring to a boil and boil 5 minutes. Cream butter, 1/2 cup sugar and egg. Add flour and milk alternately until it's a smooth batter. Pour batter into greased baking dish. Mix blackberries with sugar syrup and spoon over batter. Bake at 375 degrees for 30 minutes or until golden brown.

APPLE COBBLER

8 cups apples, peeled and
   sliced thin
3/4 cup sugar

1/2 tsp. cinnamon
1/4 tsp. nutmeg

Place apples in bottom of 9 x 13-inch pan. Mix sugar, cinnamon and nutmeg. Sprinkle over apples.

1 cup flour
1 cup sugar
1 tsp. baking powder

3/4 tsp. salt
1 egg, well-beaten
1 stick margarine, melted

Mix together the flour, sugar, baking powder and salt; add egg and mix. Spread over apples. Drizzle margarine over top. Bake at 350 degrees for 1 hour.

BLUEBERRY ICE CREAM

3 cups fresh frozen blueberries
1/2 cup water
2 pints half & half
1 quart milk
3 cups sugar

Crush blueberries, place in saucepan with water and boil until berries are soft, stirring to prevent scorching. Strain to remove hulls. Place fruit in a one-gallon freezer churn, add remaining ingredients; stir to dissolve. Freeze. **Note: Any of your favorite berries may be used.** Yield: 3 quarts.

FRESH PEACH ICE CREAM

12 fresh peaches
2 cups sugar
1 cup sweetened condensed milk

2 quarts milk
1 8-oz. carton sour cream
2 tsp. vanilla

Peel and slice peaches. Mix peaches and sugar together in blender. Add peaches and sugar mixture to other ingredients and churn until frozen. Yield: 4 quarts.

BLUEBERRY BUCKLE

1/4 cup butter or margarine
1 cup sugar, divided
1 tsp. vanilla extract
1 egg, lightly beaten
1-1/3 cups sifted all-purpose
   flour, divided

1/4 tsp. salt
1/3 cup milk
2 cups blueberries
1/2 tsp. ground cinnamon
1/4 cup margarine
1 tsp. baking powder

Preheat oven to 375 degrees. Cream butter, 1/2 cup sugar and vanilla and add beaten egg. Sift together 1 cup flour, baking powder and salt. Add dry ingredients alternately with milk to the creamed mixture. Pour into a 10 x 5 x 2-inch greased baking dish. Cover with berries. Combine remaining sugar, flour, cinnamon and margarine. Blend together to form a crumb topping and sprinkle over berries. Bake for 40 to 50 minutes. Yield: 6 servings.

BLUEBERRY CRUNCH

2-1/2 lb. undrained, crushed pineapple
2-3 cups fresh or frozen blueberries
3/4 cup sugar

1 box yellow cake mix
2 sticks melted margarine
1 cup chopped pecans
1/4 cup sugar

Butter a 9 x 13-inch baking dish: spread the following in layers; pineapple, blueberries, sugar (sprinkled on berries), dry cake mix, melted margarine, pecans, additional 1/4 cup sugar sprinkled on top. Bake 325 degrees for 35-40 minutes or until top is brown. Serve warm or cold, delicious with whipped cream.

PECAN CRUNCH DESSERT

1/2 cup sugar
1 cup finely chopped pecans
1 egg, beaten
1 3-1/2 oz. pkg. instant vanilla
   pudding mix

1 cup sour cream
1 cup milk
8 oz. carton whipped topping
4 bananas, sliced

Combine sugar, pecans and egg. Spread onto a cookie sheet that has been lined with foil and greased. Bake at 350 degrees for 15 minutes or until brown. Cool and crumble. Mix pudding mix, sour cream and milk. Fold in whipped topping. Place half of pecan mixture in bottom of a 9 x 13-inch baking dish, then sliced bananas. Pour pudding mixture over bananas and top with remaining pecan crunch mixture. Cover and refrigerate until ready to serve. Serves 8-10.

HEAVENLY DESSERT

1 large angel food cake, cubed
1 large pkg. strawberry gelatin
1 quart fresh strawberries, quartered

2 cups boiling water
Whipped topping

Place cubed angel food cake in an 8 x 12-inch baking dish. Dissolve gelatin in boiling water; add strawberries and pour over cake. Let set in refrigerator 30 minutes. Serve with whipped topping.

STRAWBERRY DELIGHT

1 large container whipped topping
1 small pkg. vanilla instant pudding
1-1/2 cups frozen strawberries, thawed

1 graham cracker pie crust
3/4 cup shredded coconut

Mix together whipped topping, dry pudding and strawberries. Stir until well blended and the pudding mix is fully dissolved. Pour into pie crust and garnish with coconut; chill one hour. Yield: 6 servings.

BLUEBERRY DELIGHT

2-1/2 cups graham cracker crumbs
1/4 cup sugar
1 stick margarine, melted
2 cups blueberries
1 cup sugar

1/4 cup sugar
1/4 cup water
1 (8 oz.) cream cheese,
   softened
1 pkg. dream whip

Mix crumbs, 1/4 cup sugar, and melted margarine together. Reserve 1/2-3/4 cup for top. Press into 13 x 9-inch pan. Prepare filling, cook berries, 1/4 sugar and 1/4 cup water until berries are done on medium high. Add 1/4 cup water mixed with 2 heaping tsp. cornstarch into filling. Bring to a boil. Cool. Mix cream cheese and 1 cup sugar. Prepare box of Dream whip according to pkg. directions. Mix Dream Whip and cream cheese together. Layer 1/2 mixture on crust, then all berry filling, other 1/2 cheese mixture. Top with reserved crumbs. Chill overnight or 3 hours

MARK'S BLUEBERRY DELIGHT

CRUST:
1 stick margarine   1 cup flour
1/4 cup brown sugar   1/4 cup chopped pecans

Melt margarine then mix other ingredients into the melted margarine. Pour into a baking dish and press down to cover the bottom of dish. Bake at 350 degrees for 15 minutes then remove from oven and let cool.

FILLING:
8 oz. cream cheese   1/2 cup lemon juice
1 can sweetened condensed milk 1-1/2 tsp. of vanilla
1 can blueberry pie filling

Let cheese become room temperature. Beat cheese then add milk and other ingredients. Pour over cooled crust and chill 2-3 hours before adding pie filling. Spread pie filling over top and refrigerate.

FROZEN STRAWBERRY SQUARES

1 cup all-purpose flour
1/2 cup butter, melted
1/2 cup chopped pecans
2 eggs whites
1/4 cup brown sugar
1 cup sugar
2 Tbs. lemon juice
1 cup heavy cream, whipped (may use whipped cream)
2 cups sliced, fresh strawberries or 2 (10 oz.) pkg. frozen strawberries (thawed)

Mix together flour, nuts, sugar and butter. Spread in a 13 x 9 x 2-inch pan or baking dish. Bake at 350 degrees for 20 minutes stirring every 5 minutes. Remove from oven and stir again. Remove crumbs from pan and cool. Sprinkle 2/3 of crumbs back in same pan to cover bottom. Combine egg whites, strawberries, sugar, and lemon juice in large mixing bowl. Beat at high speed until stiff peaks form, about 10-15 minutes. Fold in whipped cream. Spread lightly over crumbs in pan and sprinkle remainder of crumbs on top. Freeze until firm and cut into squares. Yield: 12-16 servings.

OLD-FASHIONED EGG CUSTARD

1 cup sugar	1 cup milk
2-1/2 Tbs. flour	2 Tbs. melted butter
1/8 tsp. nutmeg	2 egg whites
4 egg yolks	2 Tbs. sugar
2 egg whites	1 9-inch unbaked pie crust

Combine sugar, flour, and nutmeg. Beat 4 egg yolks and 2 egg whites; add to dry ingredients, beat well, add milk, and stir in melted butter. Pour in crust and bake at 400 degrees for 10 minutes. Reduce heat to 325 degrees and bake 30 minutes longer. Beat egg whites and sugar to make meringue. Spread on custard and brown.

CHOCOLATE TOFFEE CRUNCH

1 sleeve saltines	2 sticks real butter (no margarine)
1 cup brown sugar	1 12 oz. bag milk chocolate chips

Line 15 x 10 x 1-inch cookie sheet with foil. Grease well. Line with saltines (edge to edge). Boil sugar and butter 3-5 minutes and pour over saltines. Cook 12 minutes at 350 degrees. Pour chocolate chips on top of hot sugar/crackers and spread until completely melted. Refrigerate 30-60 minutes. Break into pieces. Store at room temperature.

THREE-LAYER PEACH TRIFLE

1 angel food cake mix
3-1/2 cups fresh peaches, peeled and sliced
2 (3-oz.) boxes of French vanilla pudding
1 (16-oz.) container of whipped topping

Prepare Angel Food Cake as directed on box. Break cake into bite-size pieces. Place 1/3 of cake pieces in bottom of trifle dish. Place 1 cup peaches on top of cake. Prepare pudding as directed on box. Drizzle 1/3 of pudding over peaches. Spoon 1/3 of whipped topping on top. Repeat this process twice. Use the remaining 1/2 cup peaches to garnish top and sides. Serves 12.

PEACH BOWL

2 cups sliced peaches   1 pint strawberries, hulled
1 cup fresh blueberries   1 kiwi fruit, peeled and sliced
2 cups cubed watermelon   1 (6 oz.) can frozen orange juice, thawed
1 fresh banana, sliced
1 medium cantaloupe, cubed

In a decorative glass bowl, layer fruit. Pour orange juice over all; cover and let marinate in refrigerator two hours.

LEMON ICEBOX DESSERT

2 lemons (juice from both and graded rind from one)
1 cup sugar
1 large can evaporated milk, chilled
1 lb. box vanilla wafers

Combine lemon juice and rind with sugar in a small saucepan and bring to a boil. Cool. In a large mixing bowl, whip chilled milk until very stiff. Slowly add lemon mixture to milk and beat slowly. Place a layer of wafers in the bottom of a 9 x 13 inch baking dish. Spread half of lemon and milk mixture over wafers. Repeat layers ending with vanilla wafers. Cover and freeze until ready to serve. Serves 10.

FRUIT DELIGHT

1 20 oz. can pineapple chunks, drained (reserve juice)
1 17 oz. can mixed fruit chunks, drained
3 bananas, sliced
1 (3-1/2 oz.) box instant vanilla pudding mix
3 Tbs. instant breakfast orange drink mix

Place fruit in large bowl. Combine vanilla pudding mix, orange drink mix and pineapple juice. Pour over fruit and stir gently. Chill before serving. Serves 6.

DIRT DESSERT

20 oz. pkg. Oreo cookies
1/2 stick margarine
8 oz. cream cheese
1 cup powdered sugar

2 small pkg. instant vanilla pudding mix
3/5 cups milk
12 oz. cool whip

Use 8-inch diameter plastic planter flower pot. Wash and cover holes with tape. Put cookies through the food processor (do not scrape off cream center). Set aside. Cream together; margarine, cream cheese, and powdered sugar. Set aside. Mix pudding with milk according to directions until thickened. Add pudding mixture to creamed cheese mixture. Add cool whip. Layer the pudding mixture and cookie crumbs in the flower pot, start and end with cookie crumbs. Refrigerate until chilled. Top with long stem silk flowers just before serving. If you're really daring add a few gummy worms on top of the cookie crumbs.

AMBROSIA

8 or 10 oranges peeled, diced
1 cup coconut
1/2 cup pecans chopped (optional)

1/2 cup cherries
1/2 cup sugar
Small can crushed pineapple

Combine all ingredients and chill.

FLUFFY COOKED ICING

2 egg whites
1/2 cup water
1-1/2 cups sugar
1 Tbs. corn syrup

1 tsp. cream of tartar
1 tsp. vanilla
Dash of salt

Place all ingredients in top of double boiler and cook over boiling water, beating with electric mixer or rotary egg beater until mixture forms stiff peaks (about 8 or 10 minutes). Very good for coconut cake.

PUMPKIN ROLL

3 eggs	2/3 cup pumpkin
1 cup sugar	1 tsp. lemon juice

Beat eggs at high speed for 5 minutes. Add sugar. Stir in pumpkin and lemon juice. In separate bowl, stir together:

3/4 cup plain flour	2 tsp. cinnamon
1 tsp. baking powder	1 tsp. ginger
1/2 tsp. salt	

Fold into pumpkin mixture. Spread batter in a well greased 15 x 10 x 1 cookie sheet and bake at 325 degrees for 15 minutes. Turn out on wax paper covered in powdered sugar or Pam. Roll wax paper and cake together lengthwise and let cool. After cool, unroll and spread filling; then roll back up and chill.

FILLING:

1 cup powdered sugar	4 Tbs. margarine
1 (8 oz.) pkg. cream cheese	1 cup nuts
1 tsp. vanilla	

Beat until smooth.

CARAMEL FROSTING

1 cup milk	1/2 cup butter or oleo
2-2/3 cups sugar	1 tsp. vanilla

Cook milk and 2 cups sugar until it forms soft ball when tested in cold water. Brown remaining 2/3 cups sugar in heavy skillet. Add butter and let simmer until sugar dissolves. Combine two mixtures, add vanilla and cool. Stir and spread on cake.

STRAWBERRY PUDDING

Prepare the same way as banana pudding, except use fresh strawberries instead of bananas.

TOMATO PUDDING

4 cups white bread crumbs (about 6 slices) 1/2 cup water
1 cup melted butter   1 cup light brown sugar
2 cups tomato puree   1/2 tsp. salt

Put bread cubes in a baking dish and pour melted butter over them. Mix remaining ingredients and simmer together for five minutes then mix with buttered bread cubes. Set baking dish in a pan of hot water and bake for 45-50 minutes or until top is well browned. Serves 6.

CHOCOLATE 4-LAYER DELIGHT

1st layer: **1-1/2 sticks butter, melted**
                1 1/3 cups self-rising flour
                1 cup chopped pecans

Blend together and spread in bottom of 9 x 13 dish; bake at 375 until browned.

2nd layer: **1 (8 oz.) pkg. cream cheese, softened**
                1 cup 4X powdered sugar
                1 cup Cool Whip

Beat cheese and sugar until creamy; fold in Cool Whip and spread over first layer while slightly warm.

3rd layer: **1 large pkg. instant chocolate pudding**

Prepare pudding according to directions on package; spread over 2nd layer.

4th layer: **Cool Whip**

Top with Cool Whip and refrigerate several hours before serving.

LEMON CHEESE FILLING

1 Tbs. cornstarch   2 grated apples, peeled
2 cups sugar   2 egg yolks, or 1 whole egg
2 Tbs. butter or oleo   A yellow food coloring will add
Juice of 2 lemons   color
Grated rind of 1 lemon

Mix all ingredients and cook slowly in heavy pan for 5 minutes. If too thick, a little milk or cream may be added before spreading on layers.

LEMON CHEESE FILLING

2 cups water
4 egg yolks
Juice of 2 lemons
Grated rind of 1 lemon

2 Tbs. cornstarch
1/4 cup butter or oleo
1 cup sugar

Let water boil in heavy pan. Mix sugar and cornstarch together. Add egg yolks and lemon juice. Beat well. Add enough hot water to mixture to thin. Then pour mixture into boiling water over low heat and stir until it thickens. Add butter and stir. Remove from heat and cool. If egg yolks are pale, a little yellow food coloring will add to filling. The whites of the eggs used in this filling can be used in place of 2 whole eggs in cake batter.

FLOATING ISLAND

2 cups milk
5 eggs (reserve 1 egg white)
1/2 cup sugar
1 tsp. vanilla

Let milk heat to boiling and add eggs, sugar and vanilla that have been whipped together. Stir constantly. As soon as the mixture thickens, pour into dessert dishes. Whip egg white until very stiff and add a little sugar and drop a teaspoonful in center of each dish of custard. Whipped cream is also a very good topping. Yield: 4 servings.

HEAVENLY HASH

1 (8 oz.) can crushed pineapple, well drained
2 cups thawed Cool Whip
1 cup coconut
1 cup miniature marshmallows
1/4 cup chopped maraschino cherries
3 Tbs. milk

Mix all ingredients and chill about 1 hour. Yield: 6 servings.

BAKED STUFFED PEACHES

6 ripe peaches
1/2 cup sugar
1/2 lb. almond macaroons, crushed (about 2 cups crumbs)
4 egg yolks

Peel and halve peaches; scoop out about 1 teaspoon of the center pulp of each half, Mash pulp; mix with sugar, crushed macaroons, and egg yolk. Place halves close together, cut side up, in greased baking dish, about 8 x 12. Spoon macaroon mixture into center of each. Bake in a slow oven (300 degrees) for about 30 minutes or until peaches are tender. Yield: 6 servings.

BROWNIE FROSTING

2 heaping Tbs. cocoa
2 Tbs. butter or other shortening
2 cups confectioner's sugar
3 Tbs. cream – more if needed
1 tsp. vanilla

Blend well and beat until creamy. Spread over brownies.

BROWNIES

2/3 cup plain flour
1/2 tsp. baking powder 2 heaping Tbs. cocoa
1/4 tsp. salt
1/3 cup butter or other shortening
1 cup sugar
2 eggs, beaten
1 tsp. vanilla
1/2 cup chopped nuts

Mix sugar, shortening and cocoa. Add well beaten eggs, then flour, baking powder and salt that have been sifted together. Add vanilla and nuts. Bake in greased pan for 25 minutes at 350 degrees. Square or oblong pan is best. When cool, cut in small squares.

MINUTE FUDGE FROSTING

1/2 cup butter   2 cups sugar
2/3 cup cocoa   Dash of salt
1/2 cup milk

Melt butter in pan, add remaining ingredients and stir over low heat until sugar dissolves. Then boil for 1minute. Remove from heat until creamy enough to spread.

PISTACHIO PUDDING FROSTING

1 (4 serving size) pkg. instant pistachio pudding mix
1-1/2 cups milk
1/2 cup butter or margarine
1/2 cup shortening
1 cup sifted powdered sugar

Prepare the pudding mix according to package directions using the 1-1/2 cups milk. Set aside the pudding—will thicken as it sits. In a small mixer bowl, beat the butter or margarine and shortening with electric mixer on medium speed for 30 seconds. Add powdered sugar to beaten butter mixture; beat until light and fluffy. Gradually add pudding mix, beating well. Yield: 3-3/4 cups frosting. A real frosting for just a plain cake.

ICE BOX COOKIES

2/3 cups butter or other shortening   1/2 tsp. salt
1 cup brown sugar   1/2 tsp. cinnamon
1 tsp. baking powder   2 eggs
2-1/2 cups plain flour   1/2 cup chopped nuts

Cream shortening and sugar. Add well beaten eggs. Beat mixture thoroughly. Sift dry ingredients together and add to first mixture. Add nuts. Shape in rolls and wrap in wax paper. Store in refrigerator for at least 6 hours. Slice 1/4-inch thick as needed and place on ungreased baking sheet. Bake at 375 degrees for 5 minutes.

OATMEAL COOKIES

1 cup shortening
1 cup brown sugar
1/2 cup white sugar
2 eggs
1 tsp. cinnamon
1 tsp. vanilla

2 cups oatmeal
1 cup chopped nuts
2 cups plain flour
1/2 tsp. soda
1/2 tsp. baking powder

Blend all ingredients well. Drop on greased cookie sheet from teaspoon 2 inches apart. Bake at 375 degrees for 10 minutes or until slightly browned.

SUGAR COOKIES

3 2/3 cups sifted all-purpose flour
2-1/2 tsp. baking powder
1/2 tsp. salt
2/3 cup shortening

1-1/2 cups sugar
2 eggs, unbeaten
1 tsp. vanilla or lemon
    flavoring
4 tsp. milk

Sift flour, baking powder and salt together. Cream shortening, add sugar gradually, add eggs one at a time, add vanilla. Chill 3 or 4 hours or over night (more crisp if chilled over night). Roll out very thin and cut with cookie cutter; sprinkle with sugar. Bake on ungreased sheet in oven (375 degrees) for 5 to 8 minutes or until done.

OLD-FASHIONED SOUTHERN TEACAKES

2 1/4 cups sifted plain four
1/4 tsp. salt
2 tsp. baking powder
1/2 cup butter

1 cup sugar
2 eggs beaten
1/2 tsp. vanilla
1 Tbs. milk

Sift flour, salt and baking powder together. Cream butter, sugar and eggs. Add vanilla, milk and dry ingredients. Blend well. Place dough on a lightly floured board, sprinkle little flour over the dough and roll to about 1/2-inch thick. Cut with cookie cutter. Place on cookie sheet and bake n a moderate over 350 or 375 degrees about 12 to 15 minutes or until lightly browned on top.

EASY PEANUT BUTTER COOKIES

1 (14 oz.) can sweetened condensed milk
3/4 cup peanut butter
2 cups biscuit baking mix
1 tsp. vanilla extract
Granulated sugar

Preheat oven to 375 degrees. In large mixer bowl, beat sweetened condensed milk and peanut butter until smooth. Add biscuit mix and vanilla; mix well. Shape into 1-imch balls. Roll in sugar. Place 2 inches apart on ungreased baking sheets. Flatten with fork. Baking 6-8 minutes or until lightly browned. Do not over bake. Cool. Store tightly covered at room temperature.

PEANUT BUTTER COOKIES

1 cup sugar
1 cup peanut butter
1 egg
1 tsp. vanilla

Bake at 350 degrees.

PEANUT BUTTER OATMEAL COOKIES

3/4 cup butter-flavored
1 cup peanut butter
1-1/2 cups firmly packed
   brown sugar
1/2 cup water
1 egg

Crisco 1 tsp. vanilla
cups oats, uncooked
1-1/2 cups all-purpose flour
1/2 tsp. baking soda
Granulated sugar

Beat first three ingredients until creamy. Beat in water, egg and vanilla. Add combined dry ingredients; mix well. Cover; chill about 2 hours. Heat oven to 350 degrees. Shape into 1-inch balls. Place on ungreased cookie sheet; flatten with tines of fork dipped in granulated sugar to form crisscross pattern. Bake 9 to 11 minutes or until edges are golden brown. Cool 1 minute on cookie sheet; remove to wire rack. Cool completely. Store tightly covered. Yield: 7 dozen cookies.

SINGLE PIE CRUST

1-1/3 cups flour	1/2 cup shortening
1/2 tsp. salt if plain flour is used	3 Tbs. cold water

Mix flour and salt in mixing bowl. Cut shortening into flour with two forks or pastry blender until mixture is very fine. Sprinkle water over mixture one table-spoon at a time mixing lightly. When all water has been added work dough into firm ball with the hands. Roll on lightly floured board to cover pie pan.

COCOA CLOUD PIE

2 (3 oz.) pkgs. c ream cheese softened
1 cup confectioner's sugar
1/2 cup unsweetened cocoa
1/4 cup milk
2 cups (1 pint) cold whipping cream
1 (6 oz.) packaged graham cracker crumb crust

In large bowl, using an electric mixer, beat cream cheese, sugar and vanilla until well-blended. Add cocoa alternately with milk, beating until smooth. Gradually add whipping cream; beat until very stiff, but not curdled. Spoon into crust. Cover; refrigerate leftover pie.

NO BAKE PEANUT BUTTER PIE

4 oz. cream cheese	8 oz. frozen whipped topping,
1 cup confectioner's	thawed
sugar, sifted	1 deep-dish graham cracker or
1 cup crunchy peanut butter	chocolate flavored crust
1/2 cup milk	1/4 cup chocolate syrup (optional)

In large bowl, combine cream cheese and confectioner's sugar; mix well. Add peanut butter and mix. Slowly add milk and mix well. Fold in whipped topping. Pour into pie shell and cover. Freeze for at least 30 minutes. If desired, drizzle each serving with chocolate syrup. Yield: 8 servings.

CHOCOLATE CARAMEL PECAN PIE

CRUST:

1 cup finely crushed chocolate wafer cookie crumbs (half of a 9 oz. box)
1 Tbs. granulated sugar
2 Tbs. unsalted butter, melted

Caramel-Pecan LAYER:

2/3 cup granulated sugar
2 Tbs. water
1 Tbs. dark corn syrup
1/4 cup (1/2 stick) unsalted butter
1/3 cup whipping cream
3/4 cup chopped pecans
Chocolate Cream FILLING:

6 oz. semisweet chocolate
2 cups whipping cream
1/4 cup (1/2 stick) unsalted butter

For crust, mix crumbs and sugar; add butter; mix well. Press into bottom and up sides of 9-inch pie plate. Bake in preheated 350 degrees oven for 10 minutes, or until set. Cool. For caramel, combine sugar, water and corn syrup in small, heavy saucepan. Bring to boil over high heat, swirling pan so sugar crystals from sides wash down. Watching closely, boil until mixture takes on rich honey color, 4 to 5 minutes. Remove from heat; stir in butter. Add cream, return to high heat; cook until smooth. Cool. Reserve 3 tablespoons caramel for garnish. Pour remainder into crust; sprinkle on pecans. For filling, chop chocolate, reserving 1 ounce. Heat cream and butter to boil. Remove from heat; add 5 ounces chopped chocolate. Whisk until smooth. Remove 1/2 cup and whisk in reserved 1 ounce chocolate; leave at room temperature to use as glaze. Refrigerate rest for at least 4 hours. Whip well-chilled cream mixture with electric mixture until it holds soft peaks. Spread over caramel layer. Refrigerate at least 2 hours before serving.

BUTTERFINGER CANDY BAR PIE

8 (2/1-oz.) Butterfinger candy bars
3 large eggs
1-1/2 cups granulated sugar
1/2 cup water
1/4 cup all-purpose flour

1/4 tsp. salt
1/2 cup unsalted butter, melted
1 unbaked 9-inch pie shell
Whipped cream

Preheat oven to 325 degrees. Chop 6 candy bars; set aside. Chop remaining 2 candy bars; set aside. Whisk eggs in a large mixing bowl. Add sugar, water, flour and salt; mix to blend. Stir in melted butter, and then stir in 6 chopped candy bars. Pour filling into unbaked pie shell. Bake 45 to 50 minutes. Cool on a wire rack, then refrigerate 12 hours or overnight. Serve garnished with whipped cream remaining candy bars. Yield: 8 servings.

BLUEBERRY BUCKLE

1/2 cup shortening
3/4 cup sugar
1 egg
2 cups sifted all-purpose flour
2-1/2 tsp. baking powder
1/4 tsp. salt

1/2 cup milk
2 cups fresh blueberries
1/2 cup sugar
1/2 cup sifted all-purpose flour
1/2 tsp. ground cinnamon
1/4 cup butter

Thoroughly cream shortening and 3/4 cup sugar; add egg and beat until light and fluffy. Sift together 2 cups flour, baking powder and salt; add to creamed mixture alternately with milk. Spread in greased 11 by 7 1-1/2 pan. Top with berries. Mix 1/2 cup sugar, 1/2 cup flour and cinnamon; cut in butter till crumbly; sprinkle over berries. Bake at 350 degrees for 45 minutes. Cut in squares. Serve warm.

GEORGIA PECAN PIE

3 whole eggs
2 Tbs. melted butter or margarine
2 Tbs. flour
1/4 tsp. vanilla
1/4 tsp. salt

1/2 cup granulated sugar
1-1/2 cups dark corn syrup
1-1/2 cups broken pecans
1 unbaked 9-inch pie shell

Preheat oven to 425 degrees. Beat eggs in a large bowl, then blend in melted butter, flour, vanilla, salt, sugar and syrup. Sprinkle pecans over bottom of unbaked pie shell. Gently pour syrup mixture over pecans and bake at 425 degrees for 10 minutes. Reduce heat to 325 degrees and bake for 30 minutes.

PUMPKIN CHIFFON PIE

Mix 1 envelope unflavored gelatin, 3/4 cup brown sugar, 1/2 tsp. salt, 1/2 tsp. nutmeg, 1 tsp. cinnamon, 1 tsp. vanilla together in top of double boiler. Stir in 3/4 cup milk, 3 egg yolks beaten and 1-1/2 cups pumpkin. Mix thoroughly. Cook over boiling water, stirring occasionally, until gelatin dissolves (about 10 minutes). Remove from heat, chill until mixture mounds when dropped from a spoon. Beat egg whites until stiff; beat in 1/2 cup sugar. Fold in gelatin mixture. Turn into baked pie shell and chill. Serve with whipped cream.

EXCELLENT PECAN PIE

1 cup white corn syrup
1 cup dark brown sugar
1/3 tsp. salt
1/3 cup melted butter

1 tsp. vanilla
3 whole eggs
1 heaping cup pecans

Mix syrup, sugar, salt, butter, vanilla. Add slightly beaten eggs. Pour into a 9-inch unbaked pie shell. Sprinkle pecans over filling. Bake in 350 degrees oven for approximately 45 minutes.

PUMPKIN PIE

1 cup sugar
Dash of salt
1-1/2 cup pumpkin
3 eggs

1 tsp. cinnamon
1 cup milk
1 tsp. vanilla

Combine all ingredients and beat well. Pour on pie shell that has been heated and mashed flat on pan. Bake at 350 degrees for 45 minutes or until done.

SWEET POTATO PIE

2 cups cooked,
  mashed sweet potatoes
1 cup sugar
2 eggs
1/4 cup melted butter or margarine
1/4 tsp. salt

3/4 cup milk
1 tsp. cinnamon
1 tsp. pumpkin pie spice
  or allspice
1 tsp. of vanilla
9-inch pie shell, unbaked

Mix all ingredients well and pour into pie shell. Bake at 350 degrees for 60 minutes or until knife comes out clean.

COCONUT PIE

5 eggs
2-1/2 cups sugar
2 Tbs.. flour
1-1/2 stick margarine

3/4 cup buttermilk
Dash salt
1 tsp. vanilla
1 large can coconut

Pour mixture into unbaked pie crust. Bake for 55 minutes. Oven temp. at 300-325 degrees.

LEMON OR LIME PIE

6 oz. lemon-de or lime-ade, frozen
9 oz. cool-whip
15 oz. sweetened condensed milk
1 ready-made pie crust

Mix ingredients and add to pie crust. Chill and serve.

PEANUT BUTTER PIE

CRUST:
1-1/4 cups chocolate cookie crumbs (20 cookies)
1/4 cup sugar
1/4 cup butter or margarine, melted

FILLING:
1 pkg. (8 oz.) cream cheese, softened
1 cup creamy peanut butter
1 cup sugar
1 Tbs. butter or margarine, softened
1 tsp. vanilla extract
1 cup heavy cream, whipped
Grated chocolate or cookie crumbs, optional

Combine crust ingredients; press into a 9-inch pie plate. Bake at 375 degrees for 10 minutes. Cool. In a mixing bowl, beat cream cheese, peanut butter, sugar, butter and vanilla until smooth. Fold in whipped cream. Gently spoon into crust. Garnish with chocolate or cookie crumbs if desired. Refrigerate. Yield: 8-10 servings.

MOLASSES PECAN PIE

3/4 cup brown sugar
3 eggs, well beaten
1 cup dark corn syrup

1 Tbs. butter
1 cup chopped pecans
Dash of salt

Blend 3/4 cup firmly packed brown sugar with 1 tablespoon butter. Add 1 cup dark corn syrup, eggs well beaten, and a dash of salt, add teaspoon of vanilla. Mix well, add 1 cup coarsely chopped pecan meats and turn into a pie plate lined with pastry. Bake 10 minutes at 450 degrees, reduce heat to 350 degrees and bake until pie is set, about 35 minutes longer.

PEANUT BUTTER CHOCOLATE PIE

1 cup confectioner's sugar
1/2 cup crunchy peanut butter
1 deep dish baked 9-inch pastry shell
    shell
3 Tbs.. cornstarch
2/3 cup granulated sugar
2 Tbs.. cocoa
1/4 tsp. salt

2 cups milk, scalded
3 eggs yolks, beaten
2 Tbs.. butter
1 tsp. vanilla
3 egg whites
2 Tbs.. granulated sugar

Combine confectioner's sugar and peanut butter, blend until the appearance of biscuit mix. Spread 3/4 of this mixture on baked pie shell. Combine cornstarch, granulated sugar, cocoa and salt; add scalded milk and mix well. Pour small amount over beaten egg yolks. Mix well, then return to milk mixture. Cook in top of double boiler until mixture thickens; add butter and vanilla. Pour into prepared pie shell. Top with meringue.

For meringue, beat egg whites, adding sugar a little at a time until sugar is all dissolved and the meringue is stiff and glossy. Pile onto hot pie filling and sprinkle remaining peanut butter and sugar mixture over the meringue. Bake at 350 degrees until the meringue is lightly browned. Yield: 6-8 servings.

GRANDMOTHER'S COCONUT PIE

6 Tbs. butter, melted
3 eggs, beaten
1 cup sugar

1/4 cup buttermilk
1 cup flaked coconut
9-inch unbaked pie shell

Combine first 5 ingredients and pour into pie shell. Bake at 350 degrees for 30-40 minutes.

NEW PEACH PIE

1 unbaked pie shell 9-inch
4 large peaches
1-1/2 cups sugar
1/3 cup flour

2 eggs beaten
1/2 stick butter, melted
1/4 tsp. almond flavoring

Peel and slice peaches. Put into pie crust. Mix sugar and flour well. Add beaten eggs, melted butter and flavoring. Pour over peaches. Bake at 350 degrees until crust is brown and custard thick.

COCONUT CREAM PIE

1 cup sugar
1/4 cup cornstarch
3 eggs, separated
1-2/3 cups milk
4 Tbs. butter

1 tsp. vanilla flavoring
1-1/4 cups coconut
9-inch pie shell, baked
4 Tbs. sugar

Combine sugar and cornstarch, beat egg yolks until lemon colored, add milk and stir into sugar and cornstarch. Cook over medium heat, stirring constantly until thick. Remove mixture from heat, add butter, vanilla and coconut. Pour into cooled pie shell. Top with meringue. Make meringue using egg whites and 4 tablespoons sugar. Serves 6.

CREAMY CHOCOLATE PIE

1 (9-inch) baked pastry shell
3 (1-oz.) squares unsweetened chocolate
1 (14-oz.) can sweetened condensed milk
1 cup (1/2 pint) whipping cream

1/4 tsp. salt
1/4 cup hot water
1 tsp. vanilla extract

In saucepan, over medium heat, melt chocolate with sweetened condensed milk and salt. Cook and stir until thick and fudgy, 5 to 8 minutes. Add water; cook and stir until mixture thickens and boils. Remove from heat; add vanilla. Cool 15 minutes. Chill 20 to 30 minutes; stir. Fold in whipped cream. Pour into shell. Chill 3 hours. Garnish as desired.

JAPANESE FRUIT PIE

2 egg yolks (save whites)
1 cup sugar
1 stick butter, melted

Beat this together, add:

1/2 cup coconut
1/2 cup pecans
1/2 cup raisins

Beat the two egg whites and fold in mixture. It will soften up enough to pour into unbaked pie shell. Bake one hour at 300 degrees.

FUDGE PIE

1/2 cup butter or margarine
1/4 cup plus 2 Tbs. cocoa
1 cup sugar
2 eggs, slightly beaten

1/4 cup all-purpose flour
Dash of salt
1 tsp. vanilla extract
Whipped cream or ice cream
(optional)

Melt butter in medium saucepan; remove from heat. Add cocoa, sugar, eggs, flour, salt and vanilla; beat well. Pour into a well-greased 9-inch pie pan. Bake at 350 degrees for 15-20 minutes; cool. Serve plain or topped with whipped cream or ice cream, if desired. If served warm, spoon into compotes. If chilled, cut as pie wedges. Yield: 6 servings.

STRAWBERRY PIE

1 cup sugar
2 Tbs. cornstarch
1 quart strawberries

Heat 1 pint strawberries and mash (add a little red food coloring as berries lose color when cooked). Add sugar and cornstarch that have been mixed. Cook 1 minute and cool. Pour over 1 pt. fresh whole berries and put mixture in baked pastry shell. Cover top of pie with whipped cream and chill before serving.

EASY AND QUICK TO MAKE BASIC CUSTARD FOR PIES

2-1/2 cups milk	**Dash of salt**
1 cup sugar	**1 tsp. vanilla**
3 heaping Tbs. cornstarch or flour	**2 Tbs. butter or oleo if desired**
3 egg yolks	

For quick method heat milk in heavy pan or boiler to boiling on medium heat. In another bowl put sugar, egg yolks, cornstarch or flour, dash of salt and vanilla. Mix well together adding enough of the hot milk to make smooth paste. After beating good add enough hot milk to make thin mixture and pour this mixture back into hot milk over heat. Turn to low and stir until thickens well and remove from heat. The butter or oleo may be stirred into hot mixture if rich custard is desired. It is better to let custard cool before placing on crust.
For variety add coconut to mixture. For chocolate pie add 3 tablespoons cocoa to mixture before adding milk. For caramel brown 1/4 of sugar and let melt in 1 cup of the water (do not burn sugar too brown).

PECAN PIE

3 eggs beaten	**1 cup nuts, chopped**
3/4 cups sugar	**1 tsp. vanilla**
3/4 cup corn syrup	**2 Tbs. melted butter**

Beat eggs and syrup together. Add sugar, butter, vanilla and pecans. Mix well and pour into pastry shell that has been heated in pie pan and pressed down. Bake in 325 degrees oven for 1 hour.

LEMON PIE

1 cup sugar	**2 cups water**
Dash of salt	**3 egg yolks**
3 heaping Tbs. cornstarch or flour	**1/4 cup lemon juice grated rind of**
2 Tbs. butter	**1 lemon**

Let water boil and in mixing bowl place sugar, salt, cornstarch, egg yolks and lemon juice. Beat until smooth. Into this mixture pour enough boiling water to thin. Mix thoroughly and pour mixture into boiling water over low heat. Stir until thick and remove from heat. Add 2 tablespoons of butter and stir. Let cool before placing on crust. Top with meringue. Beat egg whites until stiff enough to hold peak. Add 6 tablespoons sugar and beat in. Add 1 teaspoon vanilla and stir.

LEMON CRÈME CHEESE PIE

1 pkg. cream cheese
3 egg yolks
1 pack lemon instant pudding mix
1 can condensed milk

1 carton cool whip
Lemon juice to taste
2 graham cracker crust

Cream cheese and eggs together, add condensed milk and pudding mix. Lemon juice, then the cool whip. Mix well, then pour into crust.

NO-CRUST COCONUT PIE

4 eggs, beaten
1-3/4 cups sugar
2 cups whole milk
3/4 stick butter, melted

3/4 cup all-purpose flour
1 tsp. vanilla
2 cups shredded coconut

Preheat oven to 350 degrees. Combine all ingredients and mix well. Pour into a greased, 9-inch, deep-dish pie pan. Bake 30 to 40 minutes.

SKY-HIGH STRAWBERRY PIE

3 quarts fresh strawberries, divided
1-1/2 cups sugar
6 Tbs. cornstarch
2/3 cup water Red food coloring, optional

1 deep-dish pastry shell (10-inch), baked
1 cup heavy cream
1-1/2 Tbs. instant vanilla pudding mix

In a large bowl, mash enough berries to equal 3 cups. In a saucepan, combine the sugar and cornstarch. Stir in the mashed berries and water; mix well. Bring to a boil over medium heat, stirring constantly. Cook and stir for 2 minutes. Remove from the heat; add food coloring if desired. Pour into a large bowl. Chill for 20 minutes, stirring occasionally, until mixture is just slightly warm. Fold in the remaining berries. Pile into pie shell. Chill for 2-3 hours. In a small mixing bowl, whip cream until soft peaks form. Sprinkle pudding mix over cream and whip until stiff. Pipe around edge of pie or dollop on individual slices. Yield: 8-10 servings.

LEMONY PIE

3 eggs
5 Tbs. flour
1 cup sugar
1 pie shell, cooked

2 lemons
1/4 cup butter
1-1/4 cup milk

Separate eggs, beat egg yolks. Mix flour with sugar gradually. Add flour and sugar to beaten egg yolks. Add grated rind of 2 lemons and juice of 1 lemon. Add butter, beat, then add milk. Cook in a double boiler until thick, pour into baked pie shell and top with meringue and brown.

MACAROON PIE

3 egg whites-beat to firm peak
1 tsp. almond extract
12 saltines-crumbled

6 dates-chopped
1 cup nuts
1 cup sugar

1. Beat egg whites, add sugar and almond extract.
2. Crumble crackers and add to dates and nuts.
3. Fold crackers, etc. with egg whites.
4. Bake at 350 degrees for 20 minutes or until straw comes clean.
5. Serve topped with whipped cream and cherry.

Note: Pie crumbles when cut—don't panic—pry loose from pie pan.

FAMOUS PUMPKIN PIE

1 unbaked 9-inch deep-dish
   pie shell
3/4 cup granulated sugar
1/2 tsp. salt
1 tsp. ground cinnamon
1/2 tsp. ground ginger

1/4 tsp. ground clove
2 eggs
1-3/4 cups (15-oz. can)
   solid pack pumpkin
1-1/2 cups (12 oz. can)
   evaporated milk

Combine sugar, salt, cinnamon, ginger and cloves in small bowl. Beat eggs lightly in large bowl. Stir in pumpkin and sugar-spice mixture. Gradually stir in evaporated milk. Pour into pie shell.

Bake in preheated 425 degrees oven for 15 minutes. Reduce temperature to 350 degrees; bake for 40 to 50 minutes or until knife inserted near center comes out clean. Cool on wire rack for 3 hours. Serve immediately or chill (do not freeze).

FRIED FRESH PEACH PIES

FILLING:
3 Tbs. cornstarch
3/4 cup water
3/4 cup sugar
pinch of salt
1/4 tsp. almond flavoring (optional)
2 cups chopped, fresh Georgia peaches

Combine cornstarch and water in measuring cup and stir until dissolved. Place sugar and salt in medium saucepan, add water and cornstarch mixture. Stir over low heat until thick and clear. Add flavoring and peaches and set aside while preparing pastry.

Pastry:
1 large can refrigerator biscuits (20 to a can)
vegetable oil

On a lightly floured board, roll each biscuit individually very thin. Set aside and allow to rise for 10 minutes. After dough has risen, roll each biscuit thin again. Place approximately 1-2 tsp. of peach filling over one-half of each biscuit. Fold dough over and press edges together with a fork being careful to seal filling inside. Heat oil in skillet. Place each pie in hot oil and fry for approximately 2 minutes on each side or until brown. Drain on paper towels. Serve warm. Yield: 20 pies.

CHOCOLATE NUT PIE

1/4 cup butter
1-1/2 cups sugar
3 Tbs. cocoa
1 (5 oz.) can evaporated milk
2 eggs, beaten

1 tsp. vanilla
1 unbaked 8-inch pie shell
1/2 cup chopped pecans

In a medium saucepan over low heat, melt butter and add sugar, cocoa and milk, stirring constantly. Stir a small amount of hot chocolate mixture into eggs, then add eggs to mixture in saucepan. Remove from heat, add vanilla and pour into pie shell. Sprinkle nuts on top and bake at 300 degrees for 40 to 50 minutes, until knife inserted comes out clean.

FRENCH SILK CHOCOLATE PIE

1 cup all-purpose or unbleached flour
1/2 tsp. salt
1/3 cup shortening
2 to 3 Tbs. cold water

Chocolate FILLING:

1/2 cup margarine or butter (see note)
3/4 cup sugar
1 square, 1 oz., unsweetened chocolate, melted and cooled
1 tsp. vanilla extract
2 eggs
Whipped cream and walnuts, optional

Heat oven to 425 degrees. Lightly spoon flour into measuring cup; level off. In medium bowl, combine flour and salt. Using pastry blender or mixer at low speed, cut in shortening until particles are size of small peas. Sprinkle flour mixture with water, 1 tablespoon at a time, while tossing and mixing lightly with a fork. Add water until dough is just moist enough to hold together. Form dough into ball; place on floured surface. Flatten ball slightly; smooth edges. Roll out dough to circle 1-1/2 inches larger than inverted 8-inch pie plate. Fold pastry in half; place in pan and unfold, easing into pan. Trim edge of pastry 1 inch from rim of pan; fold pastry under, even with rim and flute. Prick bottom and sides generously with fork. Bake at 425 degrees for 10 to 12 minutes. In small bowl, combine margarine or butter and sugar; blend well. Stir in chocolate and vanilla. Add eggs, one at a time, beating 5 minutes after each addition. Pour into cooled pie shell. Chill six hours or until firm. Before serving, top with whipped cream and walnuts, if desired. Yield: one 9-inch pie.

Note: Butter, not margarine, was used in the original recipe.
Tips: If using self-rising flour, omit salt.

MILLION DOLLAR PIE

1 9 oz. container of cool whip
1 large (20 oz.) can crushed pineapple
1 can sweetened condensed milk

Juice of 1 lemon
1 cup of chopped nuts
2 pie shells (baked)

Blend lemon juice into the condensed milk, add cool whip, pineapple and nuts. Spoon into the two pie shells and refrigerate overnight or at least 3 hours before serving.

STRAWBERRY PIE

1-2/3 cups water
1 cup sugar
4 Tbs. cornstarch
1 tsp. red food coloring

1/2 pkg. strawberry Jell-O
1 baked 9-inch pie shell
Fresh strawberries

Boil first 4 ingredients until thick. Add Jell-O. Fill pie shell with fresh strawberries. Pour mixture over strawberries and chill. Top with whipped cream.

MILLIONAIRE'S PIE

2 graham cracker crusts
1 large can crushed pineapple
    (without sugar in natural juices)
1 large carton whipped topping

1 can condensed milk
1/4 cup lemon juice
Chopped pecans (optional)

Mix pineapple with whipped topping, condensed milk, and lemon juice. Add chopped pecans, if desired. Fill two graham cracker crusts and refrigerate for several hours before serving. Sprinkle nuts on top.

EASY APPLE PIE

2 cans apple pie filling
1/2 pkg. white or yellow cake mix

1-1/2 sticks margarine

Pour pie filling into 9 x 13-inch greased pan. Sprinkle cake mix on top, then dot top with margarine. Bake at 350 degrees for approximately 30 minutes or until brown and bubbly.

APPLE BUTTER PUMPKIN PIE

1 cup mashed cooked pumpkin
1 cup apple butter
3/4 cup brown sugar
1/2 tsp. salt
1/2 tsp. ground cinnamon

3 slightly beaten eggs
2/3 cup evaporated milk
1/3 cup milk
1 9-inch pastry shell

In a large mixing bowl thoroughly combine pumpkin, apple butter, brown sugar, salt and cinnamon. Blend in eggs, evaporated milk, and milk. Turn into baked pastry shell. Bake in 400 degrees oven for 45-50 minutes or until knife inserted in center comes out clean.

FROZEN STRAWBERRY YOGURT PIE

2 containers (8 oz. each) strawberry flavored yogurt
1 tub (12 oz.) cool whip, whipped topping, thawed
1 cup sweetened finely chopped strawberries
1 prepared graham cracker crust

Stir yogurt gently into 3-1/2 cups of the whipped topping until well blended. Stir in strawberries. Spoon into crust.
Freeze 4 hours or overnight until firm. Let stand in refrigerator 15 minutes or until pie can be cut easily. Garnish with remaining whipped topping, if desired. Store leftover pie in freezer. Yield: 8 servings.

STRAWBERRY PIE

Combine:
1 cup water
1 cup sugar
3 Tbs. cornstarch

Boil until thick, add 1 pkg. strawberry Jell-O. Let cool. Add fresh strawberries and pour into a baked pie-shell (cooled). Chill for 2 hours before serving and top with cool whip.

MISSISSIPPI MUD PIE

1 stick (1/4 lb.) margarine
1 cup all-purpose flour
1/2 cup chopped pecans
1 (8-oz.) pkg. cream cheese
1 cup powdered sugar
1 8-oz. carton frozen whipped
   topping, divided

Grated coconut
Chopped pecans
2 (3-1/2 oz.) pkg. instant
   chocolate pudding
3 cups milk

Cream together the margarine, flour and pecans to form a dough. Press into bottom of a 9 x 13-inch pan and bake at 350 degrees for 20 minutes. Cool. Mix together the cream cheese, powdered sugar and 1 cup of the whipped topping. Spread over crust. Sprinkle with some coconut and a few chopped pecans. Prepare the instant pudding using only 3 cups of milk. Immediately pour and spread over whipped-topping layer. Spread the remainder of the whipped topping over pudding and sprinkle with more coconut and chopped pecans. Refrigerate for 5 or 6 hours or overnight.

KEY LIME PIE

1 small can frozen limeade
1 can eagle brand milk
1 (9 oz.) cool whip

Let limeade thaw a few minutes, add eagle brand milk and stir with spoon, then add cool whip and stir well again. Pour into graham cracker crust. For best results make day before serving.

Substitute lemonade if desired.

CHOCOLATE-PEANUT BUTTER SWIRL PIE—

2/3 cup sugar
2 Tbs. all-purpose flour
1 Tbs. cornstarch
1/4 tsp. salt
2-1/2 cups milk
3 egg yolks
1/2 cup creamy peanut butter
1/2 tsp. vanilla extract

1/2 cup semisweet chocolate morsels
Chocolate Pastry Shell
1/2 cup heavy cream
1 Tbs. sifted powdered sugar
2 Tbs. dry-roasted peanuts, coarsely chopped

Combine the 2/3 cup sugar, the flour, cornstarch and salt in a heavy saucepan. Gradually add milk; cook over medium heat, stirring constantly, until mixture is thickened and bubbly. Beat egg yolks. Gradually stir 1/4 of hot mixture into yolks. Add remaining hot mixture, stirring constantly. Cook, stirring constantly, until mixture thickens. Remove from heat and add peanut butter and vanilla. Stir until peanut butter melts. Stir in semisweet chocolate morsels until distributed but not melted. Pour mixture into prepared Chocolate Pastry Shell. Let stand 3 minutes, gently swirling with knife. Beat heavy cream until foamy; gradually add powdered sugar, beating until soft peaks form. Pipe whipped cream around edge of pie and sprinkle with peanuts. Yield: one 9-inch pie.

FRUIT PIES

1 cup sugar
1 cup flour
Quart of fruit or 2 cans pie filling

1 cup milk
1 stick margarine

Melt margarine in pan. Mix flour, milk, and sugar together and pour into buttered pan. Add fruit and bake for 30 minutes at 400 degrees.

CHOCOLATE PASTRY SHELL

1 cup all-purpose flour
1/4 tsp. salt
1/4 cup firmly packed brown sugar
1/2 cup vegetable shortening
2 Tbs. cocoa
3 to 4 Tbs.. cold water

start
Combine flour, brown sugar, cocoa and salt; cut in shortening with pastry blender until mixture resembles coarse meal. Sprinkle cold water, 1 tablespoon at a time, evenly over surface. Stir with a fork until all dry ingredients are moistened. Shape pastry mixture into a ball; chill 30 minutes. Roll out pastry into 1/8-inch thickness on a lightly floured surface. Place in a 9-inch pie plate; trim excess pastry from edges and flute. Prick bottom and sides of pastry with fork. Bake at 450 degrees for 8 minutes or until browned. Set aside to cool. Yield: 1 (9-inch) pastry shell.

CHOCOLATE PEANUT BUTTER PIE

1 cup confectioner's sugar
1/2 cup crunchy peanut butter
1 baked deep-dish 9-inch
   pastry shell
3 Tbs. cornstarch
2/3 cup granulated sugar
2 Tbs.. cocoa
1/4 tsp. salt

2 cups milk, scalded
3 egg yolks, beaten
2 tablespoons butter
1 tsp. vanilla
3 egg whites
2 tablespoons granulated
   sugar

Combine confectioner's sugar and peanut butter, blending until it has the appearance of biscuit mix. Spread 3/4 of this mixture on baked pie shell.
Combine cornstarch, granulated sugar, cocoa and salt; add scalded milk and mix well. Pour small amount over beaten egg yolks. Mix well, then return to milk mixture. Cook in top of double boiler until mixture thickens. Add butter and vanilla. Pour into prepared pie shell.
For meringue, beat egg whites adding sugar a little at a time until sugar is dissolved and meringue is stiff and foamy. Pile onto hot-pie filling and sprinkle remaining peanut butter and sugar mixture over the meringue. Bake at 350 degrees for 10 to 15 minutes or until the meringue is lightly browned.
Yield: 6-8 servings.

HELPFUL HINTS

CAKES

Cake mixes: To improve, add 1/4 cup (no more) cooking oil per box of mix.

Sprinkle cake lightly with powdered sugar to keep filling from soaking into layer cake.

Always have ingredients at room temperature.

Cool cake on rack for at least 10 minutes before removing from pan. (Longer will make it soggy.)

Cool cake before icing.

Tests to see if cake is done: Angel and sponge cake will sing if not done, so listen. Cake is done if it pulls away from edge, if it springs back when lightly touched in center, if straw or uncooked piece of spaghetti will come out clean after being inserted.

Add a pinch of salt to uncooked icing to keep from graining.

Cut a square from center of layer cake before slicing—will keep from crumbling.

To cut cake with fruit filling, dip knife in hot water before cutting each slice. Cut quickly.

To keep cakes from sticking to pan: Grease pan, then place waxed paper in bottom and reuse it. Dust with flour if recipe calls for it.

When mixing a cake: To speed creaming, mix butter and sugar and add 1/2 cup of the required flour and one of the required eggs.

When only a small amount is eaten at one time, cut in half, slice pieces from center and push cake together to keep fresh for several days.

If top of cake is sprinkled with flour as soon as it is taken from oven, icing will spread more easily and not be so likely to run off.

The layers of a cake will come out of their pans without sticking if you will set the hot pans on a damp cloth when they come out of the oven.

CUSTARD

When recipe calls for scalding milk, put a little water in pan to cover bottom and bring to a boil before adding milk, and this will keep it from sticking.

COOKIES

Arrange cookies on waxed paper or foil and place on a baking sheet. When done, slide paper with cookies off to cool. Have another batch on paper ready to slide on.

For soft cookies, place in earthen jar while slightly warm. Cover tightly.

Toast uncooked oatmeal and use in making cookies. Gives a nutty flavor.

When rolling out cookies, use powdered sugar instead of flour on cutting board.

May be quickly made by spreading out batter in pan and cutting it in squares after baking.

PIES

Brush pastry shell with egg white before baking. Will help to keep it from absorbing filling.

Cool pies on rack to prevent bottom pastry from becoming soggy.

You can cut a meringue pie cleanly by coating both sides of the knife lightly with butter.

To keep icings moist and to prevent cracking, add a pinch of baking soda to the icing.

When rolling cookie dough, sprinkle board with powdered sugar instead of flour. Too much flour makes the dough heavy. When freezing cookies with a frosting, place them in freezer unwrapped for about 2 hours—then wrap without worrying about them sticking together.

Place on piece of waxed paper in double boiler when melting chocolate to save chocolate and dish washing.

1-4 cup cocoa may be substituted for each ounce chocolate and 1/2 table-spoon butter added to recipe.

When you are creaming butter and sugar together, it is a good idea to rinse the bowl with boiling water first. They will cream faster.

To melt chocolate, grease pan in which it is to be melted.

Dip the spoon in hot water to measure shortening, butter, etc., the fat will slip out more easily.

When you buy cellophane-wrapped cupcakes and notice that the cellophane is somewhat stuck to the frosting, hold the package under the cold-water tap for a moment before you unwrap it. The cellophane will then come off clean.

When you are doing any sort of baking, you get better results if you remember to preheat your cookie sheet, muffin tins, or cake pans.

A clean clothespin provides a cool handle to steady the cake tin when removing a hot cake.

Try using a thread instead of a knife when a cake is to be cut while it is hot.

Meringue will not shrink if you spread it on the pie so that it touches the crust on each side and bake it in a moderate oven.

If you want to make a pecan pie and do not have any nuts, substitute crushed cornflakes. They will rise to the top the same as nuts and give a delicious flavor and crunchy surface.

To prevent crust from becoming soggy with cream pie, sprinkle crust with powdered sugar.

Cut drinking straws into short lengths and insert through slits in piecrusts to prevent juice from running over in the oven and permit steam to escape.

Put a layer of marshmallows in the bottom of a pumpkin pie, then add the filling. You will have a nice topping, as the marshmallow will come to the top.

If the juice from your apple pie runs over in the oven, shake some salt on it, which causes the juice to burn to a crisp so it can be removed.

Use cooking or salad oil in waffles and hot cakes in the place of shortening. No extra pan or bowl to melt the shortening and no waiting.

To cut a pie into five equal pieces, first cut an Y in the pie and then two large pieces can be cut in half.

To keep icing soft, add pinch of baking soda to egg whites before beating them.

CASSEROLES
&
MAIN DISHES

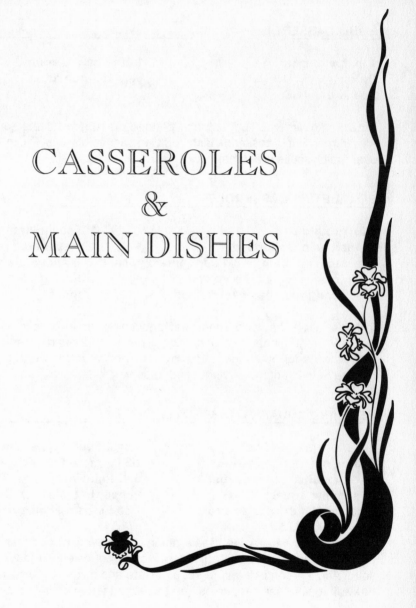

CASSEROLES

HOBO CASSEROLE

1 lb. hamburger
Onion
Salt and pepper

1 cup tomato soup
Veg-All, drained

Brown hamburger, onion, salt and pepper; drain. Add tomato soup and Veg-All; simmer. Put in casserole dish; top with canned biscuits. Put in 250 degrees over until biscuits are done.

ELIZABETH'S CASSEROLE

1 lb. ground beef
1 small onion, chopped
1 can tomato soup or 3/4 cup tomato juice
1 can cream of mushroom soup
Small can green peas, undrained

1/2 cup instant rice
1/8 tsp. garlic powder
Salt and pepper to taste
1/2 cup grated cheddar
  cheese

In large skillet, brown ground beef and onion, drain off excess liquid. Add remaining ingredients, except cheese. Pour into a 2-quart casserole and bake 350 degrees for 30 minutes. Remove from oven and top with cheese. Allow cheese to melt before serving. Yield: 6 servings.

BEEF AND SQUASH CASSEROLE

1-1/2 lbs. ground beef
1 large onion, chopped
10-12 medium (or 1-1/2 lbs.)
  summer squash
1 can cream of celery soup

1 small bell pepper chopped
1/2 lb. grated cheddar cheese
Salt to taste
Pepper to taste
1 can cream of mushroom soup

Brown beef and set aside. Sauté onion until clear. Cook squash until tender. Drain beef and squash. In a bowl, mix cream of celery soup with mushroom soup. Add 1/4 can of water to soup mixture and mix well. Combine soup mixture with onion, bell pepper, salt and pepper; then mix with squash.

Layer beef, then squash in a large buttered casserole dish. Top with grated cheese. Put into a 350 degrees oven until brown on top---approximately 20 minutes or until bubbly.

BEEF-A-RONI CASSEROLE

1-1/2 cup cooked macaroni
1 lb. ground chuck
1 (8 oz.) can tomato sauce
1 small onion

Brown ground chuck, onion, bell pepper in skillet; add flour, tomato sauce and 2 tomato sauce cans water. Add salt, pepper and garlic powder to taste. Simmer 5 minutes. Add to meat mixture the cooked macaroni. Pour mixture into casserole dish and cover top with grated cheese. Bake for 15 minutes at 375 degrees.

CORNED BEEF AND CABBAGE

1 small head cabbage, shredded   Mayonnaise
1 small onion, shredded   Salt and pepper to taste
1 (12 oz.) can corned beef, shredded
1/2 tsp. celery seed

Combine ingredients and toss with mayonnaise to taste. Refrigerate before serving. Serve with rye bread.

CHICKEN CASSEROLE—I

I chicken, boiled and deboned
1 pkgs. chopped broccoli
1 jar pimento
1 can white whole kernel corn
Sliced mushrooms
1 cup Half & Half
Cornstarch

Boil chicken and debone. Keep remaining broth. Cook broccoli, corn, pimento, and mushrooms. Add chicken and Half & Half. Thicken mixture with cornstarch. Better warmed over second time

CHICKEN CASSEROLE—II

1 can cream of celery soup
1 soup can milk
3/4 cup rice, uncooked
Salt and pepper to taste

1 (4 oz.) jar mushrooms, undrained
1 envelope onion soup mix
6 boneless chicken breasts

Combine soup and milk in a medium sized mixing bowl (reserve half of mixture for top of casserole). Combine rice, mushrooms with liquid and half of onion soup mix with half of soup and milk mixture. Pour into a large greased casserole; place chicken breasts on top. Pour reserved soup mixture over top and sprinkle with remaining dry soup. Cover with foil and bake at 350 degrees for one hour. Remove foil and bake an additional 15 minutes. Yield: 6 servings.

CHICKEN DINNER CASSEROLE

1 (10-oz.) pkg. frozen broccoli cuts
1/3 cup chopped onion
1 cup grated, cheddar cheese
2 eggs, slightly beaten
1/2 cup mayonnaise
Paprika

1 can cream of mushroom soup
1 soup can of water
3/4 cup converted rice, uncooked
1/2 cup sliced mushrooms
6 chicken breasts (boneless, if
   desired)

Cook onions with broccoli according to package directions, drain. Mix together next 7 ingredients. Add broccoli and onions and stir. Pour into a 9 x 13-inch baking dish and place chicken on top. Sprinkle with paprika. Bake at 350 degrees for 1 hour. Yield: 6 servings.

CHICKEN DRESSING CASSEROLE

1 (8 oz.) pkg. herb stuffing
1/2 cup butter, melted
1 cup chicken broth
2-1/2 cups diced chicken or turkey
1/2 cup chopped onion
1/4 cup chopped green onion
1/2 cup chopped celery

1/2 cup mayonnaise
3/4 tsp. salt
2 eggs
1 cup milk
1 can cream of mushroom soup,
   undiluted
1/2 cup grated cheddar cheese

In a large bowl, combine first nine ingredients. Pour into a 9 x 12-inch baking dish. Combine eggs and milk and pour over chicken mixture. Spread soup over all; bake at 350 degrees for 40 minutes. Sprinkle cheese over casserole and bake additional 5 minutes.

CHICKEN & DRESSING CASSEROLE

2 lbs. boiled chicken, boned & chopped
1/2 stick oleo
1/2 (10 3/4 oz.) can cream of celery soup
1/2 (10 3/4 oz.) can cream of chicken soup
1/2 (13 oz.) can evaporated or whole milk
1 box cornbread stuffing mix
1-1/2 cup chicken broth

Put chicken in a 2-quart casserole. Melt oleo; add soup and milk. Pour over chicken. Mix stuffing with broth and spoon over mixture in casserole. Do not stir together. Bake 425 degrees for 25 minutes or until brown. Yield: 6 to 8 servings.

CHICKEN AND RICE CASSEROLE

2 cups Minute Rice
4 chicken breast halves
1 (10-3/4 oz.) can cream of chicken soup
1 (10-3/4 oz.) can cream of celery soup
3 cups milk
Salt and pepper to taste

Preheat oven to 350 degrees. Place rice in a greased 13 x 9-inch baking dish. Add chicken breasts, skin up. Add salt and pepper. Mix together milk and soups. Heat mixture (do not boil) and pour over chicken. Cover pan with foil and bake in preheated oven for 45 minutes, or until chicken breasts test done. Yield 4 servings.

SOUTHWEST CHICKEN CASSEROLE

1 cup Extra Long Grain Rice
2 cups chicken stock
1 lb. cooked chicken, cut into strips
1 medium onion, chopped
Salt and pepper
1 tsp. chili powder
1 can cream of chicken soup
1 cup sour cream
16 oz. cheddar Cheese
1 (10 oz.) can Ro-Tel tomatoes &
Green Chilies

Combine rice and chicken stock in medium saucepan. Line bottom of 13-1/2 x 9 x 2-inch casserole with one-half of cooked rice. Layer in the following order: Chicken, onion, salt and pepper, chili powder, soup, sour cream, cheese. Just before baking, top with Ro-Tel tomatoes. Bake at 350 degrees for 45 minutes. Yield: 6 servings.

PORK APPLE CASSEROLE

5 oz. uncooked egg noodles (about 3 cups)
1 lb. boneless pork, cubed
1 Tbs. cooking oil
1 Tbs. flour
1 apple, peeled and chopped
1 small onion, sliced
1 clove garlic, minced
1/2 cup sliced celery
1/4 cup water
1/4 tsp. salt
1/2 cup sour cream
Dash pepper

Cook noodles as directed on package; set aside. Heat oil in glass casserole over medium heat; coat pork with flour and brown. Add apple, onion, garlic, celery, water, salt and pepper. Cover and microwave on 30 percent power for 8-10 minutes; stir once. Stir in sour cream. Serve over noodles, potatoes or rice.

PORK CHOP CASSEROLE

4-6 pork chops
1 can cream of celery soup
1 soup can milk
3/4 cup uncooked rice
1 envelope onion soup mix
Salt & pepper to taste

Lightly brown pork chops, drain on absorbent paper. In a medium-sized bowl, combine soup and milk and reserve 1/2 cup for topping; add rice and half of dry soup mix. Pour mixture into a lightly greased 12 x 9-inch baking dish. Place pork chops on top, pour reserved soup mixture over chops and sprinkle with remaining dry soup mix. Cover with aluminum, foil and bake at 350 degrees for one hour. Remove foil and bake 15 minutes longer.

HAM BROCCOLI CASSEROLE

1 (10 oz.) pkg. frozen broccoli
    spears, partially cooked
1-1/2 cups cubed cooked ham
1 can cream of mushroom soup
1/2 cup mayonnaise
1/4 tsp. turmeric
1/2 cup grated cheddar cheese
1/2 cup bread crumbs
2 Tbs. butter, melted

Lay broccoli in an 8-inch square baking dish. Sprinkle ham over broccoli. Combine soup, mayonnaise and turmeric; pour over ham. Sprinkle grated cheese over soup mixture. Mix bread crumbs with butter and top casserole. Bake at 325 degrees for 30 minutes. Yield: 4 servings.

SPAM-MAC CASSEROLE

1 (7 oz.) pkg. elbow macaroni
2 Tbs. margarine or butter
1/2 cup chopped onion
2 Tbs. flour
1 tsp. Dijon mustard
Buttered bread crumbs
1/4 tsp. pepper

2 cups milk
1 cup (4 oz.) shredded swiss cheese
1 (12 oz.) luncheon meat, cubed
1 cup frozen peas and carrots,
    thawed and drained

Prepare macaroni according to package directions; drain. In medium saucepan, melt margarine. Add onion, cook until tender. Stir in flour, mustard and pepper. Blend in milk. Cook, stirring constantly, until thickened and bubbly. Add cheese; stir until melted. Combine macaroni, luncheon meat, peas and carrots, and cheese sauce. Pour into a 3-quart baking dish. Top with bread crumbs. Bake in a 350 degrees oven until hot and bubbly, about 30 minutes.

CORN AND SAUSAGE CASSEROLE

4 eggs, beaten
1 (17 oz.) can creamed corn
1 tsp. salt
1 cup bread crumbs

1 lb. pork sausage, cooked and crumbled
1/2 cup cracker crumbs
1/4 tsp. pepper

Combine all ingredients, except cracker crumbs; mix well. Spoon into lightly greased 10 x 6 x 1-3/4 inch baking pan. Sprinkle with cracker crumbs. Bake at 350 degrees for 50 minutes

MINI SHRIMP CASSEROLES

1/2 lb. mushrooms, sliced
2 medium tomatoes, diced
1/2 bell pepper, chopped
2 Tbs. flour
1 Tbs. cooking Worcestershire sauce
1 cup cream, 1/4 cup butter, 1/3 cup cooking sherry

4 green onions, chopped
2 lbs. boiled, peeled shrimp
Salt and pepper to taste
Seasoned bread crumbs

In a large skillet, melt butter; add mushrooms and sauté add onions, tomatoes, and pepper, simmer 10 minutes. Stir flour into cream and add sherry and Worcestershire sauce; pour over vegetables. Add shrimp. Pour mixture into eight 6-ounce custard cups and top with bread crumbs. Bake at 350 degrees for 20 minutes or until brown. Yield: 8 mini casseroles.

BROCCOLI CASSEROLE—I

1/4 cup finely chopped onion
6 Tbs. butter
2 Tbs. flour
1/2 cup water
1 8-oz. jar cheddar cheese spread

2 10-oz. pkgs. frozen, chopped
broccoli, thawed and well drained
3 eggs, beaten
1/2 cup soda cracker crumbs
Slivered almonds

Sauté onion in 4 tablespoons of the butter until soft. Stir in flour, add water. Cook over low heat, stirring until mixture thickens and becomes like paste. Remove from heat. Blend in cheese. Combine this sauce and broccoli. Add eggs and mix gently. Pour into greased 1-1/2-quart casserole. Cover with cracker crumbs, and dot with remaining butter. Bake at 325 degrees for 30 minutes. Garnish with slivered almonds.

BEST BROCCOLI CASSEROLE

1/2 tsp. salt
1 cup water
1 cup instant rice
1 can (10 3/4 oz.) cream of mushroom soup, undiluted
1 can (10-3/4 oz.) cream of celery soup, undiluted
1 pkg. (10 oz.) frozen, chopped broccoli, thawed
1/2 cup diced process American cheese

1/4 cup butter or margarine
1/4 cup chopped onion
1/4 cup chopped celery

Bring water and salt to a boil. Add rice; cover and remove from heat. Let set for 5 minutes. Melt butter in skillet; sauté onion and celery until tender. In large mixing bowl, combine rice, celery and onion with remaining ingredients. Pour into a greased 1-1/2 qt. casserole. Bake at 350 degrees for 1 hour.
Yield: 6 servings.

BROCCOLI CASSEROLE—II

2 pkgs. chopped broccoli, cooked, drained
1 medium onion, chopped fine
1 can cream of celery soup
1 cup shredded cheddar cheese
2 eggs, slightly beaten
1 cup mayonnaise

Mix all ingredients together, pour into buttered casserole dish. Top with dry Pepperidge Farm stuffing mix. Bake at 350 degrees for 30 minutes.

BROCCOLI CASSEROLE—III

1 small onion, chopped
1/2 cup chopped celery
1 pkg. (10 oz.) frozen chopped broccoli, thawed
1 Tbs. butter or margarine
1 jar (8 oz.) process cheese spread
1 can (10-3/4 oz.) condensed cream of mushroom soup, undiluted
1 can (5 oz.) evaporated milk
3 cups cooked rice

In a large skillet over medium heat, sauté' onion, celery and broccoli in butter for 3-5 minutes. Stir in cheese, soup and milk until smooth. Place rice in a greased 8-inch square baking dish. Pour cheese mixture over; do not stir. Bake, uncovered, at 325 degrees for 25-30 minutes or until hot and bubbly. Yield: 8-10 servings.

BROCCOLI CASSEROLE—IV

2 10 oz. pkgs. frozen, chopped broccoli, cooked & drained
2 eggs, slightly beaten
1/2 cup mayonnaise
1 can cream of celery soup
4 oz. sliced Swiss cheese
Bread crumbs
Butter

Combine first 4 ingredients, then top with cheese slices, and then crumbs and butter on top of cheese. Place in a greased 8-inch casserole. Top with bread crumbs and butter. Bake at 325 degrees for 45 minutes. Yield: 6 servings.

SHOE PEG CORN CASSEROLE

1/2 cup chopped celery
1/2 cup chopped green pepper
1/2 cup chopped onion
1 can French cut green beans, drained
1 can shoe peg corn
1/2 cup grated cheese
1 can mushroom soup
1 cup sour cream
1 stick oleo
1 stack Ritz crackers

Mix first 8 ingredients and put in casserole, 8-1/2 x 13 inch. Crush Ritz crackers and mix with melted oleo. Cover top of casserole with cracker mixture. Bake at 350 degrees for 45 minutes.

CORN CASSEROLE

Two 14-1/2 oz. cans whole kernel corn, drained
1/4 cup sugar
1-1/2 Tbs. flour
1/4 cup butter or margarine
1/2 pint of heavy cream
Salt and pepper to taste

Place corn in a 1-1/2-quart casserole. Mix together sugar, flour and salt. Mix dry ingredients with corn and pour cream over mixture. Cut margarine into chunks and place over top. Bake at 350 degrees for 35 minutes. Stir twice while baking. (Note: 2 pints fresh corn when in season can be substituted for canned corn.) Yield: 6-8 servings.

DEVILED CORN CASSEROLE

1 can niblets whole kernel corn
1 cup corn liquid and milk (sweet)
2 Tbs. chopped onion
3 slices diced bacon
2 Tbs. butter

2 Tbs. flour
1 tsp. dry mustard
1/2 tsp. Worcestershire sauce
1/2 tsp. salt

Drain corn; save liquid, add enough milk to make 1 cup. Brown onion and bacon; add butter and flour, then add milk and cook until thick. Fold in corn, dry mustard and Worcestershire sauce. Turn into buttered baking dish. Top with bread crumbs. Bake in 375 degrees oven until crumbs are brown.

NITA'S EGGPLANT CASSEROLE

1 medium eggplant
1 can cream of chicken or cream of mushroom soup
8-oz. pkg. cream cheese, softened
20 saltine crackers, crushed
1 lb. of mild cheddar cheese

Peel eggplant and slice 1/4 inch thick. Cook in salted water until tender. Drain, but reserve liquid. Combine soup and cream cheese, set aside. In an 8-inch slightly greased casserole, layer 1/2 of eggplant, cracker crumbs, soup mixture and cheese. Repeat layers ending with cheese. Spoon 4-5 Tablespoons of eggplant liquid into casserole. Bake at 350 degrees for 30-45 minutes. Or until bubbly. Yield: 6 servings.

EGGPLANT CASSEROLE

1 medium size eggplant
2 Tbs. butter or oleo
1 egg
1 chopped onion
1/2 grated cheese

1 cup milk
1 cup bread crumbs or crushed saltines
Salt and pepper to taste

Peel and cut in chunks and boil eggplant until tender. Drain and mash with butter. Add slightly beaten egg and onion (optional) grated cheese, milk and seasoning. Mix well. Bake 30 or 40 minutes at 350 degrees.

GREEN BEAN CASSEROLE

1 16 oz. can French green beans, drained
1 16 oz. can whole kernel white corn, drained
1 8 oz. can sliced water chestnuts, drained
1 can cream of celery soup
1/4 cup sour cream
1/4 cup cottage cheese
1 medium onion, chopped
1 cup grated cheddar cheese

TOPPING:
1/2 cup melted margarine
1 pkg. (individual roll) crackers
Garlic powder, salt and pepper to taste
1 pkg. slivered almonds (optional)

FIRST LAYER—green beans
SECOND LAYER—corn
THIRD LAYER—water chestnuts

Combine the next four ingredients and spread over water chestnuts to form fourth layer. Sprinkle grated cheese over chestnuts; crush crackers and add margarine and seasoning. Sprinkle almonds over topping. Bake 30 to 40 minutes at 350 degrees. NOTE: 1/2 cup sour cream may be used in place of 1/4 cup cottage cheese and 1/4 cup sour cream. Yield: 6 servings.

237

VIDALIA ONION CASSEROLE

5 large Vidalia onions thinly sliced
25 round butter crackers
1/2 cup grated Parmesan cheese
1/2 cup margarine, melted

Preheat oven to 350 degrees. Place half of onions in a 13 x 9-inch baking dish. Top with half of crackers and half of Parmesan cheese. Repeat with remaining ingredients. Pour melted margarine over casserole. Bake uncovered for 45 minutes. Yield: 16 servings.

ENGLISH PEA & CHESTNUT CASSEROLE

1/2 cup butter or margarine
1 small onion, chopped
2 Tbs. green pepper, chopped
1 cup sliced celery
Two 17 oz. cans English peas
1 cup sliced water chestnuts, drained
1 can cream of mushroom soup, undiluted
Cracker crumbs

Melt butter in large skillet. Add onion, pepper, and celery; sauté' over medium heat until tender. Remove from heat, add peas and chestnuts. Arrange half of vegetable mixture in bottom of a 2-quart buttered casserole; top with half of soup. Repeat layers. Sprinkle with buttered cracker crumbs. Bake at 350 degrees for 30 minutes. Yield: 6-8 servings.

ENGLISH PEA CASSEROLE

1 can cream of mushroom soup, undiluted
1 can cream of asparagus soup
3 hard boiled eggs, chopped
1 can English peas, drained
1 cup grated cheese
Cracker crumbs

Mix all ingredients and top with cracker crumbs. Bake in covered casserole at 350 degrees until top is brown, about 30 minutes.

POTATO CASSEROLE

2 lbs. frozen hash brown potatoes
1 cup diced onions
1 can cream of chicken soup
6 oz. sour cream
1/2 cup melted margarine
8 oz. of grated sharp cheese
Salt and pepper to taste

Thaw potatoes about 30 minutes, then mix all ingredients in a large bowl. Place in a 9 x 13-inch baking dish. Bake at 350 degrees for one hour. Yield: 8 servings.

SWEET POTATO CASSEROLE

3 cups mashed sweet potatoes
1/8 cup orange juice
1 cup sugar
1 tsp. vanilla

2 eggs
1 stick margarine
1 tsp. salt

TOPPING:
1 cup pecans
1 cup brown sugar
1 stick butter
1 cup self-rising flour

Mix ingredients with sweet potatoes; mix well. Pour in baking dish. Mix topping ingredients well; sprinkle on potatoes and bake 45 minutes at 345 degrees.

SQUASH CASSEROLE—I

3 cups squash after cooked and drained
1 can cream of mushroom soup
12 saltines, crushed
3/4 cup grated cheddar
1 bell pepper, chopped and sautéed
1 onion, chopped and sautéed
Salt and pepper to taste

Mix all ingredients together. Put in baking dish. Top with crushed saltines and grated cheese. Bake at 400 degrees until bubbly and brown.

SQUASH CASSEROLE—II

About 2 lbs. of squash
1 small onion, chopped
1 small can pimento in strips
1 egg
1 scant cup grated cheese

2 Tbs. butter
1 tsp. salt
2 Tbs. sugar

Cook squash and onion in small amount of water in covered pan until tender. Add milk, eggs slightly beaten, cheese, butter, salt, sugar and pimento. Blend well. Pour in greased baking dish and bake for 25 minutes at 350 degrees.

SQUASH CASSEROLE—III

2 lbs. squash (frozen or fresh)
2 carrots, grated
2 onions, chopped
1 can cream of chicken soup

1/2 pint or 8 oz. sour cream
1 pkg. herb stuffing mix
1 stick butter

Cook squash; season lightly with salt and pepper. Add carrots, onions, sour cream, and chicken soup. Pour melted butter over stuffing mix and mix well. Add 1/2 of stuffing mix to squash mixture and put in buttered or Pam sprayed 2-quart casserole dish. Cover with remaining stuffing mix. Bake at 375 degrees for 25 to 30 minutes.

CHEESY ZUCCHINI CASSEROLE

2 lbs. zucchini, thinly sliced
One 4-oz. can sliced mushrooms,
  undrained
1 Tbs. butter
2 eggs, separated
One 8-oz. carton sour cream

2 Tbs. all purpose flour
1/2 tsp. salt
1-1/2 cups shredded cheddar cheese
6 slices bacon, fried and crumbled
1/4 cup fine dry bread crumbs
1 Tbs. butter, melted

In a large skillet, combine zucchini, mushrooms, and butter; simmer over medium heat until tender. Beat egg yolks; add sour cream, flour and salt; stir until blended. Beat egg whites until stiff; fold into sour cream mixture. In a large baking dish, layer half the zucchini, half the sour cream mixture, half the cheese and bacon. Repeat layers. Combine bread crumbs and melted butter; sprinkle over casserole. Bake at 350 degrees for 25 minutes. Yield: 8 servings.

ZUCCHINI CASSEROLE

4 eggs, slightly beaten
1/2 cup vegetable oil
1 clove garlic, minced
3 cups thinly sliced zucchini
1 cup biscuit mix
1/2 cup chopped onion

1/2 cup Parmesan cheese
2 Tbs. snipped parsley
1/2 Tbs. oregano
1/2 Tbs. salt
Dash black pepper

In a large bowl, beat eggs and oil; stir in remaining ingredients. Pour into a 2-quart casserole. Bake at 350 degrees for 30-40 minutes or until set. Yield: 6 servings.

VEGETABLE CASSEROLE

1 sleeve (about 12-15) cheese flavored crackers, crushed
3 Tbs. butter, melted
1 can (15 oz.) whole kernel corn, drained
1 can (16 oz.) French cut green beans, drained
1 can (8 oz.) sliced water chestnuts, drained
1/2 cup chopped celery
1/4 cup chopped green pepper
1/2 cup grated cheddar cheese
1 can cream of celery soup
1/2 sup sour cream

Mix cracker crumbs with butter; set aside. In a 2-quart casserole, combine remaining ingredients; top with reserved cracker crumbs. Bake at 350 degrees for 35-40 minutes. Yield: 6 servings.

VEG-ALL CASSEROLE

2 cans Veg-All, drained
3/4 cup mayonnaise
1/2 cup onion
1 cup grated cheddar cheese
1 stick butter or margarine
1 sleeve Ritz crackers

Mix all ingredients, except crackers and butter, together. Pour into baking dish. Crush one roll of Ritz crackers, and sprinkle over mixture. Melt one stick butter or margarine and pour over crackers. Bake 30 minutes at 350 degrees.

241

MAIN DISHES

BUFFALO CHICKEN WINGS

12 chicken wings, separated at joints tips discarded
Oil or shortening for frying
3 Tbs. margarine or butter
2 Tbs. to 1/4 cup hot pepper sauce
Blue Cheese Dressing (recipe follows)
Celery sticks

Cut off and discard tips of chicken wings. Cut wings at joints to form 24 pieces. Fry a few wing pieces at a time in deep 375 degrees cooking oil or shortening for 8 to 10 minutes or until golden brown. Drain on paper towels. In small saucepan, melt margarine or butter. Stir in hot pepper sauce. Pour mixture over wings, turning them to coat. Serve wings with Blue Cheese Dressing and celery sticks.

CHICKEN AND CORN

Tender stewing hen and take from broth and remove bones. This mixture should be salted to taste. In 1 pint of boiling broth add 3 cups fresh for frozen corn. Cook slow for 30 minutes. More broth can be used as needed to thin mixture; the corn will determine the amount. The chicken may be young and tender and take less broth; or the chicken may be older and require more broth. Stir often. Cook 30 minutes longer. Salt and pepper to taste.

CHICKEN PIE

Cook chicken in salted water until tender. Mix a dough of 1 cup water, 1/3 cup shortening an enough flour to make stiff dough. Roll dough on floured board and line sides of deep pan lightly greased. Put half the chicken in pan. Cut strips of the dough that has been rolled thin and place over chicken. Cut 3 hard boiled eggs over dumplings, add remaining chicken and cover with dumplings rolled thin. Sprinkle with black pepper. Pour chicken broth over all and pour 1/4 cup melted butter over top. Bake at 400 degrees until golden brown and done.

DUTCH OVEN CHICKEN

1-3 lb. chicken, cut in pieces   Oil
Salt and pepper   1 can of mushroom soup
Flour   1/2 can water

Sprinkle chicken with salt and pepper, roll in flour. Brown in deep fat. Pour up fat and add sour and water that has been stirred well. Bake at 300 degrees for 1 hour. Steak may be substituted for chicken.

BUTTERMILK FRIED CHICKEN WITH GRAVY

I broiler-fryer chicken   1-1/2 tsp. salt
1 cup buttermilk   1/2 tsp. pepper
1 cup all-purpose flour   Salt and pepper to taste
Cooking oil for frying

GRAVY:
3 tbs. all-purpose flour   1-1/2 to 2 cups water
1 cup milk

Place chicken in a large flat dish. Pour buttermilk over; refrigerate 1 hour. Combine flour, salt and pepper in a double strength paper bag. Drain chicken; toss pieces, one at a time, in flour mixture. Shake off excess; place on waxed paper for 15 minutes. Heat 1/8 to 1/4 inch of oil in a skillet; fry chicken until browned on all sides. Cover and simmer, turning occasionally, for 40-45 minutes, or until juices run clear. Uncover and cook 5 minutes longer. Remove chicken and keep warm. Drain all but 1/4 cup drippings; stir in flour until bubbly. Add milk and 1-1/2 cups water; cook and stir until thickened an bubbly. Cook 1 minute more. Add remaining water if needed. Season with salt and pepper. Serve with chicken. Yield: 4-6 servings.

EASY BARBECUED CHICKEN

1 chicken (cut-up, skinned)
2 cups cola
1 cup barbecue sauce

Combine cola and barbecue sauce. Pour into skillet, add chicken and bring to just boiling. Cover and reduce heat. Simmer for 1 hour. Yield: 4 servings.

LEMON BARBECUED CHICKEN

1/4 cup butter
2-1/2 lbs. or 6 breasts chicken
1 cup all-purpose flour
2 tsp. salt
1/4 tsp. pepper
2 tsp. paprika
1 small clove garlic, minced

1/2 tsp. salt
1/4 cup vegetable oil
1/2 cup lemon juice
2 Tbs. minced onion
1/2 tsp. thyme
1/2 tsp. pepper

Preheat oven to 400 degrees. In a shallow baking dish, melt butter. Dip chicken in mixture of flour, salt, pepper and paprika; place in baking dish. Bake at 400 degrees for 30 minutes. Combine remaining ingredients. Turn chicken after 30 minutes, pour sauce over chicken and bake additional 30 minutes. Delicious served over rice.

SUPER CRISP COUNTRY FRIED CHICKEN

1/2 cup milk
1 egg
2 tsp. freshly ground black pepper
1/2 poultry seasoning
2 cups all-purpose flour
1 frying chicken, 2-1/2 to 3 lbs.
3 tsp. garlic salt
Shortening or butter (for frying)
2 tsp. paprika

Combine the milk and egg in a medium bowl. Combine the flour, garlic salt, paprika, pepper an poultry seasoning in a paper bag or plastic bag. Add a few pieces of the chicken to the bag at a time and shake to coat. Dip the chicken in the milk-and-egg mixture, then shake a second time in the flour mixture.
To skillet-fry the chicken, place enough shortening in the skillet to come 1/2 to 1-inch up the sides of the pan. Heat the shortening to 365 degrees in an electric skillet or over medium-high heat in a large heavy skillet. Brown the chicken on all sides, then reduce the heat to 275 degrees or to medium-low heat and continue cooking until the chicken is tender, about 30 to 40 minutes, turning the chicken several times. Drain on paper towels.

To deep-fry, heat 2 or 3 inches of the shortening to 365 degrees in a deep fryer or deep saucepan. Fry the chicken for 15 to 18 minutes, or until the meat near the bone is no longer pink. Yield: 4 servings.

CONTINENTAL CHICKEN

6-8 deboned chicken breasts	1 can cream of mushroom soup
1 jar or pkg. dried beef	1/4 cup flour
1/4 cup sour cream	6-8 slices bacon

Grease crockpot. Put dried beef in bottom and around sides. Wrap each chicken breast with bacon. Stick with toothpick to hold. Place in crockpot. Mix soup with sour cream and flour. Pour over chicken. Cook with lid on 8-10 hours on low or 3-5 hours on high. Serve over rice.

GARDEN STUFFED CHICKEN BREASTS

2 Tbs. butter	1/4 tsp. thyme
1/4 cup chopped celery	1-1/2 Tbs. chopped parsley
1/4 cup chopped carrot	3 whole chicken breasts, flattened
1/4 cup chopped green pepper	Salt and pepper
1 medium Georgia sweet onion	3 Tbs. white wine or cooking wine
1/4 tsp. salt	Paprika
1/4 tsp. coarsely ground black pepper	

In a small skillet, melt butter and sauté' vegetables until tender. Stir in salt, pepper, thyme, and parsley. Place chicken breasts skin side down on squares of aluminum foil. Slightly salt and pepper each chicken breast. Place approximately 2 Tablespoons vegetable mixture in center of each breast. Fold and secure with a toothpick. Pour 1 tablespoon of wine over each breast and sprinkle with paprika. Wrap each securely with foil. Bake 350 degrees for 1 hour. Yield: 3 servings.

JUICY ROASTED CHICKEN

3 cups water	1 onion, chopped
1/2 cup soy sauce	1 tsp. salt
1 Tbs. sugar	1 4-5 lb. chicken
1/2 cup cooking sherry	
1 tsp. ginger	

Combine together all ingredients except chicken and bring to a boil. Add chicken, cover and boil for 15 minutes. Remove from heat and let stand covered for 20 minutes. Remove chicken from liquid, place in a shallow pan with rack and roast at 400 degrees for 45 minutes or until done.

MOTHER'S STICKY ROASTED CHICKEN

2 tsp. salt
1/4 tsp. white pepper
1 tsp. paprika
1/4 tsp. garlic powder
3/4 tsp. cayenne pepper
1/4 tsp. black pepper
1/2 tsp. onion powder
3 lbs. chicken
1/2 tsp. thyme
1 cup chopped onions

In small bowl, thoroughly combine salt, paprika, cayenne pepper, onion powder, thyme, white pepper, garlic powder and black pepper. Rub mixture into chicken, inside and out, patting mixture into skin to make sure it is evenly distributed and deep into skin. Place in plastic bag, seal and refrigerate overnight. When ready to roast chicken, stuff cavity with onions. Roast uncovered, at 250 degrees about 5 hours, basting occasionally with pan juices, or until pan juices start to caramelize on bottom of pan and chicken is golden brown. Yield: 4 servings.

CHICKEN AND MACARONI DINNER

1 macaroni dinner, cooked according to box
1-1/2 cup stewed chicken
2 Tbs. onion
1 can cream of chicken soup
1 cup corn
Salt and pepper to taste

Cook at 350 degrees for about 30 minutes until it bubbles.

QUICK CHICKEN & DUMPLINGS

1 large can of biscuits
1 can cream of chicken soup
1 can water
Pepper
1 can chunk chicken

Bring mixture to a boil, drop a can of biscuits one by one (cut each biscuit into 4 pieces), on top of above mixture. Boil gently with cover on until done.

SAUCY CHICKEN AND ASPARAGUS

1-1/2 lbs. fresh asparagus spears, halved
4 boneless skinless chicken breast halves
1 (10-3/4 oz.) can cream of chicken soup, undiluted
1 cup (4 oz.) shredded cheddar cheese

2 Tbs. cooking oil   1 tsp. lemon juice
1/2 tsp. salt   1/2 tsp. curry powder
1/4 tsp. pepper   1/2 cup mayonnaise

If desired, partially cook the asparagus; drain. Place the asparagus in a greased 9-inch square baking dish. In a skillet over medium heat, brown the chicken in oil on both sides. Season with salt and pepper. Arrange chicken over asparagus. In a bowl, mix soup, mayonnaise, lemon juice and curry powder; pour over chicken. Cover and bake at 375 degrees for 40 minutes or until the chicken is tender and juices run clear. Sprinkle with cheese. Let stand for 5 minutes before serving. Yield: 4 servings.

SPANISH CHICKEN WITH RICE

1 broiler/fryer chicken, cut in 8 pieces
1 tomato, chopped
Salt and pepper
1 pkg. (10 oz.) yellow rice mix
1 Tbs. vegetable oil
1 medium onion, chopped
1-3/4 cups chicken broth
1 green pepper, chopped
1 jar (4 oz.) chopped pimiento, reserved liquid
1 pkg. (10 oz.) frozen peas, thawed
2 cloves garlic, minced

Pat chicken pieces thoroughly dry with paper towels, sprinkle with salt and pepper. Heat oil in a large saucepan or dutch oven. Brown chicken pieces on all sides over medium heat (about 15 minutes).
Remove chicken and drain on paper towels. Stir onion, green pepper, and garlic into chicken drippings; sauté over medium heat until tender. Stir in chopped tomato and rice. Drain pimiento liquid into a 2-cup measure; add enough broth to make 2 cups and stir into rice mixture. Return chicken pieces to skillet. Bring mixture to a boil, reduce heat, cover and simmer for 15 minutes. Add pimientos and peas; cover and simmer additional 10 minutes. Let stand covered for 5 minutes more.

STIR FRY

2 lb. chicken breasts
1 lb. carrots
2 zucchini squash
1 lb. yellow squash
2 large Vidalia onions
2-3 ribs celery

3/4 lb. mushrooms
1/2 lb. snow peas (may use frozen)
2 pkgs. Stir Fry mix

4 Tbs. cooking oil

Dice chicken and vegetables. Heat oil in large, deep skillet or wok. Sauté' chicken and carrots until chicken is done. Add remaining vegetables. Prepare stir fry mix according to package directions. Add to vegetables, along with lemon pepper seasoning. Stir until vegetables are tender. Yield: 6 servings.

SUPER EASY CHICKEN

1 cut-up chicken
1 can cream of chicken soup
1 can milk

Rinse chicken under cold water. Put soup and milk in crockpot, stirring well. Add chicken, stir until coated with soup mixture. Cook on low for approximately 6 hours or until done. Serve over your favorite noodles. (No seasonings necessary!) Yield: 4 servings.

WILD RICE CHICKEN SUPREME

1 6-oz. pkg. wild and white rice
1/4 cup butter
1/3 cup chopped onions, optional
1/3 cup all-purpose flour
1 tsp. salt
Dash black pepper

1 cup milk or half-and-half
1 cup chicken broth
2 cups cubed, cooked chicken
1/3 cup diced pimento
1/3 cup chopped fresh parsley
1/4 cup chopped, slivered
    almonds

Cook rice according to directions. While rice is cooking, melt butter in a large saucepan. Add onion and cook over low heat until tender. Stir in flour, salt and pepper. Gradually stir in milk and chicken broth. Cook, stirring constantly, until thickened. Stir in chicken, pimento, parsley, almonds and cooked rice. Pour into a greased 2-quart casserole. Bake uncovered at 400 degrees for 30 minutes. Yield: 6 to 8 servings.

ONE DISH DINNER

1 lb. ground beef, browned
4 cups cabbage chopped
1/2 cup of onions
1/4 cup green peppers
1 cup of rice, uncooked

1 can tomato paste or puree
1 can of water
Salt & pepper to taste

Combine and cook until rice is done.

BEEF ENCHILADA RICE

1/2 lb. lean beef, diced
1 Tbs. vegetable oil
1/3 cup diced onion
1 clove garlic, minced
1-1/2 to 2 tsp. chili powder
1/2 tsp. oregano
1/2 tsp. salt
1 can (3 oz.) green chilies, diced

1 can (8 oz.) whole tomatoes in juice
3/4 cup water
1-1/2 cups dry instant Rice
2 tsp. chopped fresh parsley
2 slices (1 oz. each) American Cheese,
    cut in triangles

Brown beef in oil. Add onions and garlic and sauté' until tender. Add chili powder, oregano, salt, green chiles, tomatoes and water. Bring to a boil, breaking tomatoes into pieces. Stir in rice, cover and remove from heat. Let stand 5 minutes. Sprinkle with parsley and arrange cheese on top. Cover until ready to serve. Yield: 4 servings.

EASY-DOES-IT-SPAGHETTI

1 lb. ground chuck
1/2 cup chopped onion
2 cloves garlic, minced
6 oz. dry spaghetti, broken into 4 inch to 5 inch pieces
1 to 1-1/2 tsp. Italian seasoning

1 4-oz. can sliced mushrooms
3 cups tomato juice
2 8-oz. cans tomato sauce

Brown ground chuck in skillet, drain and put in Crock-Pot. Add all remaining ingredients except dry spaghetti; stir well. Cover; cook on Low 6 to 8 hours (High: 3 to 5 hours). Turn to High last hour and stir in dry spaghetti. Yield: 4 servings.

FLUFFY MEATLOAF

1 lb. ground beef
3 medium slices bread, torn in pieces
1/4 tsp. each pepper, dry mustard, sage, celery salt, garlic salt
1 cup milk
1-1/2 tsp. salt
1 Tbs. Worcestershire Sauce
1/4 cup chopped onion
1 egg beaten

Combine all ingredients, shape into loaf pan. Bake at 350 degrees for 1-1/2 hours or until done.

GROUND BEEF PIE

1-1/2 lbs. ground beef
8 oz. tomato sauce
1/4 cup chopped onion
1 jar (4.5 oz.) mushrooms—don't drain
1 can (8 oz.) crescent rolls

1 egg
2 cups cheddar cheese, grated
Paprika

Preheat oven to 350 degrees. Brown ground beef and drain. Simmer beef, tomato sauce, onion and mushrooms until onion is cooked an liquid is reduced by about a third. Pat crescent roll dough into the bottom of a 10-inch pie plate to form crust. Beat egg; mix with 1 cup of cheese and place in crust as the first layer. Add the meat mixture and cover with 1 cup remaining cheese. Sprinkle with paprika. Bake at 350 degrees for 20 minutes. Let stand for 10 minutes before cutting. Yield: 8 servings.

HAMBURGER STROGANOFF

1/2 cup chopped onion
1 lb. hamburger meat
2 Tbs. flour
1 pint sour cream
1 (8 oz.) can mushrooms (optional)
1 can cream of mushroom or chicken soup, undiluted

1/2 cup margarine
Pepper
Garlic salt

Sauté onion, garlic and margarine over medium heat and add meat and brown. Add flour, salt and pepper; cook for 5 minutes. Add soup and simmer 10 minutes, uncovered. Stir in sour cream and heat (don't cook, just warm). Serve over noodles or rice.

HUSBAND'S DELIGHT

Brown:

1 lb. ground beef	**Salt and pepper**
1 onion	**2 small cans of tomato sauce**
1 clove garlic	**8 oz. fine noodles**

Brown first 4 ingredients. Add 2 small cans tomato sauce. Simmer 15 minutes. Cook 8 ounces of fine noodles and drain. Mix 1 cup sour cream and small cake cream cheese. Cover casserole with 1/2 noodles, cover with meat sauce, cheese sauce, cover with rest of noodles and top with 1 cup grated sharp cheddar cheese. Bake at 350 degrees for 20-25 minutes.

MAGIC MEAT LOAF

2 lbs. ground beef
2 eggs
2/3 cup quick cooking oats
1 pkg. dry onion soup mix
1/2 cup ketchup

Reserve 2 tablespoons ketchup. Combine ground beef, eggs, oats, soup mix and remaining ketchup. Shape into a loaf. Put in Crock-Pot. Top with remaining ketchup. Cover; cook on Low 8 to 10 hours (High: 4 to 6 hours). May be doubled for 5-quart models. Yield: 8 servings.

MEAT LOAF—I

1-1/2 lbs. ground beef or turkey	**1/2 cup bread crumbs**
3/4 cup milk	**1 egg or 2 egg whites**
1 1-1/2 oz. pkg. beef onion soup mix	
1/4 cup ketchup	

TOPPING:
3 Tbs. brown sugar
3 Tbs. ketchup
1 Tbs. prepared mustard

Combine meat, soup mix, bread crumbs, milk, egg and ketchup. Pat into 8 or 9-inch round glass dish. Combine brown sugar, ketchup and mustard and mix well. Spoon topping over loaf. Cover with plastic wrap and microwave on high for 20 minutes. Slice down the middle, then across.

MEAT LOAF—II

1-1/2 lbs. ground beef
1 lb. ground pork
2/3 cup bread crumbs
1 cup milk
2 eggs beaten

1 onion chopped
1/2 tsp. sage
1 can tomato sauce
Salt and pepper to taste

Mix beef and pork together. Soak bread crumbs in milk. Add all ingredients except tomato sauce. Mix well. Turn into loaf pan; cover with tomato sauce. Bake 1 hour at 350 degrees. Baste occasionally.

MINI BEEF LOAVES

1 lb. ground beef
1 egg, beaten
1/4 cup milk
2 Tbs. dry bread crumbs
1/2 tsp. salt

1/8 tsp. pepper
1 medium onion, chopped
1 small green pepper
3/4 cup shredded cheese

In a large bowl combine ground beef, egg, milk, bread crumbs, salt and pepper. Press half the mixture in the bottom and half way up sides of 12 ungreased muffin cups. Fill each with onion, green pepper an cheese. Top with remaining beef mixture, pressing edges to seal. Place muffin tin on a cookie sheet and bake uncovered at 350 degrees for 30-35 minutes. Yield: 6 servings.

ONE POT DINNER

1/2 lb. ground beef
1/2 lb. bacon, cut into small pieces
1/2 cup chopped onion
1 can pork-n-beans
1 can kidney beans
1 can lima beans

1/2 cup ketchup
1/4 cup brown sugar
1 Tbs. liquid smoke
1-1/2 Tbs. vinegar
1 tsp. salt
Dash of pepper

Brown ground beef in skillet, drain and add to crockpot. Brown bacon and onion, drain. Add bacon, onions and remaining ingredients to crockpot, stirring well.

POOR MAN'S STEAK

1-1/2 lbs. lean ground beef
1/2 cup chopped onion
1/2 cup milk
1/2 cup cracker crumbs
1 (10.75 oz.) can cream of mushroom soup

Flour
Vegetable cooking spray
1/2 tsp. salt

In large bowl, combine first 5 ingredients. Pat mixture on a cookie sheet. Refrigerate overnight. Cut into 6 squares, roll each square in flour and brown in large skillet coated with vegetable cooking spray. Place in 9x13-inch baking pan, cover with mushroom soup. Bake 40 to 50 minutes at 350 degrees. Yield: 6 servings. Each serving contains 388 calories (53% from fat).

SATURDAY NIGHT SPECIAL

1 lb. ground beef
1 1-lb. can pork and beans
1 No. 303 can tomatoes, drained
1/4 cup brown sugar

1 tsp. salt
1 large onion, thinly sliced
2 slices bacon

Brown meat in hot skillet. Add beans, tomatoes and salt. Pour half of the mixture into a baking dish. Layer onions on top and cover with remaining beef mixture. Top with strips of bacon. Sprinkle brown sugar over all and bake at 350 degrees for one hour.

SIMPLE SALISBURY STEAK

1 lb. ground beef
1/2 cup dry bread crumbs
1 egg beaten
1 (10-oz.) can cream of mushroom soup, condensed

1/4 cup finely-chopped onion
1-1/2 cups sliced mushrooms

In a large bowl, thoroughly mix 1/4 cup soup, beef, bread crumbs, egg and onion. Shape firmly into 6 patties. Cook patties in skillet over medium high heat a few at a time until browned on both sides. Remove patties from skillet. Spoon off fat; stir in remaining soup and mushrooms into skillet. Return patties to skillet. Reduce heat to low. Cover and simmer 20 minutes or until done. Yield: 6 patties.

SKILLET MACARONI AND BEEF

1 lb. ground beef
1/8 tsp. garlic powder
2 Tbs. chopped onion
2 cans (8 oz. each) tomato sauce
1 can (4 oz.) sliced mushrooms, drained
1/2 tsp. dried oregano leaves 1/2 cup shredded mozzarella cheese
8 oz. MUELLER'S elbow macaroni cooked, drained
1/4 tsp. pepper

In large skillet, stirring frequently, brown beef and onion over medium-high heat. Add tomato sauce, oregano, pepper and garlic powder. Bring to boil. Reduce heat. Stirring occasionally, cook 5 minutes. Add macaroni and mushrooms; stir until heated. Top with cheese. Cover; heat 1 minute or until cheese is melted. Yield: 6 servings.

SPICY HOMINY SKILLET

1/4 cup coarsely, chopped onion
1/2 cup coarsely chopped green pepper
1 Tbs. butter, melted
1(14-1/2 oz.) can white or golden hominy, drained
1 (16 oz.) can tomatoes, undrained
1 (1-1/4) oz. pkg. taco seasoning mix
1/8 tsp. hot pepper sauce
1/2 cup water
1 cup grated cheddar cheese (top with half of cheese)
Ground beef

Combine all ingredients and bake 30 to 35 minutes at 350 degrees or prepare on stovetop.

TEXAS HASH

1 lb. ground beef	2 tsp. salt
1 large bell pepper, chopper	1 tsp. chili powder (more if desired)
1 large onion, chopped	1/8 tsp. pepper
1 16-oz. can tomatoes	1/2 cup uncooked rice

In large skillet, brown meat; add pepper an onion. Cook until tender. Add remaining ingredients and heat through. Place in a 2-quart casserole. Bake at 350 degrees for 1 hour.

TRI-HI MEAT LOAF

1 cup cracker crumbs
1-1/2 lbs. ground beef
1 can (6 oz.) tomato paste
2 eggs, beaten
1 cup finely chopped onion
1/3 cup finely chopped green pepper

3/4 tsp. salt
1/8 tsp. pepper
1-1/2 cups small curd cottage cheese
1 can (4 oz.) mushroom pieces
1 tsp. dried parsley

In an 8-inch square dish, combine 1/2 cup cracker crumbs with beef, tomato paste, eggs, onion, green pepper, salt and pepper. Pat half of the mixture into the bottom of square dish. Combine remaining 1/2 cup cracker crumbs with cottage cheese, mushrooms and parley. Spread over meat mixture in dish. Top with remaining meat mixture in dish. Bake in a preheated 350 degrees oven 1 hour. Let stand 10 minutes. Yield: 6 servings.

GREEN PEPPER STEAK

1 lb. beef chuck or round, fat trimmed
1/4 cup soy sauce
1 cup green onion, thinly sliced
1 cup red or green peppers cut into 1-inch squares
1 clove garlic
1-1/2 tsp. grated fresh ginger or
1 Tbs. cornstarch
2 stalks celery, thinly sliced
1/2 tsp. ground
1 cup water
1/4 cup salad oil
2 tomatoes, cut into wedges

1. With a very sharp knife cut beef across grain into thin strips 1/8-inch thick.
2. Combine soy sauce, garlic, ginger. Add beef. Toss and set aside while preparing vegetables.
3. Heat oil in large frying pan or wok. Add beef and toss over high heat until browned. Taste meat. If it is not tender, cover and simmer for 30 to 40 minutes over low heat.
4. Turn heat up and add vegetables. Toss until vegetables are tender crisp, about 10 minutes
5. Mix cornstarch with water. Add to pan; stir and cook until thickened. 6
6. Add tomatoes and heat through.
7. Serve over rice. Yield: 4 servings.

BEEF STROGANOFF

Mix:

3 Tbs. flour	1 lg. or 3 sm. cans mushrooms
1-1/2 tsp. salt	1/4 tsp. pepper
1 clove garlic	1 cup sour cream (do not use light)
1/2 onion, minced	1 lb. round steak
1/4 cup butter	1/4 cup water
1 can undiluted cream of chicken soup	

Rub both sides of steak with garlic. Lb. flour, salt and pepper into steak. Cut meat into 1-inch squares. Brown in butter. Sauté' onions. Add water and stir; add soup and mushrooms. Cook uncovered. Use low heat and cook until meat is done. Add sour cream at last minute. Pour over top and fold through mixture. Do not boil. Serve over rice (Minute Rice is fine). Yield: 4 to 6 servings.

BEEF AND BROCCOLI STIR-FRY

8 oz. boneless beef steak	3 Tbs. soy sauce
1 Tbs. cornstarch	1 cup water
1 tsp. sugar	3 Tbs. peanut oil
1 Tbs. soy sauce	Flowerets of 1 lb. broccoli
2 tsp. minced fresh gingerroot	1 onion, coarsely chopped
1 clove garlic, minced 1 carrot, sliced	
1 Tbs. cornstarch	

Cut beef across grain into thin slices. Combine 1 Tablespoon cornstarch, 1 Tablespoon soy sauce, sugar, gingerroot and garlic in bowl. Add beef. Let stand for 15 minutes. Combine 1 Tablespoon cornstarch and 3 tablespoons soy sauce with water in bowl; set aside. Heat 1 Tablespoon oil in wok. Add beef; stir-fry for 1 minute; remove beef. Heat remaining 2 tablespoons oil in wok. Add broccoli, onion and carrot; stir-fry for 4 minutes or until tender-crisp. Add beef and reserved cornstarch mixture. Cook until sauce is thickened.

MY FAVORITE SUPPER

1 lb. stew beef
1 pack dry onion soup
1 can cream of mushroom soup

Cook all day in crock pot. Serve over rice or potatoes.

SWEET & SOUR BEEF AND VEGETABLES

2 lbs. stew meat, cut into cubes
2 Tbs. oil
2 8 oz. cans tomato sauce
2 tsp. chili powder
2 tsp. paprika
1/4 cup sugar

1 tsp. salt
1/2 cup vinegar
1/2 cup light Karo syrup
2 cups fresh carrots, sliced
1 onion, quartered
1 green pepper, cut into chunks

Brown meat in hot oil in skillet, transfer to crockpot. Add rest of ingredients and mix well. Cook on low 7-8 hours. Serve over shell macaroni or rice. Yield: 4-6 servings.

ORIENTAL BEEF AND NOODLES

1-1/2 lbs. lean, boneless sirloin,
   cut into thin strips
1 red bell pepper, chopped
3 cloves garlic, minced
3 carrots, chopped
2 Tbs. rice vinegar

1/4 cup tomato sauce
1/4 cup sherry
1 Tbs. oyster sauce
1 tsp. sugar
2 Tbs. chopped peanuts
12 oz. hot cooked vermicelli

Combine all ingredients, except noodles, in crockpot. Cover; cook on Low 8 to 10 hours (High: 4 to 5 hours). Serve over noodles. May be doubled for 5-quart models. 6 servings.

LIVER PUDDING OR MUSH

1 fresh hog liver
1-1/2 lbs. fresh fat pork
2 cups corn meal
Red pepper
Salt
Black pepper
Sage

Cook liver and fat pork until tender. Remove from broth the liver only and mash with potato masher or grind. Add meal, peppers and sage to taste. Add enough of the broth to soften mixture and cook in saucepan until meal has cooked, stirring constantly. Put in mold. Press down until cold. Slice and serve cold or broil.

COUNTRY-STYLE POT ROAST

3 to 3-1/2 lb. boneless chuck roast
1 Tbs. Shortening
1 envelope onion soup mix
2 cups water
4 medium sized potatoes, cut into
    1-inch cubes

4 carrots, thinly sliced
2 Tbs. all purpose flour
1/2 cup water

In a dutch oven, brown roast in shortening. Combine onion soup mix with 2 cups water, pour over roast, simmer turning occasionally for 1-1/2 to 2 hours or until tender. Add vegetables and cook 30 minutes or until potatoes are tender, remove roast onto serving platter. Blend flour and remaining water, stir into gravy, bring to a boil, reduce heat and simmer until thickened. Yield: 6 servings.

SAUERKRAUT ROAST

1 lean, boneless 3-lb. roast
1 15-oz. can sauerkraut, rinsed and drained
1 15-oz. can tomatoes, drained
1/4 cup packed brown sugar
1 large apple, cored and sliced
1 envelope onion gravy mix (not soup mix)

Put apple slices in crockpot. Cut roast in half and put on top of apples. Mix other ingredients, except gravy mix, and pour over meat. Cook on low 8 hours or until done. Then stir in gravy mix, cover and cook 15 minutes longer. Serve over hot mashed potatoes with fresh carrots on the side. Yield: 6 servings.

HOPPIN' JOHN

1 bag (16 oz.) black-eyed peas
1 cup chopped onion
1 cup rice, uncooked
Salt and pepper to taste

1 lb. sausage, browned
1/2 green pepper, chopped
1/2 red pepper, chopped

In a large saucepan, cook peas according to package directions until two-thirds done. Add remaining ingredients to peas and simmer until peas are tender, about 30 minutes. Add warm water so there is enough "pot-liquor". Serve with cornbread.

BREAKFAST CASSEROLE

1 lb. sausage, cooked
6 slices white bread
1-1/2 cups cheddar cheese
5 eggs
2 cups half and half

1 tsp. dry mustard
1 tsp. salt
1/2 tsp. pepper

Spread bread with butter; cube. Place cubes in a 9 x 13-inch baking dish; sprinkle with crumbled sausage, top with shredded cheese. Combine remaining ingredients; beat well, and pour mixture over cheese. Chill at least eight hours or overnight. Remove from refrigerator and bake in a 350 degrees oven for 40 to 50 minutes.

CLASSIC SWISS STEAK

1 round steak
2 cups flour
1/4 tsp. salt and pepper
1 green pepper, sliced

2 Tbs. butter
1 onion, sliced
1 4-oz. can tomato sauce

Cut steak into serving portions. Combine flour, salt and pepper in medium bowl. Roll steaks in flour mixture, coating both sides. Melt butter in skillet. Brown on both sides, but do not cook. Place browned meat in crockpot. Add tomato sauce, onion and green pepper. Cook on low for 6-12 hours, or on high for 6 hours.

OVEN SWISS STEAK

6 Tbs. all purpose flour
1 tsp. dry mustard
1-1/2 tsp. salt
1/4 tsp. pepper
2 lbs. round steak, 1-inch thick

1 cup onion slices
3 Tbs. butter
1/2 cup water
1/2 cup chili sauce
1 clove garlic, grated (optional)

Combine flour, mustard and salt & pepper and rub into steak, set aside. In a large skillet, sauté' onions in butter until clear, remove from pan. Add steak n brown on both sides. Place in 9 x 12-inch casserole and add onions, water and chili sauce, cover tightly. Bake at 325 degrees for 1-1/2 to 2 hours or until tender. If using electric skillet, prepare same as above and cook on low for 2 hours or until tender, turn often to prevent sticking (more water may need to be added). Yield: 4 servings.

COUNTRY SHORT RIBS

3 lbs. short ribs of beef
Flour to dredge meat
3-4 Tbs. vegetable oil
3 Tbs. flour
2 cups water
1/2 cup tomato sauce

1/4 cup chopped carrots
1/4 cup chopped onions
1/4 cup chopped celery
1/2 tsp. minced garlic
1-1/2 tsp. salt
1/8 tsp. pepper

Preheat oven to 350 degrees. Have ribs cut individually and remove any excess fat. Dredge in flour and brown in oil. Place browned ribs in a 3-quart baking dish. Blend flour into pan drippings, gradually add water, stirring constantly. Add remaining ingredients and pour over ribs. Cover and bake 1-1/2 hours or until tender. Yield: 8 servings.

BAKED HAM AND BROCCOLI

1 pkg. (10 oz.) frozen broccoli spears
1-1/2 cups cubed, cooked ham
2 pkgs. (3 oz. each) cream cheese, softened
3/4 cup milk
1/4 tsp. salt
Dash of garlic salt
3 Tbs. Parmesan or Italian style cheese

Cook broccoli according on package directions, until barely tender. Drain and arrange in bottom of buttered 1-quart baking dish. Spread ham on top. Place cream cheese, milk, alt and garlic salt in top of double boiler. Stir over medium heat until blended and thickened. Remove from heat; stir in cheese. Pour over ham and broccoli. Bake in preheated 350 degrees oven for 30-35 minutes or until heated through and sauce is bubbly.

CATFISH CHOWDER

1 lb. fish cooked until tender in 1-quart water. Take fish from liquid and remove bones; add to liquid 2 chopped onions, cooked 2 cups chopped potatoes, 5 slices of bacon cooked crisp and crumbled, salt and pepper to taste. Ad fish that has been sprinkled with 1 heaping tsp. flour; cook slowly for 30 minutes. Add 1 cup of milk just before serving and do not let boil. Serve with saltines.

MEXICAN PORK CHOPS

4-6 pork chops, approximately 1/2-inch thick
1 large green pepper, sliced
1 medium onion, sliced
1 6-oz. can tomato paste
1/2 tsp. cayenne pepper, optional
1/2 tsp. garlic, optional
1 cup plus 1 6-oz. can water
Salt and pepper to taste

Salt and pepper pork chops and brown in a large skillet or electric frying pan. Place a slice of onion and green pepper on each. Mix tomato paste and water, pour over chops. Simmer for 45 minutes or until tender. Serve over rice. Yield: 4-6 servings.

SALMON LOAF

1 can pink salmon
1 cup bread crumbs
3 eggs
Juice of lemon
1 tsp. salt
2 Tbs. melted butter or other shortening

Remove bones and break in chunks. Add bread crumbs, beaten eggs, seasoning, butter and liquid from salmon. Mix thoroughly and shape in loaf in greased pan. Rub top of loaf with butter or other shortening. Bake at 325 degrees for 1 hour or until done.

BAKED BEAN SUPPER

1/4 cup chopped onion
1 Tbs. margarine
2 1-lb. cans pork & beans
1/4 cup catsup
1/4 cup brown sugar
2 Tbs. prepared mustard
2 5-oz. cans.
Vienna Sausage
1 can refrigerator biscuits

Cook onion in margarine until soft. Place beans, catsup, mustard, onions and brown sugar in a shallow 1-1/2-quart baking dish. Arrange sausage on top of the beans. Place biscuits on top of the meat. Bake at 375 degrees about 15 minutes, or until biscuits are done. Yield: 6 servings.

BAKED BEANS

8 slices bacon
2 cans baked beans
1 can kidney beans, drained
1 (15 oz.) lima beans
1 chopped onion 1/2 tsp. minced garlic, real
3/4 cup brown sugar

1/2 cup catsup
pepper to taste
1/4 cup vinegar, white
2 Tbs. Worcestershire
2 tsp. mustard
1 tsp. salt

Sauté' bacon and crumble. Reserve 4 tablespoons grease. Cook onions in grease until tender. Add garlic and bacon, cook and stir. Add remaining ingredients. Bring to boil. Transfer to crock pot, bring to boil on high. Turn crockpot off and let set until ready to serve.

FRIED CABBAGE

Bacon grease
6 bacon strips
1 cabbage

Soy sauce
Accent

Cut your cabbage into pieces 1-inch wide. Get 4-6 strips bacon and lay horizontally on cutting surface and cut vertically about 1 inch wide. Get skillet hot and add bacon and stir fry for 3-4 minutes on medium heat. Pour bacon and grease into separate bowl. Put 4 tablespoons bacon grease into pan. Turn stove to high heat, put cabbage in and cook, stirring occasionally, for 8-10 minutes. Add Accent. Add bacon to cabbage and mix it. Add soy sauce; simmer for 5 minutes with cover on skillet.

CORN MEDLEY

Mix together:
2 cans yellow corn, drained
2 cans white corn, drained
1 green pepper, chopped

1 jar (4 oz.) pimientos
1 large onion, chopped

Bring to a boil:
1-1/2 cup sugar
1 cup oil

1 cup vinegar
2 tsp. salt & 1 tsp. pepper

Pour over vegetable mixture. Refrigerate at least 4 hours. Overnight is better.

CORN AND BACON

Fry 6 or 8 slices of bacon crisp. Remove from drippings and let cool and crumble. Pour up drippings except about 2 tablespoons   Add 1 cup water. To boiling mixture add 2 cups fresh or frozen corn. Stir often and cook slow for 30 minutes. Salt and pepper to taste and add crumbled bacon. More water may be added if needed to thin mixture.

GEORGIA GUMBO

Combine the following ingredients:

2-1/2 cups chopped ripe tomatoes　　**1/4 tsp. pepper**
1/2 cup diced celery　　**1 Tbs. vinegar**
1/4 cup diced onion　　**1 Tbs. sugar**
1-1/2 cup cut okra　　**2 Tbs. butter**
1 Tbs. salt

Cook in open pan on low heat about 45 minutes.

ONION-ROASTED POTATOES

1 envelope Lipton Recipe Secrets Onion or Onion-Mushroom Soup Mix
2 lbs. all-purpose potatoes, cut into large chunks
1/3 cup olive or vegetable oil

Preheat oven to 450 degrees. In large plastic bag or bowl, add all ingredients. Close bag and shake, or toss in bowl, until potatoes are evenly coated. Empty potatoes into 13 x 9-inch baking or roasting pan; discard bag. Bake uncovered, stirring occasionally, 40 minutes or until potatoes are tender and golden brown. Garnish, if desired, with chopped fresh parsley. Yield: About 4 servings.

SWEET POTATO PUDDING

3 cups sweet potatoes, grated　　**1 stick butter, melted**
1-1/2 cups sugar　　**1 cup nuts, chopped**
3/4 cup buttermilk　　**1/2 tsp. salt**
1/2 cup sweet milk　　**2 eggs, well beaten**
1/2 tsp. cinnamon　　**Grated orange rind**
1/2 tsp. cloves

Mix ingredients in order. Bake for 1 hour at 300 degrees. Yield: 10-12 servings.

SCALLOPED POTATOES

6 medium sized potatoes peeled and sliced thin
2 medium onions chopped
1 can pimiento, cut in strips (optional)
1 stick butter or oleo
2 cups bread crumbs
1-1/2 or 2 cups whole milk or light cream
Salt and pepper to taste

Into greased casserole dish place a layer of sliced potatoes, sprinkle with salt and pepper, add a few strips of pimiento and over this spread a layer of bread crumbs and a portion of the melted butter or oleo. Repeat until all ingredients are used. Over the dish pour enough milk or cream to cover potatoes completely. Top with bread crumbs and butter. Bake at 375 degrees about 1-1/2 hours. Heating the milk or cream will lessen cooking time.

SENATOR RUSSELL'S SWEET POTATOES

3 cups cooked and mashed sweet potatoes
1 cup sugar
2 eggs
1/2 cup butter

TOPPING:

1 cup brown sugar
1/2 cup flour

1/2 cup butter
1 cup chopped pecans

Mix first set of ingredients until thoroughly blended. Combine topping ingredients and crumble over all. Bake 30 minutes at 350 degrees.

SWEET POTATO PONE

3 cups grated raw sweet potato
1/2 cup brown sugar
1 cup cane syrup
3 eggs
2 cups sweet milk
1/2 cup melted butter

Combine all ingredients, add 1/2 tsp. each of cinnamon, allspice and a dash of salt. Place mixture in greased baking dish and bake in 350 degrees oven for about 1-1/2 hours.

SWEET POTATO SOUFFLÉ

4 medium potatoes or about 3 cups canned potatoes
1 tsp. vanilla
1 cup sugar
1 egg
1/4 cup milk
3 Tbs. flour
1/2 cup butter or oleo
1 tsp. cinnamon

Cook and mash potatoes, add sugar, butter, flour, well beaten egg, milk, vanilla and cinnamon and mix thoroughly. Put into greased baking dish and cook for 45 minutes at 350 degrees. Marshmallows may be placed on top when done and browned slightly.

ORANGE RICE

3 Tbs. butter
2/3 cup sliced celery
2 Tbs. chopped onions
1-1/2 cups water
1 cup orange juice

2 Tbs. grated orange peel
1-1/4 tsp. salt
1 cup uncooked rice

Melt butter in sauce pan with cover, add celery and onions and cook until tender and light brown. Stir in water, orange peel, juice. Add salt. Bring to boil and add rice. Cover and steam on very low heat 25 to 30 minutes or until rice is tender. Use with ham or poultry. Yield: 6 servings.

TOMATO PUDDING

1 10-oz. can of tomato puree
3/4 cup boiling water
1 cup brown sugar
1/2 tsp. salt
1 quart bread cubes with crust removed
1/2 cup melted butter

Add sugar, water, and salt to puree. Boil 5 minutes. Place bread cubes in casserole and pour melted butter over cubes. Add hot tomato mixture and place cover on casserole. Bake at 350 degrees for 30 minutes.

HELPFUL HINTS

Put a tablespoon of butter in the water when cooking rice, dried beans, macaroni, to keep it from boiling over. Always run cold water over it when done to get the starch out. Reheat over hot water, if necessary.

To make bread crumbs toast the heels of bread and put in blender or food processor.

When preparing a casserole, make additional batches to freeze. Then, when there is not time to plan a meal or when unexpected guests appear, simply take the casserole from the freezer and pop it in the oven.

Glazed pottery, earthenware, glass, metal...takes your pick. All can be used for casseroles. Many of these casserole containers come in bright colors and pleasing designs to contrast or complement your kitchen décor or tableware. The type of container you use makes very little difference, as long as it is heatproof. Some of the earliest casseroles were made of earthenware and were glazed inside. They had cover and were similar to those that are still used today.

Soufflé dishes are especially designed to help your soufflé climb to magnificent heights. A soufflé dish has straight sides. Ramekins are good for serving individual casseroles.

Add a small amount of chopped nuts to ground meat for hamburger or meatloaf. Nuts are a delicious meat extender and, since they are relatively high in protein and vitamin E, more nutritious than most bread crumbs.

HEALTHY HINTS

FIRST AID

1. Keep victim lying down, lower head or raise feet (except for chest or head injuries).

2. Cover only enough to keep him from losing body heat.

3. Get medical help as soon as possible. Water may be given if medical help will be delayed. DO NOT give water if stomach injury is present or if victim is unconscious or having convulsions.

4. DO NOT move victim if injuries or the neck or lower spine are suspected.

5. Insure airway is open for breathing and give artificial respiration if neces sary.

MOUTH TO MOUTH METHOD

1. Wipe any foreign matter from mouth quickly.

2. Tilt victim's head backward so that his chin is pointing upward.

3. Pinch the victim's nostrils shut with the thumb and index finger of your hand that is pressing the victim's forehead.

4. Blow air into victim's mouth with your mouth widely opened and sealed around his mouth (on small children cover their mouth and nose with your mouth). Use deep breaths blowing at least once every five seconds.

5. Watch victim's chest to see when it rises. Stop when it has expanded and listen for exhaustion. Watch for chest to fall.

6. Repeat cycle until victim begins breathing on his own or until trained medical help arrives.

HELPFUL HINTS WITH CHILDREN

Child's Party

- ❖ Push animal shaped cookie cutters lightly into icing. Fill depressed outlines with chocolate icing.
- ❖ Fill ice cream cones (flat bottoms) with cake batter half full and bake. Decorate with icing topped with colored sugar.
- ❖ Small marshmallows can be used for candleholders on cakes.

OTHER USEFUL TIPS

❖ To teach a child how to put the right shoe on the right foot, mark or tape the inside of the right shoe only.

❖ Has your child outgrown his favorite sweater? Don't throw it away. Chances are it is only the sleeves that are too short. Cut off the sleeves and finish the armholes and he will have a great sweater vest to wear.

❖ Want an inexpensive way to stretch your baby powder? Mix the baby powder with a box of cornstarch and it will go much further. Cornstarch is safe and will stretch your money also. Cornstarch is just fine to use alone.

❖ Want a good way to wean your baby from his or her bottle? Take the lid off the bottle and let the baby drink from the "old favorite" bottle, then start using a cup from there. Make sure you start with baby's favorite drink.

❖ Here is a good way to keep your baby's bottle warm when you go some where. After the baby's bottle is warmed, just pop it into a wide mouth thermos that has been "warmed" with hot water. Put on the lid. This will keep the bottle just right.

❖ Remember this simple tip when going to outings. A child in colorful clothes is easier to find. Nothing stands out in a crowd like a toddler in red, purple, or yellow.

❖ If your child has trouble swallowing a pill, place it in a teaspoon of apple sauce and see how easily it goes down.

❖ Spoon for baby: A tablespoon of your measuring spoons set is ideal for baby to eat soup or cereal. The short handle and deep scoop helps them to get more into their mouths as they learn to feed themselves.

❖ Eliminating drink spills: Your child will be able to hold onto a glass better if you place two tight rubber bands around the glass an inch or so apart. This makes it easier for little hands to hold.

❖ Hints for a sick child: A penny sucker makes an excellent tongue depressor when checking for a sore throat.

OLD-TIME MOUNTAIN REMEDIES

ASTHMA:

Burn chicken feathers and inhale smoke.

Pick and dry leaves from the Mullen plant (grows in the woods), crush leaves very fine and roll into a cigarette and smoke. This will open the bronchial tubes.

Cut a stick from a sourwood tree, lay the stick in a completely dry place, the stick must be as tall as the child; when the child outgrows the stick, the asthma will leave.

Take the child out to the sourwood tree and bore a hole in the tree, put a wisp of hair cut from the child's head into the hole. Cut a peg and seal up the hole. When the child grows taller than the hole in the tree then the child will be cured of asthma.

UPSET STOMACH:

Scrape the bark down from a peach tree, make a cold water tea, and drink.

Boil coke and drink it as hot as you can stand it.

DIARRHEA:

Scrape the bark up from a peach tree and make a cold water drink.

SHINGLES:

Hunt up a black chicken, pull its head off and let the head bleed into a saucer. Rub the blood on the shingles and don't wash it off. Let it wear off. Shingles will dry up with treatment of blood for 3 days in a row. You will need 3 black chickens.

STINGS:

Use strong tobacco and make a moist plaster on the sting. This will draw the poison out and relieve the pain.

ULCERS OF THE MOUTH:

Go to the creek bank to get yellow root. Boil the root and make a tea or chew the root.

BOILS:

Take a piece of fat pork and put on to boil to make a poultice. This will bring the boil to a head.

MEASLES:

Boil the Red Alder bark and make a hot tea. This tree grows along the creeks and branches. Drinking this tea will bring the measles out.

EARACHE:

Cut a sourwood stick when the sap is up. Put one end in fire, juice will run out, let it drip into a spoon. Put this into the ear while it is still hot

Blow smoke from a pipe into the ear and it will relieve the earache.

CUT FINGER:

The more you let it bleed, the less sore the finger will be.

BLISTER FROM WALKING:

Open the blister after the sun goes down, let it drain, blister will dry and heal. Under the blister the skin will peel off.

BURNS:

Put plain mayonnaise on burn, takes the burning out.

RUSTY NAIL TREATMENT:

Person stepping on a nail, pull nail out, grease nail with pork skin, lay nail up in a dry place.
No infection.

HICCUPS:

1 teaspoon. peanut butter taken as needed.

CHEST COLD AND PNEUMONIA:

Fry onions and put into a cloth bag, put on your chest.

INSECT STING:

Dab snuff on sting to take the poison out.

HEADACHE:

Soak a paper bag in yellow homemade vinegar, pour table salt on bag, place on forehead and tie a cloth real tight around your head.

BABIES WITH HIVES:

Use ground ivy, make a tea, strain, sweeten with sugar, cool and give to baby.

ITCH:

Mix sulfur with homemade lard and rub on affected areas.

NOSEBLEEDS:

Force a large cylinder of bacon into affected nostrils to get almost immediate relief.

RINGWORM:

Yellow root or leaves steeped in vinegar to cure even the worse case.

OPEN CUT:

Pour turpentine or kerosene on open cut to prevent infection or soreness.

SORE THROAT:

Gargle with strong solution of lemon juice and water.

SHOCK—EARLY SYMPTOMS:

Shock is a condition resulting from a depressed state of vital body functions. Shock may be caused by severe injuries of all types, infection, heart attack, poisoning, and lack of oxygen. The victim's skin is pale or cold to touch. It may be moist and clammy. Victim is weak. Pulse is rapid and faint.

CANNING

HOW TO CAN VEGETABLES

Points on Packing

Raw pack. Pack cold raw vegetables (except corn, lima beans, and peas) tightly into container and cover with boiling water.

Hot pack. Preheat vegetables in water or steam. Cover with cooking liquid or boiling water. Cooking liquid is recommended for packing most vegetables because it may contain minerals and vitamins dissolved out of the food. Boiling water is recommended when cooking liquid is dark, gritty or strong-flavored and when there isn't enough cooking liquid.

How to Check Canning Jars

The first step in home canning should take place long before food and equipment are assembled and ready to go. Jars and other supplies should be checked prior to the canning session. In that way, you can replace damaged supplies and purchase new ones to avoid costly delays or inconvenience. Here are some tips to help you.

Choosing mason jars. Jars manufactured especially for home canning generically are called mason jars and must be used when preserving. They are designed with a specially threaded mouth for proper sealing with mason lids. So, can with standard mason jars only.

Preparing glass jars. Check all jars, rings and lids carefully. Discard any with nicks or cracks in top sealing edge and threads that may prevent airtight seals. Ring should be free of dents or rust. Select the size of closures—widemouth or regular—that fits your jars. Wash jars in hot, soapy water and rinse well. Then place in boiling water for 10-15 minutes. Keep jars in hot water until ready to use. Boil lid according to package directions.

Closing glass jars. Always wipe jar rim clean after food product is packed. Place lid on jar with button side up. Screw rings on firmly, but don't force. Do not re-tighten rings after processing or cooling.

A new lid that snaps down and clicks as the jar cools, providing visible proof of sealing, called Magic Button ® is made by Owens-Illinois. Its red button pops up when the seal is broken. The Magic Mason jars that go with the special lids have metric measurements as well as customary U.S. measurements molded on the side.

Jar transfer. Use jar lifter or long-handled canning tongs to transfer jars to and from canner safely. Place hot jars on rack or towel, allowing 2-inches of air space on all sides for jars to cool evenly.

Processing in a Pressure Canner

Use a steam-pressure canner for processing all vegetables except tomatoes and pickled vegetables.

Directions. Follow the manufacturer's directions for the canner you are using. Here are a few pointers on the use of any steam-pressure canner:

.... Put 2 or 3 inches of boiling water in the bottom of the canner; the amount of water to use depends on the size and shape of the canner.

.... Set filled glass jars or tin cans on rack in canner so that steam can flow around each container. If two layers of cans or jars are put in, stagger the second layer. Use a rack between layers of glass jars.

.... Fasten canner cover securely so that no steam can escape except through vent (petcock or weighted-gage opening).

.... Watch until steam pours steadily from vent. Let it escape for 10 minutes or more to drive all air from the canner. Then close petcock or put on weighted gage.

.... Let pressure rise to 10 pounds (240 degrees F.) The moment this pressure is reached, start counting processing time. Keep pressure constant by regulating heat under the canner. Do not lower pressure by opening petcock. Keep drafts from blowing on canner.

.... When processing time is up, remove canner from heat immediately. With glass jars, let canner stand until pressure is zero. Never try to rush the cooling by pouring cold water over the canner. When pressure registers zero, wait a minute or two, then slowly open petcock or take off weighted gage. Unfasten cover and tilt the far side up so steam escapes away from you. Take jars from canner.

APPLE BUTTER—I

1 peck apples
4 cups water
10 cups sugar (about) 1 tsp. ground allspice

2 tsp. ground clove
2 Tbs. ground cinnamon

Wash, quarter and cook apples, unpeeled, with water. Cover and let simmer slowly until tender. Rub through coarse sieve. There should be about 5 quarts pulp. Add half as much sugar as pulp, and spices. Let simmer about 2 house, stirring frequently. An asbestos mat placed under kettle will prevent scorching. When thick pour into hot sterilized jars and seal at once. Remember that apple butter becomes stiffer when cold. Recipe makes 9 or 10 pints.

APPLE BUTTER—II

1/2 gallon apple sauce
1/2 cup dark Karo
1-1/2 lb. dark brown sugar
2 lb. white sugar
1-1/2 tsp. cinnamon
1 tsp. ground allspice

1/2 cup red vinegar
1-1/2 tsp. allspice
1-1/2 tsp. cloves

Cook in crockpot until thick. Stir occasionally. Fill and seal jars.

PEACH BUTTER

1 peck peaches
10 cups sugar (about)
2 whole sticks cinnamon
2 tsp. cloves
1 Tbs. whole anise

Scald, peel and stone peaches. Cook very slowly, without water, until soft enough to mash to a pulp. Measure about 5 quarts of pulp. Add half as much sugar as pulp, and spices, and continue to cook very slowly until thick (about 2 hours). Remove spices (which may be tied in bag) and seal.

PICKLE BEANS

Cook beans tender. Pack in quart jars. Add 1 teaspoon salt and 1 teaspoon sugar. Fill jar with hot water. Put lids on and sit jars in a cool dark place for about 10 days, then store away.

CANNED CHILI

2 pounds ground chuck
2 cups chopped onion
2 tsp. garlic salt
4 Tbs. chili powder
1/2 tsp. crushed pepper

1/2 cup bell pepper
1/4 cup oil
2-1/2 cups chopped tomatoes
4 cups kidney beans, drained

Mix together. Simmer for one hour. Pressure on 15 pounds for one hour.

CHILI SAUCE

1 peck tomatoes
6 large green peppers, seeded and finely chopped
6 white onions, peeled and finely chopped
3/4 cup sugar
1/2 cup salt
1 tsp. ground cloves
1 tsp. allspice
1 tsp. black pepper
2 cups vinegar

Scald, peel and slice tomatoes. Bring to boiling point. Add peppers and onions, sugar, salt, vinegar and spices (which may be varied to suit taste). Boil slowly until thick, about 3 hours. Seal in sterilized jars or bottles.

TOMATO CATSUP

1 peck tomatoes
8 medium-size onions
1/2 clove garlic
1-1/2 bay leaves
2 long red peppers (no seeds)
3/4 cup. brown sugar
1 Tbs. whole allspice

1 Tbs. cloves
1 Tbs. mace
1 Tbs. celery seed
1 Tbs. peppercorns
2 inches stick cinnamon
2 cups vinegar
Salt to taste (about 1 Tbs.)

Skin tomatoes, onions, garlic and red peppers. Cut into pieces, add bay leaves and boil until very soft. Remove bay leaves and strain. Add sugar (closely packed) and spices, tied in a bag. Boil quickly until quantity is reduced one-half. Add vinegar and season to taste and boil 10 minutes longer. Remove spice bag. Spices may be varied to suit individual taste. Seal at once in steril-ized bottles.

CHOW-CHOW

4 quarts chopped cabbage
2 quarts chopped green tomatoes
12 medium size onions, chopped
12 medium size green peppers, chopped
1/2 cup plain salt (not iodized)
Add 12 medium red pepers, chopped

Mix all of above listed ingredients and let stand over night. Drain liquid off before cooking. When ready to cook Chow-Chow mix following:

2 quarts apple cider vinegar
1 quart 1/2 vinegar and 1/2 water
5 1/2 cups sugar
1 Tbs. turmeric
3 Tbs. celery seeds
4 Tbs. mustard seeds

(Tie celery seeds and mustard seeds together in a small cloth). Simmer this mixture for approx. 20 minutes. After mixture has simmered approximately 20 minutes, add the chopped ingredients that have stood overnight. (leave the bag of celery seed and mustard seed in while cooking). Cook (simmer) approx. 1-1/2 hours. Put in hot cans and seal. Take the bag of celery and mustard seeds out and throw away after cooking chow-chow.

GREEN PEPPER JELLY

1 cup drained, ground green peppers
1/2 cup drained, ground chili peppers
6-1/2 cups sugar
1-1/2 cups white vinegar
1/4 tsp. salt
1 (6 oz.) bottle fruit pectin
1 tsp. red food coloring

Combine green peppers, chili peppers, sugar, vinegar and salt in 6-qt kettle. Cook, stirring constantly, until it comes to a full rolling boil. Boil 1 minute. Remove from heat. Stir in pectin and food coloring. Ladle immediately into 8 hot half-pint jars, filling to within 1/4 inch from top. Adjust lids. Process in boiling water bath 5 minutes. Makes 8 half-pints.

PICKLED OKRA

Garlic, 1 clove each jar
Hot pepper, 1 for each jar
Dill seed, 1 tsp. each jar
Okra

1/2 cup salt
1 quart white vinegar
1 cup water

Place the garlic and hot pepper in the bottom of clean, hot jars. Pack firmly with clean, young okra pods from which only part of the stem has been removed. Stem end must be open. Add dill seed after packing jars. Bring vinegar, water and salt to a boil. Simmer about 5 minutes and pour while boiling hot over the okra. Seal immediately. The above amount of pickling solution will fill from 5 to 7 pint jars.

PICKLED ONIONS

1 gallon small white onions
2 quarts cold water
1/4 cup mixed pickle spices

1 cup salt
2 quarts vinegar

Cover onions with boiling water. Let stand 2 minutes. Drain, cover with cold water. Peel Let stand in brine to cover over night (1 cup salt to 2 quarts water). In the morning drain. Add to hot vinegar and sugar mixture, with spices and pack while hot into sterilized jars. Seal at once. Omit spices when using white onions. In this case add a teaspoon of white mustard seed and a thin slice of red pepper to each pint jar.

ARTICHOKE PICKLES

3 quarts artichokes, cut not too fine
1 pint onions, chopped
1 can pimentos, chopped
1 bunch celery, chopped

Brine: 3/4 cup salt and 3 quarts hot water. Pour over all mixture except artichokes. Let stand 2 hours. Wash well.
Brine for artichokes: 1 quart water and 4 tablespoons salt. Let stand 2 hours.

Mix 1/2 cup flour, 4 cups sugar, 1 box dry mustard, 1 tablespoon tumeric, butter size of egg, 4 cups white vinegar. Put onions on; let come to boil about 10 minutes. Add celery to this mixture. Add artichokes and cook 10 to 15 minutes. Seal in jars while hot.

BANANA PEPPER PICKLES

Select crisp, full-grown peppers (hot or sweet). Split lengthwise and remove insides. Place in gallon jugs or other deep container. Cover with a mixture of 1 cup lime to 1 gallon of water. Let stand overnight or 12 hours. Remove from lime mixture and rinse well in cool water. Then place in jars and cover with a mixture of syrup and seal. Let stand about a week before using.

Syrup:
3 cups vinegar
2 cups water
2 1/2 cups sugar
1/2 tsp. salt
1 Tbs. spices (preferably mixed pickling spices)

Mix all ingredients and bring to a full boil and pour over peppers.

CABBAGE PICKLES

3 large heads cabbage	**1 stalk celery**
2-1/2 to 3 pounds onions	**5 pounds sugar**
2 red bell peppers or 1 jar pimiento	**1 tsp. salt**
1 tsp. red or black pepper	**turmeric to color**
1 quart vinegar	**1/2 box mustard seed**
1 quart mustard	**1/2 box pickling spice**

Cut cabbage, pepper, celery and onions. Put mustard seed and pickling spice in cloth bag. Mix all ingredients and boil 15 minutes. Mix 1 cup flour and water to make a thin paste. Add to pickles to thicken stirring constantly to keep from sticking. Remove from heat and seal in sterilized jars.

DILL PICKLES

1 bushel medium-sized cucumbers
7 quarts water
1 quart vinegar
3 cups salt
1 piece dill and 1 red pepper for each jar

Bring water, vinegar and salt to boil. Chop dill and red pepper and place in each jar. Pack clean cucumbers in jars and cover with hot liquid. Seal at once. Store 10 to 14 days before using.

SWEET PICKLES

300 small cucumbers
2/3 cup salt
6 Tbs. each dry mustard, salt, sugar
1 ginger root
2 quarts cold vinegar
6 cups sugar

Wash cucumbers and wipe dry. Sprinkle with salt, cover with boiling water and let stand overnight. In the morning remove from brine, wipe dry and lay in crock. Add mustard, salt, sugar and ginger root to vinegar and pour this over pickles. Set away in a cool place. Each morning after, add 1/2 cup sugar, until 6 cups have been used up. Seal in sterilized jars.

SWEET CRISP GREEN TOMATO PICKLES

8 pounds green tomatoes
2 cups lime (from builders or farm supply)
9 cups sugar
1 Tbs. salt
10 drops green food coloring (optional)
2 gallon water

Cut tomatoes into 1/4 inch slices. Mix lime and water, pour over tomatoes. Soak for 24 hours. Rinse well and soak in cold water for 2 hours. Mix sugar, vinegar, salt, and coloring. Drain tomatoes and add to vinegar-sugar mixture. Soak tomatoes in mixture overnight. Bring to boil and boil 40 minutes. Pack in clean, hot jars and seal. Yields 8 pints.

ICEBERG PICKLE

Cut up 7 pounds of cucumbers and soak in lime water for 24 hours. (2 gallons water and 3 cups lime). Rinse; soak in cold water for 4 hours changing water every hour. Cook 30 minutes in 1/2 gallon vinegar and 4 pounds sugar and 2 tablespoons mixed spices tied in bag. Seal in jars.

LAZY CUCUMBER PICKLES

6 cups cucumbers, thinly sliced, unpeeled
1 cup Vidalia onion, sliced
1 cup bell pepper, chopped
1 Tbs. salt
1 cup vinegar
2 cups sugar 1/2 tsp. celery seed

Place cucumbers, onion, bell pepper and salt in a large glass bowl. Refrigerate for two hours. (Do not drain.) Whisk together vinegar, sugar and celery seed. Pour over cucumber mixture and store in refrigerator. Makes about 10 cups.

PICKLED SWEET RED PEPPERS

Wash outside of peppers and wipe them dry. Cut slices from stem end and remove seeds. Cut into thin strips with scissors or into long ribbons, working around and around the peppers. Scald well, then drop into ice water to crisp, drain. Put the peppers into clean, hot jars; fill to overflowing with hot syrup made in the proportion of one cup sugar to 2 cups good apple vinegar. Seal immediately.

SWEET DILLED OKRA PICKLES (6 Pints)

3 pounds okra
6 cloves garlic
6 tsp. celery seed
6 pods hot pepper
6 tsp. dill seed

1/2 cup salt
1 cup sugar
1 quart vinegar
1 quart water

Pack okra in jars. Put into each jar 1 teaspoon dill seed, 1 teaspoon celery seed and 1 hot pepper. Heat to boiling vinegar, salt, sugar and water. Pour over okra, seal. Let stand 3 weeks.

BREAD AND BUTTER PICKLES

25 medium-sized cucumbers
2 cups sugar
12 onions
2 tsp. mustard seed
1/2 cup salt
2 tsp. turmeric
ice water
2 tsp. celery seed
1 quart vinegar
1 tsp. cassia buds

Slice cucumbers and onions. Soak in ice water to cover with salt for at least 3 hours. Scald vinegar, add sugar and seasonings. Add drained cucumbers and onion. Just heat through. Put in sterilized jars, covering with vinegar solution, and seal.

MIXED PICKLES

1 medium head cauliflower
1 pt. wax beans
1 pt. small green beans
4 chili peppers
4 sweet red or green peppers
1 pt. pearl onions
1 pt. large cucumbers
6 quarts water
1 oz. each whole cloves, allspice, cinnamon, mustard seed, celery seed, peppercorns

3-1/2 quarts vinegar
2 pounds sugar (white or brown)
1 small piece horseradish root
3 bay leaves
1 lemon
1 quart small cucumbers
1/3 cup salt

Wash vegetables. Slice large cucumbers, string beans, if necessary, chop peppers, separate cauliflower, peel onions and slice and seed lemon. Dissolve salt in water, add cucumbers, sweet peppers and onions. Let stand over night. Then drain and place in cold water for 2 hours. Meanwhile cook cauliflower and beans separately in boiling, salted water for 10 minutes. Drain and rinse in cold water. Add sugar and seasonings to vinegar and boil together 10 minutes. Strain over vegetables and lemon. Let stand until cold. Drain again and bring liquid to a boil. Pack vegetables in sterilized jars, pour over hot vinegar and seal tightly. Let ripen about 6 weeks.

WATERMELON RIND PICKLE

4 pounds watermelon rind
1 gallon cold water
3 Tbs. slack lime (Calcium Hydroxide
   if bought from druggist)
2 quarts vinegar
2 Tbs. whole allspice
1 Tbs. whole cloves

2 long pieces cinnamon
2 pieces ginger root
1 lemon peel
2 tsp. salt
3 pounds sugar
1 quart boiling water

Select firm, thick, melon rind; remove all pink meat and green skin; weigh; cut into cubes or strips. Dissolve lime in gallon of water; add rind and let stand several hours; rinse rind and cover with fresh water; let stand 2 or 3 hours. Change water and cook until tender. Let stand over night in cooking water. Combine all other ingredients and bring to a boil; add the drained rind and boil gently until clear. Remove spices, pack rind into sterilized jars and seal immediately.

PICKLED PEACHES

9 pounds peaches, peeled
6 cups sugar
1 pint vinegar

1 tsp. whole cloves
3 sticks cinnamon

Pour all ingredients over peaches, let set 30 minutes. Bring to a boil and seal.

PICKLED PIG'S FEET

Cut off horny parts of feet and toes, scrape clean and wash thoroughly, singe off stray hairs, place in kettle with plenty of water, boil, skim, pour off water and add fresh. Boil until bones will pull out easily. Do not bone, but pack in stone jar with pepper and salt sprinkled between each layer; cover with cider vinegar. When wanted for table, take out sufficient quantity, put in hot skillet, add more vinegar, salt and pepper if needed, boil until thoroughly heated, stir in smooth thickening of flour and water, and boil until flour is cooked. Serve hot as a nice breakfast dish. Or, when feet have boiled until perfectly tender, remove bones and pack in stone jar as above; slice down cold, when wanted for use. Let liquor in which feet are boiled stand over night; in morning remove fat and prepare and preserve for use.

STRAWBERRY PRESERVES

2 quarts ripe strawberries
8 cups sugar

Wash and cap berries. Cover with boiling water and let stand 3 minutes. Drain well. Pour 4 cups sugar over berries and bring to a boil. Boil for 5 minutes. Remove from heat and cool. When cool, add remaining sugar and bring to a boil. Boil 5 more minutes and remove from heat. Let stand overnight. Place in sterilized jars next morning. Sealing is not necessary. Do not double recipe.

RELISH

4 cups red bell pepper, chopped
2 cups vinegar
2 cups cabbage, chopped
2 cups sugar
2 cups onion, chopped
2 tsp. salt
2 pods hot pepper, chopped
few green tomatoes, chopped

Let boil, low until tender. Fill jars and seal.

SWEET RELISH FOR SALADS AND SLAW

8 large cucumbers
1/4 cup canning salt
4 sweet red peppers (can use green or both)
4 large onions
1 Tbs. celery seed
1 Tbs. mustard seed
2-1/2 cup sugar
1-1/2 cup white vinegar

Peel and slice cucumbers. Put in Glass or stainless steel bowl. Add salt. Mix well. Cover and let stand in refrigerator overnight. Drain well. Put through food chopper with peppers and onion. Use coarse blend. Place in kettle with remaining ingredients. Bring to a boil and simmer uncovered 30 minutes, stirring occasionally. Put into hot jars and seal. Yield: 3 pints.

CHOW CHOW RELISH

3 medium cabbages
1/2 peck tomatoes
6 green peppers
6 red bell peppers
3 pounds onions
1/2 cups plain salt
1 cup plain flour

3 pounds sugar
3 Tbs. mustard seed
3 Tbs. turmeric
2 Tbs. celery seed
4 Tbs. ground mustard
1/2 gallon vinegar

Chop vegetables. Dissolve salt in 8 cups of water and pour over vegetables. Let stand 1 hour. Drain (if too salty, rinse and drain again.) Mix dry ingredients and spices. Add vinegar and cook just to boiling point. Add drained chopped vegetable to sauce and simmer for 20 minutes. Do not boil; just simmer. Pack in hot jars and seal.

CORN RELISH

1 dozen ears corn
6 white onions
4 red peppers
6 green peppers
2 cups sugar
1 quart vinegar
1/2 pt. water

1 Tbs. salt
4 Tbs. mustard seed
2 Tbs. turmeric
1 large head cabbage, cut fine
2 hot peppers (if liked)

Cut corn from ears, slice onions and peppers and cut cabbage fine. Add other ingredients except flour. Boil together 20 to 25 minutes. Thicken with flour, mixed with a little water. Boil 15 minutes longer Seal in sterilized glass jars.

PEAR RELISH

1 peck pears
5 onions
6 bell peppers
2 pounds sugar

5 cups vinegar
1 Tbs. salt
1 Tbs. spices
1 Tbs. turmeric

Grind and boil for 30 minutes. When thick, pour into sterilized jars and seal.

PEPPER RELISH

12 sweet green peppers
  cored, seeded and minced
12 sweet red peppers
  cored, seeded and minced
2 cups minced yellow onions
1 cup minced celery

3 cups white vinegar
1-1/2 cups sugar
1 Tbs. pickling salt
1 Tbs. mustard seed
1 tsp. celery seeds

Can put in chopper to save time. Mix all ingredients in large enamel or stainless steel kettle. Cover and simmer 15 minutes. Ladle into jars 1/8 inch of top and make sure liquid covers vegetables – or leave 1/2 inch head space. Seal and process in hot water bath 15 minutes.

RAW RELISH

9 red peppers (sweet)
9 green peppers (sweet)
12 medium onions
5 pounds cabbage
1 cup salt
3 hot peppers

Chop all ingredients very fine or grind in food chopper, add salt and let stand over night. Drain all water off next morning and add two level tablespoons white mustard seed and one tablespoon of celery seed, one quart and one pint vinegar, one quart sugar. Pack in jars cold and seal.

SWEET RELISH

8 large cucumbers
1/4 cup canning salt
4 sweet red peppers
  (can use green or both)
4 large onions, quartered

1 Tbs. celery seed
1 Tbs. mustard seed
2-1/2 cup sugar
1-1/2 cup white vinegar

Peel and slice cucumbers, place in glass or stainless steel bowl. Add salt, mix well. Cover and let stand in refrigerator over night. Drain well, put through food chopper with peppers and onions, using coarse blade. Place in kettle with remaining ingredients. Bring to a boil and simmer 30 minutes, uncovered, or until mixture is thickened and vegetables are cooked, stirring occasionally. Spoon into hot sterilized jars, seal immediately. Makes 3 pints.

VEGETABLE RELISH (Uncooked)

8 large carrots
12 white onions
12 large sweet red peppers
12 large sweet green peppers
2 large heads cabbage
3/4 cup salt

1-1/2 quarts vinegar
6 cups sugar
3 Tbs. celery seed
3 Tbs. mustard seed
1/2 tsp. red pepper

Peel carrots and onions, seed peppers. Chop all vegetables together until fine. Add salt and let stand 3 hours. Drain well. Add vinegar, in which sugar has been dissolved, and seasoning. Pack into clean jars. Cover well with liquid and seal. No cooking required.

SALSA

Dish pan tomatoes
12 onions
6-10 hot peppers

1 cup vinegar
1/2 cup salt
3 Tbs. coriander

Cook approximately 3 hours. Fill and seals jars. Yield: About 12 pints.

PICKLED SQUASH

4 quarts squash, sliced
1/4 cup salt
5 cups sugar
6 medium onions, chopped

3 cups vinegar
1-1/2 tsp. celery seed
1-1/2 tsp. mustard seed
1 tsp. turmeric

Sprinkle salt over onions, squash, cover with ice, let stand 3 hours. Mix other ingredients and heat well. Add squash, mix , bring to full boil. Fill jars and seal.

PICANTE SAUCE

5 quarts tomatoes
5 med onions
1 cup vinegar (white)
10 peppers

2/3 cup sugar
8 tsp. canning salt
6 tsp. garlic salt

You can either chop or grind tomatoes, onions, and pepper. Mix all 7 ingredients together. Bring to boil. Boil for 30 minutes. Put in jars and seal.

TOMATO SOUP

14 quarts tomatoes
7 medium onions chopped
1 stalk celery chopped
7 Tbs. parsley flakes
3 bay leafs

Cook above ingredients until done, then run through colander.

Paste:

14 Tbs. flour
14 Tbs. butter (melted)
3 Tbs. canning salt
8 Tbs. sugar
2 tsp. pepper

Mix together and thin with tomato juice. Then add paste to juice and cook until thickens. Pour into jars and put in hot water bath for 15 minutes.

CANNED OKRA AND TOMATOES

Cut okra and peel tomatoes. Cook together until tender (approximately 20 minutes). Fill hot jars. Add 1/2 teaspoon salt to each can and seal. Good to use as soup starters or just add butter. Heat and serve.

GREEN TOMATO PICKLES

Hot pepper to taste
7 quarts tomatoes
1 cup water
1 cup vinegar
1 cup sugar

Boil tomatoes and peppers. Fill jars and seal.

HELPFUL HINTS FOR CANNING

In making pickles, use white vinegar to make clear pickles and coarse salt, which comes in 5 pound, bags. This is not rock salt. Avoid using iodized salt for pickle making. Most pickles are better if allowed to stand six weeks before using.

Liquids: Save all liquid from pickle to use for pickled beets, slaw or for moistening meat or fish sandwich fillings.

Paraffin: Melt it in old coffeepot; easily poured out. Place piece of string or tape across jars before adding paraffin; easily removed when cold.

Watermelon Rind: Color green and red when preserving to use in winter baking instead of citron and cherries.

HELPFUL HINTS FOR FREEZING

Never overcook foods that are to be frozen. Foods will finish cooking while being heated. Do not refreeze cooked thawed foods.

Do not freeze spaghetti, macaroni or noodle mixtures. These tend to lose texture and become too soft when reheated.

Green pepper may change the flavor in frozen casseroles. Clove, garlic and pepper flavors get stronger when they are frozen, while sage, onion, and salt get milder or fade out.

Do not freeze cooked egg white—it becomes tough.

When freezing foods, label each container with contents and the date it was put into the freezer. Store at zero degrees. Always use frozen cooked foods within 1 or 2 months.

ETC.

The secret of freezing okra is double bag it.

To keep apple butter from popping out, cook it in a crock pot.

A stitch in time saves nine.

Evening red and morning gray helps the traveler on his way.

Red skies in the morning, sailors take warning.